PRAISE FOR
EXTRAORDINARY CA
#1 NATIONAL BESTSELLER

"A remarkable collection of personal stories about Canadians, many of them unknown to the wider national community, who have helped make this country a better place for all."
National Post

"Three words describe the Canadians whose stories are told in this book: courage, resilience, and imagination. The courage to face the unthinkable and take on the impossible. The resilience to pick up when things go wrong and carry on. And the imagination to find new ways of living and giving. These heroes, sung and unsung, teach us what it is to be a Canadian. An entertaining and uplifting read."
BEVERLEY McLACHLIN,
former Chief Justice of Canada and bestselling author of *Truth Be Told*

"A welcome exposure to an abundance of goodness afoot in Canada."
Winnipeg Free Press

"This collection of greats shows what Canadians do: we think of others and act selflessly, and with great and quiet courage."
JESSE THISTLE, #1 bestselling author of *From the Ashes*

"A love letter to this country."
Policy Magazine

"A wide range of inspiring stories from the perspective of seventeen Canadians who aren't necessarily well known but have made a difference in their own ways across the country."
The Canadian Press

"Some would say that to brag about being extraordinary is un-Canadian. I say, it's time we celebrated ourselves. But what do I know? I wasn't extraordinary enough to be included in this book."
MARK CRITCH,
comedian and bestselling author of *Son of a Critch*

EXTRAORDINARY
CANADIANS

Stories from the Heart
of Our Nation

PETER MANSBRIDGE

WITH MARK BULGUTCH

PUBLISHED BY SIMON & SCHUSTER
New York London Toronto Sydney New Delhi

To all those extraordinary Canadians out there,
you make us who we are.

**SIMON &
SCHUSTER
CANADA**

Simon & Schuster Canada
A Division of Simon & Schuster, Inc.
166 King Street East, Suite 300
Toronto, Ontario M5A 1J3

This Simon & Schuster Canada edition April 2022

SIMON & SCHUSTER CANADA and colophon are trademarks of Simon & Schuster, Inc.

For information about special discounts for bulk purchases, please contact Simon & Schuster Special Sales at 1-800-268-3216 or CustomerService@simonandschuster.ca.

Manufactured in the United States of America

10 9 8 7 6 5 4 3 2 1

Library and Archives Canada Cataloguing in Publication
Title: Extraordinary Canadians : stories from the heart of our nation / Peter Mansbridge with Mark Bulgutch.
Names: Mansbridge, Peter, author. | Bulgutch, Mark, author.
Description: Simon & Schuster Canada edition. | Previously published: Toronto, Ontario : Simon & Schuster Canada, 2020.
Identifiers: Canadiana 20210287292 | ISBN 9781982134570 (softcover)
Subjects: LCSH: Heroes—Canada—Biography. | LCSH: Canada—Biography. |
LCGFT: Biographies.
Classification: LCC FC25 .M36 2022 | DDC 920.071—dc23

ISBN 978-1-9821-3452-5
ISBN 978-1-9821-3457-0 (pbk)
ISBN 978-1-9821-3460-0 (ebook)

Contents

Introduction

The Canadian military cemetery at Bény-sur-Mer in northwestern France is just a few kilometres from the Normandy coast. On a clear summer's day, standing among the headstones, you can see the water and the beaches. The same beaches where hundreds of young Canadian boys were cut down by German guns on June 6, 1944. D-Day.

Many of them had been out of the landing craft that had brought them across the English Channel for only a few desperate seconds. They were strafed and lay dying in the blood and sand and would never know that they had helped spearhead one of Canada's greatest military accomplishments. Our country's dead from the Normandy campaign totaled more than two thousand lads.

Now they lie in the ground at Bény-sur-Mer. It's a quiet, peaceful place, a beautiful cemetery lined with Canadian maple trees. A piece of Canada almost hidden in a tiny corner of another country.

What do we call those men? We call them heroes.

Now, keep that image in the back of your mind and come with me to another, very different front.

The Olympic hockey arena in Sochi, Russia, in 2014. Canada's formidable women's hockey team, winners of the previous three gold medals, was down 2–0 to their archrival, the United States, and there were less than four minutes to play. The end of an era was looming.

But that's not what happened. With 3:26 left on the clock, Canada's Brianne Jenner scored when the puck bounced off her leg and into the American net. Then, with less than a minute left, 54.6 seconds to be exact, Marie-Philip Poulin scored to tie the game. The unbelievable had happened. A tie is not a win. It was on to overtime, and when Canada picked up an early penalty, the nation feared the comeback was over. But, again, the fairy tale was not to be crushed. At 8:10 into overtime, Poulin took a pass to the side of the net and blasted it home.

So, what do we call those women? Actually, we call them heroes too.

These are two very different examples of what a hero is, and, no, I'm not suggesting that we are abusing the word by equating war and sports. What I'm trying to suggest is that "hero" is a description that covers a wide range of possibilities, and there are a lot of stories that fall into the space between dying for your country and winning for your country.

That's what this book is about. It's about people who have put the lives of Canadians of all walks of life first. That's what being a hero means to me.

We've all witnessed heroes very recently. Many of them. They're the frontline health-care workers who risked everything to be there for us in the battle against COVID-19: doctors, nurses, hospital staff; first responders at police, fire, and paramedic stations; grocery store clerks, truck drivers, farmers, postal workers—the list is long and we must never forget them. While we did our part by staying at home, they defined extraordinary by leaving their families every day and being on the job for us. One of the stories in the pages ahead will capture just one example of these recent extraordinary Canadians.

Before I started writing, people used to ask me, "Who's your hero, Peter?" I never hesitated. Since I am a baby boomer, much of my youth was spent revering what Tom Brokaw calls "the greatest generation," the one that preceded mine. So, of course, my father, a veteran himself, was often front and centre in my stories. But so was a lad from Winnipeg by the name of Andrew Mynarski.

On a June night in 1944, Mynarski, a mid-upper gunner on a Lancaster bomber, joined his fellow crew members on board their plane for a mission over the continent. It was supposed to be routine, but it wasn't. Once they were over the target, they were first hit by flak and then attacked by a German night fighter. With the plane crippled, listing from side to side and plummeting toward earth, the pilot ordered everyone to jump.

One after another, they bailed out until Mynarski stood alone at the doorway. He looked back and saw the tail gunner, Pat Brophy, trapped in his tiny, cramped position. Mynarski abandoned his jump and crawled back through the burning wreckage to help his buddy. With his clothes and his parachute pack on fire, he pushed and pulled as best he could, but nothing worked. Finally, Brophy yelled at him to save himself, to jump. Mynarski refused, but Brophy insisted.

Mynarski went back to the door, looked at Brophy, saluted, and said, "Good night, sir!" And then he jumped.

Andrew Mynarski didn't survive the night.

By a miracle, Pat Brophy did.

Many years later, I met Brophy while I was on assignment in northern Ontario, where he was living at the time. As I listened to his story, I got chills. Even today, it makes me tear up. But his story also made me realize that if Pat Brophy hadn't survived that night, no one would ever have learned about Andrew Mynarski's heroism. Because they did, Mynarski was awarded the country's highest medal for bravery, the Victoria Cross. His story became a *Heritage Minutes* episode. A school was named after him.

Andrew Mynarski and the other people I've mentioned in this introduction were just ordinary Canadians—everyday Canadians, if you will. They came from different provinces, communities, and backgrounds. But they became extraordinary through their actions.

When Mark Bulgutch and I set out to write this book, with the keen advice of our editor, Simon & Schuster's Sarah St. Pierre, we decided we wanted to write each story in the voice of the person we were profiling. We interviewed each person at length, for hours at times, to capture their experiences in detail. They shared everything.

Their stories will take you across the country and around the world; they'll draw on your emotions, sensibilities, and experiences. They'll make you laugh and cry. They'll make you think about the real meaning of the words "extraordinary" and "hero." Their lives may not result in medals, *Heritage Minutes*, or new names for schools, but then again, they might.

Peter Mansbridge
Stratford, Ontario

CINDY BLACKSTOCK
The Fight for Change

*I really was a child living two lives. One was much
harder and much more painful than the other. And living
the difference set me on a course for a lifetime.*

There is something magical about children. About their sense of the world, their wonder, their limitless possibilities. And how, in those opening moments of life, they're all equal. Until they're not.

I was about five years old when I overheard a discussion at my parents' dinner table that would influence the rest of my life. My mom had invited her sister and her sister's son, my cousin, to join us that night for dinner at our house in Topley, a very small town, home to a couple of hundred people, in northern British Columbia. My cousin loved to talk and it wasn't long before he had the attention of the table, and even though I was kind of running around the room, I was listening to every word he had to say. He was older than me, and he was describing what seemed, to me at least, to be an imaginary place.

"It's a wonderful spot," he said. "A place where you can learn about everything, and discuss anything, that you find interesting. A place where others join with you and share their knowledge and experience."

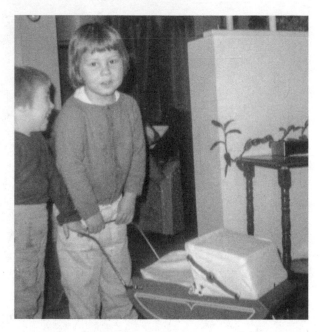

Here I am at age four with my sister, Sheila, practicing looking after "little" kids.

I decided right then and there that I wanted to go to that place. I stopped running and asked him, "What is this place?"

"UBC," he answered. He was talking about the University of British Columbia, though at the time I had no idea what he meant. To me it sounded like: "You Be See." But even at that age I was determined to find it. I was going to go there. I listened carefully as he went on.

"It's an expensive place and it costs a lot of money to go there."

My courage faltered for a moment. I knew our family didn't have a lot of money. How could I make my dream come true? This was the late 1960s, and I only knew one way to make money back then. In the part of northern British Columbia where we lived, my father, a forest ranger, had taught me to go out in the forest and pick up pine cones. If you saved enough of them to fill a gunnysack you could sell them for reforestation. In my little five-year-old mind, playing near the dinner table, I thought, "How many gunnysacks will I need to fill to go to that wonderful place called 'You Be See'?"

Despite my worry about money, even then my world seemed full of possibility. However, it was around that same age that I realized something else. Something about the way others saw my family.

My mother worked as a BC Tel operator, and between her job and my dad's, my brother, my sister, and I were always moving from town to small town to smaller town among the huckleberry bushes of British Columbia's north. No matter where we were, I noticed that when I went out with my mom everything was normal; people were friendly and talked to us openly. But when I went out with my dad, it was very different. We'd go to a local diner and sit for a long time before we got served, and even then, it seemed to me, we were served grudgingly.

You see, my dad was Gitxsan, but most people just called him Indian. My mom wasn't. She was non-Indigenous. So when I was with my mother the future seemed kind of limitless—I was seen as someone who could grow up to be a nurse or a teacher, something productive in society. But when I was with my father and associated with my First Nations family and friends, the future suddenly looked so much bleaker.

I was only five, but I was already feeling caught between two worlds.

When it was time for me to go to school, I went to public schools while almost all my Indigenous friends went to residential schools. It would be decades before we realized the horrors my friends were going through, but I was spared that experience. I was very lucky, and even to this day I'm not sure why. At the time, it was up to government-appointed Indian agents to determine where Indigenous kids like me went to school. The Indian Act dictated that those kids living on reserve went to residential schools, and those living off reserve did not. We moved a lot, sometimes living in the bush, sometimes in nearby communities, so perhaps the Indian agents lost track of me or simply didn't notice. Whatever the case, I attended public school, often the only First Nations kid in my class, and it was there, sometimes from schoolyard gossip, that I would hear non-Indigenous people say that all Indians were on welfare, that all Indians were drunks. To me, with a First Nations father, hearing this often was horrifying. It was, as I look back on it now, a constant form of bullying—in fact, constant racism.

What made these moments worse was when our family travels would take me onto a reserve because I would see so many things that backed up those stereotypes. I would see people who were drunk. I would see people whose only source of income was welfare.

From early childhood, these things shaped my views of what a First Nations person was. Of who I was. I was fighting a battle within myself, trying to determine which side of my identity I should lean to.

When I was young, a local Gitxsan reserve invited everyone in the area to come and visit in an attempt to ease tensions between the Indigenous and non-Indigenous peoples. It was a kind of festival atmosphere, and the idea was to raise awareness about traditional customs, culture, and food. I was immediately impressed, especially with the totem poles. Each giant pole told stories, and the elders would explain the legends by talking about each figure carved into the pole from top to bottom. I'd never seen one before, and the history behind the poles that had stood for decades was inspiring.

Then my sweet tooth started to have a craving. I could see one of the tables set up for visitors was serving what looked to me like strawberry ice cream. I love strawberry ice cream. I quickly manoeuvred myself to be first in line and was rewarded with a cone. I brought it to my lips and as I took a bite, I thought, "Oh my God, this is not strawberry ice cream." It sure wasn't. It was soapberry ice cream! And soap is not strawberry. It's bitter. Very bitter. That was my first taste of traditional food, and I didn't like it and I didn't finish it!

That day had its dark side as well. Again, I saw drunkenness and everything that goes with it. Even with all the fun going on around me, those were scenes I could not unsee.

On the way home, the events of the day ran through my head. Some of what I had seen and heard had made me feel very uncomfortable with half of my heritage, and I came to the conclusion that these two extremes of First Nations life were like the night sky, a profound darkness that could also include beautiful sparkles. As hard as it is for me to admit it now, I became racist against myself in some ways.

I really was a child living two lives. One was much harder and much more painful than the other. And living the difference set me on a course for a lifetime.

From my vantage point of having two childhoods, I began to realize that I was in the best possible position to ask: "Why are we different?" "Are we really different?" "Why should we be different?" "What makes us different?"

By the time I was in my mid-teens, I was reading Nelson Mandela, Martin Luther King Jr., and Mahatma Gandhi in search of the answers to those very questions. They talked about freedom in a way that I fully understood. Even though they were from a different time and place, what they were saying about equality had lasting resonance. Their power was in communicating truths that were accessible and meaningful to everyone, no matter their age, race, or circumstance.

Slowly my perception of myself began to change through education and I came to know from that early age that we, the Indigenous "we" in my blood, really weren't any different from the "we" on my non-Indigenous side. That only because we were *seen* to be different, the system treated us differently and not in a way that was good. The rules were racist, plain and simple. Why were Indigenous kids shipped off to faraway schools? Why were we living on reserves? Why were we offered different health care? How was it acceptable that we didn't have clean drinking water? The accepted image of our "difference" was echoed in the media that influenced so much of our lives. I never saw a First Nations person be a teacher or a doctor or an engineer or anything like that. The only people I saw on TV in those roles, whether they were real or dramatic, were white people.

I was determined to change things. I was convinced I could make a difference. And I knew part of my goal would have to start by getting to "You Be See."

It wasn't long after that dining room conversation with my cousin that I realized that "You Be See" wasn't some faraway, unattainable, mystical place. It was real and it was something reachable, even for me. It was, of course, UBC, the University of British Columbia. And a dozen years after I'd heard my cousin talking about it, I was there, studying and learning in the same classrooms that had educated the likes of prime ministers, Supreme Court chief justices, Olympic athletes, business leaders, authors, architects, and opera singers.

Now it was time for Cindy Blackstock.

UBC was just as wonderful as I had expected. My cousin had been correct. It *was* a place for ideas and passion. And when I walked out of that institution in 1987, I had an Arts degree in one hand and a job offer in the other. I was twenty-one and ready for work with the BC government's Child Protection Services to make a real difference in people's lives. I had been deeply affected by my experiences growing up, and I had never been able to accept that in this great country—and we have a great country—there are such historic inequities in the way we treat our citizens. As far as I was concerned those who suffer the most are those who should suffer least. Those who were here first, those who were living off this land before anyone else even knew there was land here to live off. My particular passion was for Indigenous children and to ensure they had the same basic rights as non-Indigenous kids.

I thought I was ready, but I'm not sure anyone can ever be ready for the front lines of child protection. I saw a lot of things I wished I hadn't, a lot of things that shaped my view of society.

I'd barely started working when I was confronted with what was to be an all-too-regular part of the job: making a decision about whether to take a child out of their home and away from their parent or parents.

I made it! This is my UBC graduation photo, taken in 1987.
Favourite memory of UBC? The legendary UBC cinnamon buns!

We'd received a call from a woman who was very concerned about the well-being of the kids in the apartment next door to her and I was sent to determine what should be done. It was an apartment in a low-income building in downtown Vancouver. I knocked on the door and a little First Nations girl appeared. She was barely five years old, but she had an air of confidence that suggested she was clearly in charge. Her two younger siblings were playing on the carpet behind her. One looked about three, the other about four.

"Can I see your mom?" I asked.

She said yes and began to lead me down a bleak-looking hallway, but suddenly she stopped, turned, and asked me, "Do you want to see what my mom does?"

Before I could answer, she started staggering as she walked and slurring her words. I was shocked and felt sickened. Already I was concerned that this was no place to raise a child, but now I was watching a five-year-old mimic what she saw in her mother. We got to the room where her mom was, and she was out cold. Drunk. We could not wake her and I had to call for paramedics. Later I discovered that she had severe addiction issues.

When it came time to make the decision whether to keep the children with her, my decision was easy, perhaps too easy. I took those three little First Nations girls out of their home and had them placed in foster care. It was the hardest thing I've ever done. Eventually, I was able to find an extended family member who took them in. I felt relieved about that, but I couldn't escape the fact that I'd separated them from their mother. They say you never forget your first. I don't. But sadly there were many more that followed.

What I quickly discovered was that when I was working "off reserve" doing more general child protection for non-Indigenous kids, there were food banks, youth programs, baseball diamonds, and lots of other places to provide support and a healthy environment for families who were struggling. But when I went "on reserve," none of those resources existed. There were no nonprofit groups providing food at food banks, and the schools and community centres were run-down and in disarray. The pieces that were fundamentally expected in mainstream society did not happen for First Nations. That, I decided, was driving a lot of the disadvantage.

I developed a new theme to my learning and it's stuck with me ever since. I repeat it to myself all the time: "I have to stop paying so much attention to all the stuff I can see, and instead pay more attention to the stuff I can't see." So I tried paying less attention to things like the drunkenness, and more attention to the fact that those affected by alcohol simply didn't have the services, the facilities, and the benefits that their non–First Nations counterparts did have.

It's not only about equality among citizens. It's not just about the fair treatment of Indigenous and non-Indigenous populations. This is about kids. About the most innocent and vulnerable members of our society. Children. And there are children in this country who have been treated and continue to be treated as worth less than others.

In 2002, I became the executive director of the First Nations Child and Family Caring Society, a national nonprofit organization developed by First Nations child and family service agencies to ensure the safety and well-being of our youth and their families through education initiatives, public policy campaigns, and quality resources to support communities. It's from here that I feel I can make a difference by fighting in court, by lobbying government officials both elected and unelected, and by standing up for those who can't find a way to stand up for themselves. I was convinced that a strong relationship with bureaucracy could lead to the implementation of successful new policies that would provide a solution to First Nations childhood issues.

When I started, quite frankly, I didn't know where to begin. But I went to my Indigenous strength, the one I finessed thanks to the writings of my heroes: Mandela, King, and Gandhi. Express complex things simply. That would be the best way to reach people with the truth and evoke change. This was the path I'd been on since I was a little girl. Address inequalities. Especially for children.

One case still haunts me. Just before Christmas 2012, a little four-year-old First Nations girl was admitted for dental surgery, but things went terribly wrong and she was left with terminal brain issues. The doctor asked for her to be admitted to palliative care with a special bed that would keep her at an angle to prevent suffocation. The request went through the hands of fifteen different bureaucrats, most of them in the federal public service, before someone at the end of the line wrote on the application: "Absolutely not."

If that sounds shocking, it is. If it sounds abnormal, it isn't. If she wasn't Indigenous, getting care would not be an issue; it all would have just happened. The extra costs would be covered by basic health-care funding. But not here. Why? That is the Canadian system. And it has been forever. But it doesn't make it right.

This is just one story of so many, and we at the Caring Society used these examples in our arguments before the Canadian Human Rights Tribunal to make our case that federal government laws were discriminating against Indigenous children in Canada. In February 2016, the court ruled in our favour. The settlement, it was estimated, could reach into the billions of dollars for the generations who had been discriminated against in the past. It was a stunning victory, but we're still waiting for a settlement.

As for the little girl, she was able to spend her final days in palliative care with the bed that allowed her some comfort. Who paid? The doctor did. Out of his own pocket.

It's stories like hers that illustrate how racism still exists in Canada. While I've witnessed racism firsthand by non-Indigenous people in Canada, in my view the worst offender may well be the government through its unwillingness to change its approach to decades- if not centuries-old problems. I had to change tactics and it took an unexpected source to make me realize this.

I'd been working for the Caring Society for about ten years when I traveled to India to, among other things, visit the home of one of my heroes—Mahatma Gandhi. I spent time at what I considered the museum's top five highlights, went to the gift shop, and then waited outside for my colleagues who were still on the tour inside. Within a few minutes, I found myself talking to the maintenance man who was on a smoke break.

"What do you do in Canada?" he asked.

I explained my role at the Caring Society. "I document all the inequalities between Indigenous and non-Indigenous kids. I suggest solutions. The government sometimes agrees but still does nothing. Then they ask for another report."

"How long have you been doing this?"

"About a decade."

"Let me get this straight. Every time you work with the government, you document the inequalities, you come up with solutions, they agree, they don't implement anything, and your response is to do exactly the same thing all over again?"

I nodded.

"Didn't you learn anything when you were in that house just now?" He paused and looked me straight in the eye. "Your conversation has to be with the Canadian people, not the government."

He was right. Governments don't create change. They respond to change. I'd learned the lesson from my heroes about talking simply; what I hadn't learned was *who* to talk to. So I started.

When I returned home, I immediately reached out to Canadians through speeches at a wide range of conferences for social workers, educators, lawyers, judges, and health-care workers. I was suddenly on the "speech circuit," and the audiences wanted stories and information and I was more than happy to provide them. I even spoke at the United Nations. And all the speeches led to interviews, lots of them, giving me even more opportunities to spread the word. It was difficult for everyone to understand that the inequities I outlined were actually happening because for so long they had believed that First Nations were getting the same benefits as everyone else. But the evidence started to mount.

It wasn't just about the present-day treatment of Indigenous peoples, but past treatment too. At this time, the Truth and Reconciliation Commission, led by Justice Murray Sinclair and others, conducted meetings across the country where thousands of residential school survivors shared *their* truth. The Caring Society took part in each event, bringing a stuffed bear—a child's stuffy symbolizing our spiritual leader, Spirit Bear—to each one. In 2015, the TRC released its final report, further evidence of the historical mistreatment of Indigenous people. In 2016, Gord Downie's *Secret Path* album taught us its own truth about Chanie Wenjack. Chanie was a runaway from a residential school who tried to walk hundreds of kilometres home along railway tracks in Northern

Ontario. He died trying to make it home. Slowly, attitudes have begun to change.

Now it's not only the writings of the great teachers of the past that inspire me to keep moving forward. It's the young people I've met along my journey who fight for the same advantages that their non-Indigenous brothers and sisters have.

Shannen Koostachin is one of many. Shannen grew up in Attawapiskat in northern Ontario. Attawapiskat is a remote Indigenous community on the shores of James Bay with a tortured past of bad water, alcoholism, drugs, and teen suicide, but thirteen-year-old Shannen was determined to see a different future. She wanted a new school built in her community to replace the portable trailers that had been placed on a toxic waste dump by the Canadian government. The site had been repeatedly condemned, but no replacement school was forthcoming. She took her fight to Ottawa, and I stood there on Parliament Hill on a clear, sunny May day in 2008 and watched as Shannen grabbed the microphone and challenged ministers and bureaucrats to do the right thing. She was passionate and strong and, as the cameras rolled, she pleaded for help:

"Just give us a school in our home. Just give us a chance so we can grow up and be somebody important."

Canadians watched. But nothing changed. The government said it didn't have the money. For them, they made it clear that a new school in Attawapiskat just wasn't a priority.

Shannen returned home, but she refused to give up. She chose to go to school off reserve in New Liskeard, Ontario, hundreds of kilometres away. She did it despite being terribly homesick, and whenever she had a chance to visit her family, she made the journey home and back.

On June 1, 2010, the travelling stopped. Not far from New Liskeard, Shannen was in a terrible car crash. She died that night.

In September 2014, Ottawa, perhaps out of guilt, made Shannen's dream of a new school a reality and found the money to create Kattawa-piskak Elementary School in Attawapiskat. Finally. But at such great cost. At the school, there is a plaque dedicated to Shannen. In 2019, a non-Indigenous school in Stoney Creek was named after her.

Shannen Koostachin is one of my heroes. Despite her tragic death, her dream of better education facilities for Indigenous kids continues to be acted on by children all over Canada. She inspired them, both in life and in death, to understand how inequities happen not only in education but across all different kinds of issues. And there are many more dreams still to be realized.

At the Caring Society, we host gatherings with Spirit Bear. The children think of them as teddy bear tea parties, but they are so much more than that. We believe that as the bear has been in the presence of all the stories about an era of terrible shame in Canadian history, it represents Indigenous children of both past and present. Today in our centre, children of all diversities arrive with their own bears and everyone brings books and we have readings, many of which discuss the challenges faced

In 2016, children who attended the Tribunal hearings made a beautiful book full of their drawings and wishes for a better future for First Nations children. In this picture, I am showing them the pages of the book and how much their messages mean to me.

by Indigenous kids. At these gatherings, the children express such a clear sense of fairness and understanding.

These children have something my generation of kids didn't have. They have us to make sure their voices are heard and amplified so they can make a difference. So in peaceful and loving ways they are getting involved. Over the past two decades, our kids have grown to be young adults full of passion to press for changes for First Nations kids and beyond. They are applying the same skills to fight for other disadvantaged populations and issues. That is the power of change.

There are times I think back to my first working days. Back to when I was twenty-one. Back to that home with the three little girls. Because there is a postscript to that story.

Their mom, as I learned a few months later, was a residential school survivor, although in those days we didn't know what that meant, what scars she almost certainly carried. In fact, there were still residential schools in existence the day that I took her kids from her. No one was talking about the impact the schools had had on her and on so many kids like her. Instead, across Canadian society there was a deafening silence. And there certainly were no services provided for those who were victims, as if the government didn't want to provide care because somehow that would recognize its own wrongdoing and complicity.

I often think about those three little girls and their mom, and I wonder what happened to them. It was probably the only decision that I could have made at the time, but sometimes at night I lie awake and wonder: "Was there something else I could have done?"

So while we've made progress, at least in the courts, there's still such a long way to go to ensure that court decisions are reflected in society. Some people say I complain too much. That I don't take time to celebrate even the small victories. And they're right. But small victories are just that. Small. I want big, meaningful victories that actually make a real difference. That's why I'm still fighting.

Cindy Blackstock is a Canadian-born Gitxsan activist for child welfare and the executive director of the First Nations Child and Family Caring Society of Canada. She was honoured to work with First Nations colleagues on a successful human rights challenge to Canada's inequitable provision of child and family services and failure to implement Jordan's Principle, a hard-fought litigation that resulted in hundreds of thousands of services being provided to First Nations children, youth, and families. A professor at McGill University's School of Social Work, she has a BA in psychology from the University of British Columbia, a master's in management from McGill University, a master's in jurisprudence in children's law and policy from Loyola University Chicago, a PhD in social work from the University of Toronto, and twenty honorary doctorate degrees. She has received over fifty awards, including an Atkinson Charitable Foundation's Economic Justice fellowship, a National Aboriginal Achievement Award, and an Amnesty International Ambassador of Conscience Award. In 2018, she was named an Officer of the Order of Canada in recognition of her leadership as a champion of Indigenous children and for her efforts to build a culture of reconciliation.

GINA CODY

The Power of a Name

At university, there were a few women in my classes, but looking around, it was a sea of men. Women made up roughly 10 percent of the students. There was always some skepticism about our abilities.

My birth certificate records my name as Parvaneh Baktash, but right from the beginning I was called Gina. I had big, dark eyes, and my relatives thought that made me look like one of the best-known actresses in the world at the time, Gina Lollobrigida.

I am the youngest of five children. My three brothers, sister, and I grew up in Iran in the aftermath of great political turmoil.

During the Second World War, the English and Soviets invaded Iran and forced the abdication of the Shah. Then, in 1951, Parliament elected Prime Minister Mohammad Mosaddegh, but his government was overthrown just two years later in a coup d'état organized by the US and the UK. My father supported the prime minister and, after he was deposed, went into hiding for a while to escape possible arrest. That's when my family moved to the capital, Tehran, because it was easier to go unnoticed in a big city. This was the world I was born into in 1956.

Because my parents had lived through such tumultuous times, they were focused on teaching their children survival skills, especially my sister and me. They pounded into us their understanding of life—for girls and women to survive, they have to be the equals of boys and men. My father often repeated a saying that taught me not to become a victim. It's more poetic in Farsi, but it translates roughly as "Your enemies cannot hit people until there are people who allow themselves to be hit."

My mother never finished high school, which she always regretted. She was married at sixteen and felt she lost a measure of independence. My father was a good man, but my mother hated the fact that she had to ask him for money. He would always give her the money, but that wasn't the point.

She wanted much more for me and my older sister, and she saw education as the path to a better, happier life. I remember studying all night for an exam the next day. My mother stayed up with me because getting good marks was important to us both and she didn't want me to fall asleep.

"Gina," she said. "I know you are suffering now, but you see your three older brothers? They can sleep on the street if anything happens. You cannot."

That's a very powerful thing to say to a kid. It brings tears to my eyes today.

My father was just as adamant, and his lessons touched every aspect of my life. Almost as soon as I'd learned to walk, he took me for swimming lessons. When I was five or six years old, my parents bought a bicycle for my sister. She's four years older than me, but my dad wanted me to be able to ride that bike too. It was too big for me, of course. I had to stretch for the pedals and reach up to hold the handlebars, but he taught me to ride it. Then he taught me how to ride a horse. And as soon as I was old enough to drive a car, I was behind the wheel. He always told me that I should be able to escape any situation I found myself in. The political upheaval he had seen really marked him. And he, in turn, instilled in me the unshakeable belief that a woman had to be as strong—and as capable—as a man to survive.

My mother's faith in education was almost instinctual. For my father, it was professional. He ran a private, all-boys high school. The message was clear from both, and as I grew up, nothing was more important to me than my schooling. I'll admit it got to the point where my obsession with school wasn't always healthy. I wanted to be first in my class, and I was very tough on myself. If a project or a test was graded out of 20, and I got 19, I couldn't sleep. I would cry. I never discussed my feelings with anybody, so I just suffered inside. That was my character. I studied all day and sometimes all night and ended up skipping a grade because I had learned a whole year's worth of lessons in two months at home.

When I was sixteen I was ready for university. I went to what is now called Sharif University of Technology. Often called "Iran's MIT" (Massachusetts Institute of Technology), it was the best school in the country for engineering and science. I was very good in math and physics—so much so that my father decided I should teach some courses at his school. The boys there were just a year or two younger than I was. At first my father sat at the back of the classroom to make sure the kids wouldn't give me a hard time. But once he saw I could teach, he left me alone with the boys.

"If you can manage these kids," he said, "you can manage anyone in your life. Just handle them." It was another of his lessons.

At university, there were a few women in my classes, but looking around, it was a sea of men. Women made up roughly 10 percent of the students. There was always some skepticism about our abilities. I remember an in-class physics quiz where everyone failed except one student. The professor didn't know the name of the person who passed; he just knew the student's ID number. He read it out, and I raised my hand.

"It can't be yours," he said. He asked me three times, to be certain. I then had to show him my student ID card. I know he wouldn't have done that with a male student.

In 1978, I graduated with a bachelor of science degree in structural engineering. I saw all the boys who were going further than one under-graduate degree, so I thought, "Why wouldn't I want that?" My parents had told me over and over again that I had to go as far as I could. They wanted me to get my master's degree and then a PhD. By then, I too was a firm believer in higher education and I wanted to study abroad.

I passed all the necessary government exams and was ready to leave Iran when there was a popular uprising against the Shah. The country was once again in turmoil. People were in the streets every day, fighting in a revolution they thought would bring them a democratic government. When the Shah was finally overthrown, I had all the paperwork done, and the permissions needed to leave the country, but I just couldn't. I de-cided to stay. I would rather be in the fire than watching it from the out-side. But after several months, the people's revolution became a religious revolution led by the Ayatollah Khomeini. I knew the role of women would be severely circumscribed, and I felt I had to leave.

Because I had graduated from such a prestigious university, I re-ally could have continued my education just about anywhere. But I had applied to only two schools: McGill University, in Montreal, and the University of California, in Los Angeles. Both accepted me. I had some friends in California and seriously considered going to UCLA. Also, I didn't know a lot about Canada. The strongest image I had of Canada was its United Nations peacekeepers—the blue berets. That stuck with me. I knew that anywhere there was trouble in the world, Canadians were trying to help. Canada was a country of peace. The only other thing I knew was that Canada was cold in winter.

Ultimately, two things made my decision. First, I had only two thou-sand dollars. I knew that would go further in Montreal than in Los Angeles, though it wouldn't be enough for my tuition in either place. And my brother was already living in Montreal. He had just graduated from Concordia University with an engineering degree.

I arrived in Montreal during the Labour Day weekend. I was supposed to register at McGill on the Tuesday, but my brother had mentioned me to one of his Concordia professors, who asked to meet me beforehand.

First thing Tuesday morning I went to see Professor Cedric Marsh from Concordia University. We sat down together in a room. He looked at the marks on my transcript. We talked for an hour or so. And then he said, "You should come to Concordia. I will make sure you get a scholarship. Why would you go anywhere else?"

He walked me to the registrar's office, showed them my acceptance letter from McGill, and said, "Write her a letter for Immigration Canada because I want her as a student." They typed it right up. Marsh told me to take it to Immigration Canada and get my work permit. Then I could start helping him with his projects. I didn't even know what Immigration Canada was, let alone where it was. My brother was waiting for me, though.

"What the heck happened?" he wanted to know.

"I'm not sure," I told him, "but here's a letter I have to take to Immigration Canada."

I was hyper-excited that somebody really wanted me. It didn't even enter my mind that Concordia didn't have the same reputation as McGill. To me they were equal. I got my work permit, and that very afternoon I started testing aluminum products for the professor because that was his specialty.

I loved the work. I would often stay past midnight, sometimes until 2 or 3 a.m. Then I would go home and come back at 7 a.m. I got paid by the hour, and so with my scholarship I had a pretty good life.

Concordia made me a teaching assistant too. They'd never before had a TA who was a woman in engineering courses. I was a novelty, but I was also a good teacher. My classroom was packed because I taught the material in a way students could understand. In engineering you can't memorize everything; you have to understand the underlying concepts.

As for the courses I was taking, there were even fewer women students than in Iran—I'd say no more than 5 percent. I remember hearing sexist

A close-up shot of me with the data acquisition equipment in the Concordia University laboratory in 1982.

comments all the time. But I would shrug my shoulders and walk away. If anyone said those things to me now I would be very angry, but at that time I felt I had a mission to succeed and nothing was going to stop me.

Concordia liked the idea of a woman doing well in engineering. When businesses came to see the campus or the engineering facilities, I was always asked to give the tours. I remember a brochure the school published, and I was in three or four pictures. I didn't think it was particularly noteworthy to be a woman in that faculty, but the school obviously did.

Although my days were busy and I was working very hard, I had time to meet another Concordia student, Tom Cody, who was working on his MBA. He noticed me probably because I had an office next to the student lounge where he hung out. He used to ask to use my phone as a pretext to talk to me. He knew a surprising amount about the history and geography of Iran—I remember he once started a conversation about a river in Iran. I thought, "How does anybody know about rivers in Iran?" He was well read, but I think he may have refreshed his knowledge to impress me.

My original plan was to finish my higher education and return to Iran. I thought the heat of the revolution would have dissipated by then, and there would be a democratic government in place. But it didn't turn out that way, and so going home was out of the question.

In 1981, after I graduated with my master's degree in engineering, Tom and I decided to get married. We tried to go see my parents first, but Iran was fighting a war with Iraq, and the country was in a shell. Tom was denied a visa. I went home alone, got the blessing of my parents, and was married a month later. I became a Canadian citizen shortly after that.

I began working on my PhD. My thesis was about designing buildings to be resistant to earthquakes. It was a subject close to my heart because there had been a terrible earthquake in Iran about a year before I left that killed at least 15,000 people. I finished my experiments and only had to do the write-up when I got a job offer from the government of Ontario. At the time my French wasn't that great, which would have been an obstacle to my progress in Quebec, so I welcomed the opportunity. I spoke to my thesis supervisor, and he said, "Gina, you should take the job. You can finish the PhD later."

The job was in Toronto, at the Ministry of Housing, helping to write the building code, which obviously tapped into my knowledge of how to make buildings stronger. I liked it. But I'm a very driven person, and before too long I wanted to do more. I had signed a contract with the government to work for two years, but only nine months in I got an offer with Construction Control Inc. (CCI), an engineering company that I had dealt with at the ministry. The government very nicely agreed to let me go, and CCI sent me to a small company they had just acquired, Stanford Engineering.

Going from public service to private industry was certainly different. The technical side of things was not difficult; now I was just doing more

Professor Cedric Marsh and me in the university lab testing steel structures with earthquake simulations in 1985.

consulting. A construction boom was starting in Toronto and our company was becoming very busy. The previous owner, who was the president at the time, would panic when we had a lot of jobs.

"Don't worry," I'd say. "We can handle it."

It wasn't that we couldn't do the work; he had just never tried to juggle more than four or five jobs. Now we had lots more. I would come in at seven in the morning with the coffee for everyone and get things ready. I reorganized the office. We hired and trained more draftsmen and inspectors. The owner began to rely on me. I was young and didn't yet have kids. And I had a very supportive husband. I'd stay late most nights and bring work home on the weekends. I knew that was how I would be accepted as a woman. And it paid off. When I joined Stanford Engineering, the company's revenue increased fivefold and the net profit at least tenfold within the first year.

I had a solid education and background, but I still had to learn everything as I went. There were just so many new experiences. Eventually I got into cranes and hoists. I didn't even know what cranes were; I had to learn from the president, who was retiring from the firm. He was the top guy in cranes and hoists, and for a year I became his right-hand person. I got to know all the clients in that time.

When I started doing crane inspections I was swimming in a pool inhabited only by men. Among the hundreds of crane operators there was not one woman. And they were adamant that they were not going to let a woman in—they didn't even try to hide that. They would tell me stories about past women who had somehow gotten into the group. The men gave them such a hard time that they would quit.

I remember a weekend I had to go to a construction site in Hamilton. The site had been shut down due to deficiencies in the crane and couldn't reopen until the crane had been inspected and approved. My husband, Tom, offered to drive me there, and then go out for lunch together.

When we arrived, I put on my overalls and climbed up the crane to do my inspection. Part of the process involves walking onto the boom. For obvious reasons, the crane operator isn't supposed to move anything, but this guy started moving it. I was startled at first, even a bit scared. Naively, I didn't think he was doing it deliberately. I thought, "What an idiot he is! He knows he's not allowed to move the boom because it's dangerous."

I finished my inspection and walked back to the operator, but I didn't say a word about the movement. Just "I'll write my report as quickly as I can." His smile told me everything I had to know about what he had done.

On the ground, Tom had noticed the boom move with me on it. When I told him I hadn't mentioned it to the operator on my way out, he was incredulous.

I explained that I wanted him to accept me. What would I have achieved by arguing with him? He thought I was going to be scared and

Here I am in 1992, on a crane for Stanford Engineering.

I was going to scream. I was betting that by my not getting emotional he would remember me and respect me the next time.

That was always how I operated. I was absolutely determined to say the right thing and not make mistakes. Otherwise, it would confirm what others expected of a woman—not just me but any women engineers. So my mindset was to ignore anything negative toward me and to just concentrate on my words and deeds. I knew I would have obstacles, but I was oblivious to them. I was going to make it. I was going to survive. That was all that mattered.

I was often the only woman present at industry association meetings. Whenever the question came up of who was going to take minutes, I would speak up immediately. I'd even offer to prepare the agenda for the next meeting. They'd agree, of course, and I thought that was great. The meetings became my meetings, and I came prepared. I would memorize the agenda, and I'd read every report three times so I would know every aspect of anything that might come up.

Still, I worried. Sometimes I would wake up in the middle of the night before a meeting the next day. I knew that I was going to meet people who were more experienced. Some were twice my age, and I would have to convince them to see things my way. That pressure was constant. But my preparation forced others to listen, and I earned their respect. Pretty soon, everyone in construction knew me.

I was very busy working, but three years after I left Montreal, I finally finished writing my thesis. In 1989, I became the first woman to earn a PhD in building engineering at Concordia. I was aware that I was the first, but I didn't feel any particular pride in doing something that made history. I was happy to achieve this academic pinnacle—to become Dr. Cody—something my parents had inspired me to do, but nobody else thought it was terribly significant at the time.

A little later that year, on the night of December 6, 1989, an event shook my world—and deeply affected many others too. A man shot and killed fourteen women at the École Polytechnique at the University of Montreal. Fourteen killed simply because they were women trying to become engineers! It would have been bad enough had the atrocity been committed by a deranged person who just fired at everyone, but he had separated the women from the men. It was a personal affront, and I felt distraught and frustrated that I couldn't do anything. It still burns at the back of my mind every single day.

We desperately needed more female engineers. Far too often, I was still the only woman in the room. I was at a conference once with 700 delegates and I was the only woman. The emcee opened the conference by saying, "Lady and gentlemen." It was actually funny, but it was also sad.

Meanwhile, Stanford Engineering continued to grow. We had gone from just five employees to thirty, and we were very profitable. The people in charge at CCI couldn't help but notice. They asked me to run other companies they owned until eventually I was managing more of them. I wasn't doing what you might call hard-core engineering. But I reviewed everything and had to know the subject matter. When there was a meeting, though, I was the engineer, not the manager.

Originally, the owner of CCI had given shares to a small group of engineers as part of their compensation. Over time, as they left, I bought their shares. You could say I was the last loyal employee—it came to the point where the only shareholders were the original owner and me. When he retired, I bought his shares too, and I became the sole owner. It was a big change on paper, but the workflow didn't change at all. I had already been in charge of everything.

Running a business and engineering are not exactly the same work. But engineering is common sense. If your table has four legs and you take one away, the table is going to collapse—that's common sense. The problem with a lot of engineers is they complicate things at the beginning and then they look for a solution to the complicated problem they've created. The same thing happens in business. If you simplify the business, you will succeed. Some people make it complicated for no good reason.

We weren't a giant among engineering companies, but we had a good company and our clients trusted us. Our customers were smart business-people. They watched their pennies and they watched our work. We didn't overcharge. We were honest. We earned their trust. It could take ten years to earn a client's trust, and I knew we could lose it in a day by doing one stupid thing. I was a control freak, still trying to avoid making any mistake. But it wasn't just my respect and reputation on the line. I knew it was crucially important to deliver on what we promised.

Many times a job would cost more than we'd originally quoted the client. Never ideal, but that was fine. We'd just do the work and do it well. And we'd finish the job at the price we'd agreed to. That was why we had what I called "forever clients."

Because I was running a strong and efficient company, I naturally made money, but I wasn't driven by that. I was a businessperson. I would look at every project and examine every invoice, even if there were thousands a month. I loved my job. I loved what I did and the trust that my clients gave me. Their loyalty was very rewarding.

By 2011, I had the ninth most profitable company in Canada owned by a woman. But there were still reminders that I was a woman. I can't count how many times my executive assistant would transfer a call to me and, hearing my voice, the guy would ask, "Can I please speak to your boss?" That kind of stuff never ended.

People often ask me if I went out of my way to hire women. I tried to set the same bar for men and women. I just thought the brightest should get the job. But it's true that I was probably more willing than other firms to take a chance on a woman.

I remember one of my engineers was doing some work at an apartment building. The superintendent there was a woman from Romania, an engineer who couldn't get work in her chosen profession in Canada. My employee took her CV and brought it to me. I read it and thought that maybe all she needed was someone to open the door of opportunity, just a crack. So I called her to come in for an interview the next day. I was so impressed I hired her on the spot. We no longer work together, but we keep in touch. To this day, every time she calls me she gets emotional and says, "Gina, you changed my life." But she was brilliant. I hadn't harmed my business at all by hiring her. I had improved it.

By 2016 I was ready to sell my business and retire. As much as I loved my job, I was tired. The pressure was relentless. I was reading emails at midnight. I was always "on." I knew it was time to slow down, but also I wanted to do something different. By then, I had two grown daughters: Tina, who is now a lawyer, and Roya, who has a PhD in engineering. It probably says something about the emphasis we put on education in our family that Roya once reflected, "I didn't know what a PhD was when I was a kid, but I knew I was supposed to get one."

I believe there are three chapters in life. The first is getting ready to do your life's work. The second is doing the work. The third chapter is giving back. I really believe that people who, for whatever reason, don't do the third chapter have missed out on something. I'm not just a taxpayer. I'm a citizen. I wanted to do something to earn my citizenship. I got a lot from Canada and I thought that it was only right to do what I could to acknowledge my debt and gratitude.

I thought about my education. One thing that always helped me was having a PhD. People in my industry may not have been willing to accept Mrs. Cody as an engineer, but it was impossible for them to argue with Dr. Cody. For women, education is the great equalizer and something I fiercely promoted. It was natural for me to look at how I could do something in this field.

I had maintained a close relationship with Concordia University. I had accepted their invitation to serve on the school's board of governors. So I began to think about how I could give back to this place that had been instrumental to my good life. More than being an option, I felt it was an obligation. Concordia changed my life and I wanted to change somebody else's life.

I also wanted to do something important for Canada. We are at the cusp of the fourth Industrial Revolution, and Canada is right at the centre of it. The first Industrial Revolution used water and steam power to mechanize production; the second, electric power to create mass production; and the third, electronics and information technology to automate production. Now we are in a digital revolution that is evolving so quickly that if we miss it we may never catch up. My particular fear is that if women don't get into STEM programs, if they don't learn science, technology, engineering, and mathematics, they will be left further behind. If Canada lets that happen, if it forgets about half the population, I don't know what this country will become.

I began a discussion with Concordia about what it would take to improve the future. I wanted to make a statement, but we weren't sure exactly what to do—something for inclusivity and diversity. After all, Concordia is a different kind of university. It's a blue-collar institution. You can work and get an education at the same time. People who go to Concordia tend to be go-getters, just like me. The students do not feel entitled; they work hard and they succeed. In that way, Concordia reflects what Canada is all about.

One day I started thinking about the John Molson School of Business at Concordia. It's named for someone who died in the nineteenth century. I thought, "That's a nice legacy." So I just threw it out. "What did it take for John Molson's name to be on that school?" That set off all the light bulbs.

It didn't take long for us to agree on the terms of my donation. The faculty was renamed "The Gina Cody School of Engineering and Computer Science." The most important word there is "Gina." When Concordia asked me what to call the school, I said, "People won't know the name Parvaneh—could be a man, could be a woman."

The message had to be clear: women can succeed in an engineering and computer science school. They are at no disadvantage. It takes brainpower, and there's nothing wrong with women's brains.

There is strength in numbers, so it's important for women to look around and see other women. I remember how hard it was to be the only woman in the room. Not long ago I gave a talk at an all-girls school in Montreal. I got very emotional, telling them they were strong and they were smart and they had to consider all the possibilities open to them for their futures. They see themselves as doctors or lawyers, which is of course progress from just a few generations ago. But they

*At Concordia's 2018 convocation as a member of the board of governors.
From left to right, Muthukumaran Packirisamy, Honorary Concordia University
Research Chair in Optical Bio Microsystems; Corinne Charette (Honorary Doctorate,
LLD 11), senior lecturer and former CIO of the Government of Canada; me;
Meyya Meyyappan (Honorary Doctorate, LLD 18), chief scientist, Exploration
Technology, NASA Ames Research Center; Nadia Bhuiyan, vice-provost,
Partnerships and Experiential Learning; and Amir Asif, dean, Gina Cody
School of Engineering and Computer Science.*

don't see themselves as scientists or engineers, and that has to change. Young women today are the luckiest generation that has ever lived in the history of the world. They are free to make choices about how their lives will unfold. They shouldn't be limiting themselves in any way.

I know the image of engineering students is still overwhelmingly male, and sometimes it's aggressively, even crudely, male. But that's changing in other ways as well. There's a group called "Queer Engineers Concordia" that supports LGBTQ+ students, and there are similar groups at other schools too. That was unimaginable not too long ago.

The Gina Cody School tells everyone that female engineering students will learn in a welcoming, respectful, encouraging environment. And that one day no one will find it at all unusual to see equal numbers of women and men with careers in engineering and computer science. One of the students said, "The name Gina Cody means opportunity for women." I think that's perfect.

Gina Cody came to Canada in 1979 and pursued a career in engineering at Concordia University, where she became the first woman in the school's history to earn a PhD in building engineering. During her tenure as manager and president of Construction Control Inc., the company was recognized as one of Canada's best-managed companies by the *Financial Post*. For her contributions to engineering and to women, she received an Award of Merit from the Canadian Standards Association and a Volunteer Service Award from the government of Ontario, was named an Officer of the Order of Honour of Professional Engineers Ontario and to the Order of Montreal, and was inducted as a Fellow of the Canadian Academy of Engineering. In 2020 she was named one of Canada's Top 25 Women of Influence. She lives in Toronto with her husband.

ROBB NASH

Second Chances

*I had to tell my story so that other people didn't have
to die like I did before they started to live.*

Childhood has a funny way of preparing you to be an adult, but it's only in hindsight that we understand it. Take my summer vacations, for example. I spent them in Greyhound buses, watching my dad drive hour after hour across mostly unexciting prairie landscape. I just sat there, in my free seat, staring out the window. We'd start in Winnipeg and drive east or west for a few hours. Say we went west, to Yorkton, Saskatchewan. When we got there another driver would be waiting to take the bus farther. Dad would nap while he waited for a bus to arrive to drive back to Winnipeg. I actually thought it was really cool. I had no idea that touring Canada from a bus would become part of my adult life too.

My dad didn't like his job, but he stuck it out because he had a family to support. For a long time, he used a calendar to count down to his retirement. He would cross off the days as they went by. I thought that was what life was: you found a job that you hate and you do that job until you can finally leave it.

In fact, it was worse than just not liking his job. I watched my dad sweat and shake and even cry on some days before he went to work. He was so nervous to have the lives of fifty people in his hands and worried about screwing up and having an accident. He always said, "I have nerve problems."

Mental illness was not openly discussed in those days, so now I have tried to explain to him that those were probably anxiety attacks. "No, no," he says. "Those were just nerve problems. Just nerve problems." Listening to people misunderstand mental illness became part of my adult life too.

I grew up in a tiny town in Manitoba called Kleefeld. My dad wanted me to play the guitar like my older brother Dave. That was the last thing I wanted to do, so I persuaded him to buy me an old drum set at a pawnshop for about a hundred bucks. I just banged away until, in grade five, I joined the school jazz band. My teacher gave me CDs to listen to so I could learn the drum portions. One was for the song "Stairway to Heaven" by Led Zeppelin. My brothers and sisters all grew up singing country and gospel songs. That sounded boring to me, but "Stairway to Heaven" blew me away.

Almost everyone from Kleefeld went to the same high school, just down the road in Steinbach. A week before I was supposed to start there, people from a private school, Mennonite Collegiate Institute, showed up at our house and offered me a scholarship. I was a strong, tall teenager who played volleyball, hockey, baseball, and football. I was never a super-star, but I was a good all-around athlete. I'd never heard of this school that wanted me, but did I want to go?

They brought me to the school for a tour. It was about an hour and a half from Kleefeld, close to the US border. I walked through a brand-new residence building that featured a lounge with pool tables, ping-pong tables, and a big space for watching TV. Very impressive. They told me I could live at the school. I thought, "I can move out from my parents' house at fifteen years old? Giddyup."

At this point, my place sitting behind the drums was like a second home to me, so I entered the music program at MCI. When I sat down to play for the first time, they put sheet music in front of me. It didn't take long for everyone to realize I didn't belong.

"What is this?" I asked. "Where's the CD?" They were giving me Mozart, expecting me to play the percussion parts. I had never really learned to read music (and I still haven't). Music ended up as my worst mark in grade ten. I was so deflated I quit the music program, but I taught myself to play the guitar and started a little band for talent shows.

In grade twelve we were asked to write down where we expected to be in ten years. I'm sure my fellow students wrote lofty goals like astronaut, doctor, professor, lawyer, teacher, engineer. I wasn't much of a dreamer. I wrote that I would be working at the Steinbach credit union. I thought I would get a job and count down the days to my retirement. I was so scared of the future.

Then came Wednesday, December 11, 1996. The school's Christmas social was scheduled for that night. In the afternoon three of my buddies and I went to a nearby town to buy flowers for our dates. One of my friends had just gotten his driver's license that week. He had his dad's car, a Pontiac 6000. The weather was awful. Freezing rain had shut down some highways. My best friend looked at the conditions, considered how inexperienced our driver was (not only new to driving but a city kid unused to country roads), and decided he didn't want to come with us. I convinced him to get in. My logic was one hundred percent teenager. "Come on, what's going to happen? Let's go."

We got to the flower store safely, made our purchases, and piled back into the car for the return trip. I was in the back seat, behind the driver. I can't tell you exactly what happened after that because I have no memory of it. I can only tell you what people have told me.

Most of the cars on the icy highway were going super slow, 20 kilometres an hour or less. We, on the other hand, were flying, passing cars like it was a sunny Sunday in the middle of summer. I was screaming at my friend to slow down. About half a kilometre from the school we pulled out to pass one last car. That was when we slammed head-on into a semi-trailer truck. The force of the impact crushed the front of our vehicle. The truck jackknifed. The trailer swung around and swiped the trunk right off our car. I fell back into the emptiness of where the trunk used to be.

My friends weren't hurt at all. They got up and ran because they thought the car was going to explode, like in the movies. They looked back and saw me lying there, not moving, blood pouring out of the side of my head.

Another person on the road that day, not far from the accident site, heard the thunderous crash. He was on his way home from work, planning to go to his son's Christmas play at school. He could have continued on his way; no one would ever have known. But he had just completed a course in first aid and decided to check out what had happened. He saved my life.

He immediately saw I wasn't breathing and he couldn't find a pulse. He began doing CPR to bring me back, and he succeeded. But when my heart began to beat again, the blood, which had stopped flowing, now resumed gushing out of the side of my head.

Somebody used the CB radio in the truck to call an ambulance, and my Good Samaritan started pressing my head together so I wouldn't bleed to death. He was squeezing my skull, using every muscle in his arms. I'm told he couldn't use his arms again for days after because he had exhausted them.

An ambulance finally picked me up and took me to the hospital. I was barely alive. My parents got the call no parent ever wants. "We're sorry to say your son has been in a serious car accident. You had better get here as soon as you can and bring your family." They were expecting the worst.

The doctors rebuilt the left side of my skull, and my right shoulder and collarbone too. I have a lot of titanium and stainless steel in my body today. When I awoke from my coma, my memory was gone. I didn't know who I was, where I was, or why my head hurt so much. They kept saying, "You're Robb. You were badly hurt in a car accident. You're in the hospital."

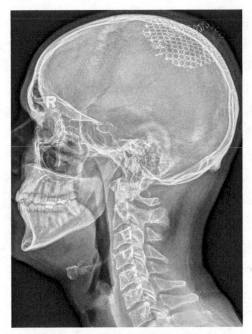

The doctors had to rebuild the left side of my skull. In this X-ray you can see the titanium on the top of my head.

There's about three months of my life I don't remember at all. I don't remember the car accident. I don't remember being in the hospital. I don't even remember coming home. I'm told I became very aggressive. The doctors warned my parents that somebody with a head injury could display new behaviours, and that was me. I would scream at my parents, which I never did before. My mother told me that I once tried to pull all the medical paraphernalia out of my head.

"Don't do that," she said.

"Leave me alone," I screamed at her, throwing in a few cuss words.

"Don't talk to me like that, I'm your mother."

"You are not my effing mother."

My old self would never have talked to her like that.

My memory picks up when I went back to school.

The doctors didn't want me to go back so quickly, but I just wanted to be around people. I was embarrassed, though, about my lack of memory. I kept a journal next to my bed because I was waking up in the middle of the night still wondering where I was and why my head hurt so much. I knew I had written something down, so I'd reach over for the journal. "You're Robb. You're in grade 12. You were in a big car accident and that's why your head hurts."

My visual short-term memory has never fully recovered. I can't retain a lot of what I see. If I try to read a book, page one is gone by the time I get to page five. On the other hand, I can enjoy watching a movie, then enjoy it again a week later because it'll be new to me.

Back at school I tried to disguise that I was having a hard time. I didn't want anyone to know I was in pain, and I just wanted to get on with my life. I had to finish a few classes to graduate, but I couldn't absorb any information from my textbooks. The Manitoba car insurance system paid people to read textbooks to me, which worked well. My auditory memory was firing perfectly.

After high school, there weren't many options for me. My mental state made university impossible, and I couldn't get a job because of my physical injuries. I moved back home. Three years had passed since I had lived in Kleefeld. My old friends had moved on. I couldn't play sports anymore—I wasn't even supposed to go into a gym. I felt so alone. Things got dark for me.

I was suicidal. I didn't want to be alive. I saw no future. I asked myself every day, "Why did this happen to me?" I didn't have an answer, but it seemed that everybody else did. People came up to me spouting clichés, trying to make everything okay. Some said, "It's fate. Those are the cards you were dealt. You had no choice in the matter." That made me angry. I don't have a say in my own life?

Some of my family told me, "God did this to you because you were bad." That also made me angry. What had I done to make God spank me with a semi-trailer? The line I heard most often was, "Everything happens for a reason." People said that with good intentions, but it didn't help. I was left to try to figure out the reason. More anger.

I hated life, but nobody knew. Not my friends, not my family. I was a big dude—6 feet 5 inches. People saw that exterior. They saw a guy who survived a terrible accident and they thought I was lucky, unstoppable. I put on a show, trying to be the fun guy. I was the loudest person in the room, always trying to be the life of the party. The truth was I was drinking to numb what I was really feeling. I was very good at putting on a mask. But that broke me. I'd get home, to my room, and feel even worse because I knew I was acting. I wasn't being myself.

Everybody thought the worst part of my accident was the physical injuries. Rebuilding my shoulder, rebuilding my skull. But that was nothing. They had no idea what was going on inside. We live in a society where men, especially, don't talk about their emotions. So I bottled them up.

I recognize now that I was obviously mentally ill. There's no other sickness like it. I felt I had nothing to offer this world. It's the lie in your head. People say suicide is a selfish act. But when you are suffering from mental illness, depression, suicidal ideation, you actually feel that the most selfless thing you can do for this world is to leave it. You actually believe that the best thing you can do for your mom and your dad is to take yourself out of their lives. You feel like a burden on the world, with nothing to offer.

I had a recurring nightmare that made me terrified to sleep. I'd see my own funeral, and no one was there. No one cared enough about me to come. No one cared if I lived or died. I couldn't shake that vision.

In my day, you didn't see many people cut themselves with a razor blade to self-harm. Instead, I smashed my fist through the door of my bedroom and sat there twisting my hand in the jagged hole until it was all cut up. It was just a distraction. I had a pain inside that I couldn't figure out. At least the physical pain I inflicted on myself was a pain I understood.

It was two terrible years before the shadows lifted. It happened after a conversation with my brother-in-law, Lewis.

"Robb," he said. "You think everything happens for a reason, right?"

I nodded. "That's what everybody says."

"Well, I know the reason you were hit by a semi-truck."

"Please tell me."

"You were hit by a semi-truck because you guys were going too fast on an icy road."

I know it sounds simple, but that's what began to set me free. I realized there was no mysterious force of nature playing with my life. I'm not a puppet. I get to make my own decisions.

Not long after that I was sitting in my car in a parking lot. I was watching rain hit the windshield, and I started to feel terrible about being so angry at life. I thought about all the young people who died every day, young people who didn't get a second chance like I did. I had done nothing to deserve my second chance, so I thought I had better make something out of it.

I didn't hear a voice telling me to go to Africa to build a well. But I did have an intense feeling that I should call the semi-truck driver involved in the accident. I wanted to tell him I was okay.

No matter how many times I asked the police for the driver's phone number, they told me they couldn't give it to me. Then one day a cop called and said, "I've done some research. The guy driving the semi hasn't been behind the wheel of any vehicle since that day. I'm not allowed to do this, and never say who I was, but here's the guy's number."

I dialed the number, and when the truck driver answered the phone, I told him I was one of the kids in the car. "I wanted to let you know I'm okay. I'm alive. I survived."

There was silence on the other end. Then, "I'm sorry about your friend."

I didn't understand. "Which friend?"

"The one who died," he said.

Then I got it. "No. That's me. I didn't die. I'm fine."

The accident hadn't been his fault, but he felt tremendous guilt nevertheless. He barely knew how to share his emotions with me. All he could really say was, "You don't know what this means to me."

It wasn't a long conversation, but by the time we'd hung up I think we had created an incredible bond. I know it did something for him, but the call did even more for me. For the first time in my entire life, it felt like I had truly done something for someone else. I had done something significant.

I wanted to have that feeling over and over again. Not just the feeling—I wanted to do meaningful things. I had to tell my story so that other people didn't have to die like I did before they started to live.

I had no idea how to get my story across to young people. Why would they listen to me? It didn't take a genius to see that every kid was walking around wearing earbuds or headphones, listening to music. I knew that was the answer. Music is a good way to tell a story.

I decided to start a band. There were five of us at first. I played guitar and was the lead singer. It was not an instant success. When people ask me today for advice on starting a project, I suggest they ask themselves why they're doing it. I tell them if you're doing it to be famous, you won't sign autographs for a very long time. If you're doing it to make money, to be rich, you won't make money for a very long time. But if you discover why you're doing it, you'll get through the days when there's nobody in the audience and no money in your bank account. And I tell them this is all from firsthand experience.

The first time our band got up on stage there were just four people in the audience. I thought, "Where's the crowd? This is supposed to be a life-changing event." But I knew why I was there—to tell my story. I said to myself, "I'm going to make this show count for those four people."

For a few years, I played in my band and we recorded music. Then I got a job as the morning DJ at a Winnipeg radio station. The owner of the station was an amazing man who became my mentor. We used the connections the radio station had with the music industry to help get my band a record deal. One of the managers there came up with a fresh name for us: Live on Arrival. Within a few months we had a top 10 song in Canada. Still, I was making no money.

Together with a team that the label put together, we started writing and working on songs for a new album. I wrote a song called "Hello Goodbye" (I know, I know—the Beatles beat me to that title, but I swear I didn't know that at the time). It was about a homeless guy I met at a soup kitchen. After writing that song, the head of the record label drove me to my hotel, looked at me with a smile, and said, "I'm glad you got this off your chest, Robb, but nobody on the radio wants to hear about homeless people. We need you to write hits." That was my first clue that maybe I wasn't going to fit in. However, that song eventually became our biggest hit. It went to number three in Canada.

We went on tour across the country. What a crazy way to live! I was twenty-eight years old, seeing a lot of musicians, with no family life. I didn't want that. It was fun watching crowds jump around, but I kept wondering, "When is this going to make an impact? When will this become meaningful?"

I was approached one day by a charitable organization to start playing at schools, just me and my guitar, telling my story while sharing their message. I thought, "There it is. That's how I can start to use my talents to make a difference."

I ripped up my record deal, my publishing deal, my management deal. Most people thought I was nuts. In fact, it looked like they were right when the deal with the charity collapsed, and I was suddenly on my own. But I had played at quite a few schools, and some called me back because I was getting through to their students. I added another guitarist and a drummer to form a new band.

The pivotal call came from a school in Ontario. "We've just lost a young girl to suicide," the principal told me. "In her suicide note we learned about a pact she had with another student. 'If you kill yourself, I'll kill myself.' We don't know who the other student is. Can you come?"

After my accident, I had to find something to live for. This is it, singing my story to those who need to hear that they are not alone. SUZANNE SAGMEISTER

I had never spoken about my own suicidal thoughts. But in my show I had always talked about never taking life for granted, making every day count because you never know what's going to happen tomorrow. I had been searching for a way to have a greater impact, and now there might literally be a life on the line. I felt this was my moment.

When I went on stage at that school there were the usual thousand students in front of me. One of them was about to kill themselves. The girl in the front row who wasn't smiling? The guy near the back who looked uncomfortable? Maybe the master of disguise, the one joking around with friends as if life were perfect?

The other members of the band knew the situation we faced, but I had never told anyone that I had struggled with thoughts of suicide. What I was about to do would surprise them as much as everyone else.

I knew in my heart I had to share that I was once in that desperate place too. I was terrified. What is the school going to think of me? Am I ever going to be welcomed back here, or to any other school? What are the students going to think of me? I opened up. "Somebody here is thinking about taking their life. I know what that's like. You're not alone. I was there once too."

As the words came out of me, I watched the reaction in the audience. I knew immediately I was doing the right thing. I just felt it. It wasn't weakness I was displaying; it was strength. Nobody would hide from their friends or parents that they have cancer. And you'd fight to stay alive. But not with mental illness. There's such stigma, you think you can't tell anybody.

When the show ended, a young girl walked up to me, pulled a note out of her pocket, and handed it to me.

"What's this?" I asked her.

"My suicide note. I was going to kill myself this weekend, but now I don't need this anymore."

I brought her over to the counselors at the school and simply said, "We found her." That was the first of more than 900 notes I've been handed after one of our shows. It's an incredibly intense experience every time.

I looked into the statistics and discovered that, in Canada, one in five teenagers has seriously considered suicide in the last twelve months. If that's the case, it meant that at every show, not just one person sitting in front of me was thinking about it but maybe dozens. That realization changed everything. Reaching out to those students became my mission.

At my next show I looked out at the crowd and said, "I know somebody out there is thinking about taking their own life. I was there once too." This time, I made the declaration with more confidence, more certainty that I could make a difference.

A young man came up at the end of the show to hand me his note. It was such a powerful thing when that happened, striking at my emotional core, but I thought, "Why do they have their suicide notes on them?" It seemed weird to me. I found out later from police officers I met at a conference that a young person's suicide note is rarely written at the last moment. They usually write the note two or three months before they take their life. They carry it with them and they wait for someone or something to push them over the edge. Or, and this is the important part, they're waiting for someone to reach out to tell them that they are not alone. That there is help out there.

We never know just how much we can affect people. I've met young people who have tattooed my song lyrics on their arms where they used to cut themselves. They cover their scars with my lyrics. It's the most moving thing I have ever seen, and I am profoundly touched that somebody could consider a song I wrote to be that important to their life.

I wanted them to know that they were just as important to me. I took the signatures from hundreds of the suicide notes I've been given and tattooed them on my arms. For me, they are a counterpoint to the many tragic suicides—the notes that don't get turned in. The signatures, which I get to see every day, are stories of victory and triumph. These kids are still here. It's a reminder to me that I've done something with my second chance. I don't think I'm the next Bono, but maybe one of these young people is, and I'll have played a small part in their life. More than anything, their survival gives hope to others that they can overcome their dark thoughts.

People often ask me what young people say in their suicide notes. I'll tell you what none of them say. I've never read, "I want to kill myself because my house isn't big enough and my car isn't shiny enough." What I do see, in almost every note, is some version of "I feel insignificant. I don't have purpose. I don't belong."

You know who's figured out how to give kids significance and purpose? Criminal gangs. They've infiltrated every middle school, every high school. They give kids a sense of belonging and purpose. They give kids a chance to be significant.

So, for a kid in trouble there are several ways things can go, and some

The tattoos on my arms are the many signatures from the suicide notes I've been given. These tattoos remind me of my purpose. JEFF GORDON

of them are bad. They could take their own life, join a gang, or become a criminal or a sex worker. We are losing some of the most gifted people to suicide and addictions. But if we can reach them first with a message of hope—give them a taste of significance, show them that they don't have to wait for rock bottom to start doing things for other people—then there is the potential for a positive ending.

It took us a while to figure out how best to reach our struggling youth. A lot of professionals are already doing amazing work. Our role is to show young people that it is okay to be vulnerable, to tell your story, to reach out for help. We tell the stories of people who have fought through the darkest times and are still here, making an impact on the world, and we bring survivors on stage to perform with us. That is a big part of what is missing in this war. We don't just talk about the tragedies; we balance those stories with the stories of victory.

I understand that musicians usually don't have good reputations and people are hesitant to let a guy like me interact with kids. But we have influence. And we can use that influence to help guide students to resources that are available. I get letters every day from parents, teachers, and counselors, letting us know that after our presentation a student opened up about their struggles for the first time.

I don't have the professional credentials to handle the ongoing counseling that an individual needs, but I have always made sure to have support staff with us so that follow-up help is available. We have partnered with the Canadian Mental Health Association, Kids Help Phone, and local resources everywhere we go. We take our shows very seriously. Our staff works for months before we come to each community, and we send videos to prepare both the staff and the students for the serious side, while getting them excited for a rock concert.

Have you ever had to keep the attention of twenty teenagers? For even ten minutes? We captivate thousands for about an hour and a half. We have a lot of bells and whistles—lights, smoke, and a ton of good music. I know that 80 percent of the kids at any concert are fine; they just want to be entertained. At the same time, I'm trying to get to the hearts of the 20 percent who are going through hell. That's a difficult thing to do. Teenagers can smell BS a mile away. They respond to us because they don't sniff it at our shows. I talk from my heart, explaining the meaning behind our song lyrics, and it sinks in.

Everybody is going to go through some tragedy in their life. It's a guarantee. I don't believe that things happen for a reason, but I think that bad things happen with potential . . . both good and bad. My accident had the potential to leave me angry, bitter, and suicidal for the rest of my life. It also had the potential to give me a story I could use to help other people.

Students react strongly to this, just as I did. "So," they ask me, "you're telling me that my dad's car accident didn't happen for a reason? That my sister didn't get cancer for some big reason?"

I try to emphasize that feeling alone and helpless doesn't make anyone unique. "Some people have a tough day and they just brush it off. Some can't. Some are like me. Some go through something tough, you wait until no one's around, and then you bawl your eyes out."

In these situations, we come to think we're cursed because we can't just keep going. But that curse is probably a gift. I've spoken at many funerals for somebody who has taken their own life. A mom or dad never tells me their son or daughter had nothing to offer this world, or that he or she was useless. It's always the total opposite. "She was so gifted, so empathetic." Or, "He was such an amazing artist."

We think we're cursed because we can't just ignore our thoughts. If you're like me, you hurt deeply. But you can see when others are hurting too. You have what I have, and it sucks. But you can help a lot of people with that depth of emotion. You hurt deeply, but you can also love deeply. I thought I was cursed by all my emotions. Then I realized I'm an artist. I write music. I am not meant to shut off my emotions. When I do, that's when things get dangerous for me. I am meant to channel my emotions into music. That's what I do.

A lot of the kids I speak to who feel this way are often people who feel deeply. I ask them, "I'm willing to bet you have a talent too—do you paint? Do you write poetry? Are you an entrepreneur?" I've talked to hundreds of thousands of young people. It's always my first question. If they're fighting their illness they might admit that, yeah, they paint—but how did I know? And I tell them, "I know because you're just like me."

It was always hard at the beginning. I'd see someone crying during a song or when I was speaking, and I thought I was seeing the tears of somebody breaking down. Now I realize they're the tears of somebody breaking through. That's a big difference.

Lots of kids write to me after they see a show. I used to try to answer every email, but it was impossible. Now, if someone is hurting at 4 a.m., they can text N A S H to 686868 on their phone and it goes directly to Kids Help Phone, where they can get anonymous and confidential help twenty-four hours a day.

We never charge for one of our shows. We will even pay for the school buses that drive the kids to the theatre or arena. We have a team that tries to find good corporate sponsors to provide the financial resources we need. For example, we found a transport company that pays for the gas in our tour bus. A tour bus that was given to us from a couple we had never even met before, who saw a show and said, "Never stop spreading this message." We have four small airlines that have provided our team with flights that allow us to perform on remote reserves. Or sometimes it goes the other way—they fly students from a northern reserve to a concert down south.

I'm not a role model because I'm a perfect person; I do this because I'm an example of a person who screwed up many times. I am flawed, and I'm willing to open up about my flaws. And I still have something to offer this world. My hope is that when people listen to me they think, "That guy has been through something tough, and so have I. He's talking about it, maybe I should too. He got help, maybe I can too."

We tour every school year from September to June. Our presentations are continuing to grow as we see many schools come together into larger venues because they have heard about the impact our tour has had on other communities or because they have seen us in the past. We play music and tell stories about the people we've met on this tour from coast to coast to coast, but we can't meet the demand. I know we can't reach every kid. That's something we have to deal with. No matter how many shows we do, there's still another community we can't get to. As a society, we have come a long way in the fight against mental illness, but there is still a long way to go and many more resources needed. And the suicide statistics keep going up. I still feel pretty helpless at times.

Then a woman recognizes me when I'm sitting at a hockey game. "Can I please see your arm?"

"Yeah, sure." I roll up my sleeve, and she starts weeping.

"That's my daughter's name there. I've always wanted to thank you for saving her."

Robb Nash and his band bring their presentation to more than 250 schools every year and have reached over one million students through school shows and social media, dealing with very difficult topics: bullying, addiction, self-harm, and suicide. Because of his work, Robb was named to the Order of Manitoba and received a Meritorious Service Medal from the governor general of Canada. When he's not touring, he lives in Winnipeg, Manitoba.

MOSES LI

On the Front Lines

Am I used to death? In a way, I am. But I'm always
affected by it. Nursing has forced me to recognize mortality.
We have a limited amount of time on this earth, but I believe each life
is valued and sacred. I don't know much about each person's life
before they come into my care, but I am part of their journey,
sometimes at the end. I appreciate that that is a privilege.

At the end of 2019, the world learned of a frightening virus wreaking havoc in faraway China. For me, a nurse at St. Paul's Hospital in downtown Vancouver, my life was about to change in a big way. I just didn't know it yet.

I was born and raised in Vancouver. My parents immigrated from Hong Kong in the 1970s, but they came separately. They met at a church group here, got married, and built a solid life for themselves and their children with careers in real estate.

I was always drawn to a helping profession. My sister Joanne is six years older than me, and she's a pediatrician. She's always been a presence in my life both as a big sister and as a role model. When I started university, I wanted to be a physical therapist, so I majored in kinesiology. My

ambitions bounced around a little bit, though. Physical therapist, paramedic, I even considered becoming a church pastor at one point.

I volunteered to do some missionary work in the Democratic Republic
of the Congo, and that's where I met a nurse who had just lost his pregnant
wife two weeks earlier and yet was working so hard, day in and day out, to
help those around him. His dedication and resilience were inspiring.

If a man becomes a nurse, there was once a stereotype that he's either
the burly psychiatric nurse who wrestles patients to the ground or he's
gay. But I saw nursing as a profession I was called to. I saw in myself
the characteristics that are important, even ingrained in nursing—caring
and compassion—and I don't think those things are exclusively feminine.

In my last semester at Simon Fraser University, I met my wife, Laura.
She was also a kinesiology major, and I may have put myself intentionally

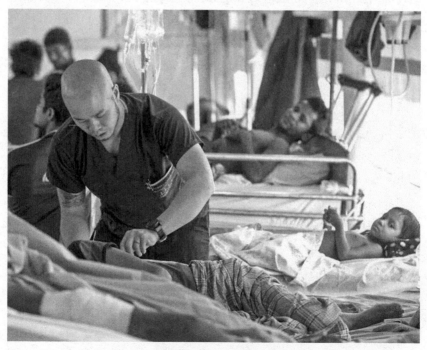

Tending to a patient on my missions trip to Bangladesh in 2017.

in her path a few times. We got married and then we both started our first year of nursing school. She went to Douglas College. I went to UBC. Laura comes from a family of nurses—her mom, her aunt, her grandmother. She pursued other options but ultimately felt led into nursing. It was like she was meant to follow in their footsteps.

By the time COVID-19 threatened in early March 2020, I had been a nurse for more than five years and had just become a clinical nurse leader, which is a leadership and educator role. On my second day in my new position at St. Paul's, the emergency operations committee met with all the hospital's departments about the mysterious new virus. My boss, in what now qualifies as a major understatement, said, "I think this COVID-19 thing is going to be a big deal."

By then, we knew it was a novel coronavirus that was highly infectious and much more lethal than the annual flu. And there was no vaccine to protect against the disease the virus caused, COVID-19. The great fear was that so many people would become infected, our hospitals would be overwhelmed and it would be impossible to treat the sick. Many people would die just because we couldn't take care of them.

Almost immediately, I started hearing references to war. It wasn't lost on me that there were parallels between being at war and fighting COVID-19. We had to adopt a mentality of pulling together, doing our part, and taking extraordinary measures beyond what we normally did. But at the same time, I was careful about using that metaphor. I didn't want to devalue what many people who experience war on a regular basis go through their entire lives. I'd seen firsthand what a "real" war was like.

It was late 2016. Just after Christmas, on our wedding anniversary, I flew off with my wife, Laura, to volunteer with an organization called Samaritan's Purse at a temporary hospital in Mosul, Iraq. As part of our Christian faith, we felt called to use the skills and training we received to serve and care for people in the world who were in greatest need.

By the time we arrived in Mosul, Iraqi troops had been fighting

ISIS terrorists for almost three full years. ISIS had blown the city apart. There was no longer any health-care infrastructure, and the Iraqi government had no ability to provide medical care for casualties of the war. Most humanitarian aid could not access the affected area at that time, but Samaritan's Purse had been in the region for six or seven years, so they were able to hastily build a hospital.

Most of us who responded had never been in a war zone before. Our own safety was a high priority, so we weren't able to start treating patients until we'd established a secure perimeter. We found this process distressing because we knew that people were suffering and dying while we were getting set up and thinking through safety measures; we were there to help, but we'd be effective only if we were properly prepared and not going to become casualties ourselves.

In Mosul, we thought we were going to be treating a lot of Iraqi military combatants, but it was mostly civilians, particularly women and children, who came through the doors of our hospital. This wasn't a war of soldiers fighting soldiers. It was soldiers fighting terrorists who were using civilians as human shields.

One minute we would be looking after a nine-year-old girl who needed an amputation because of a bomb, then the next a young, bearded male whom the security team told us to be careful around because he was probably an ISIS militant. Our policy was to treat everybody, but it was hard to maintain that neutral stance and be compassionate with people who were causing the worst injuries we had ever seen.

We heard that ISIS put explosive devices in boxes of what looked like food or children's toys, and we saw grievously injured victims of malicious violence. One morning when we opened the doors of the hospital, the first patient was a three-year-old girl who had multiple shrapnel wounds in her abdomen and a large injury to her leg. She had probably been pulled out of rubble and put into the back of a car for a long drive without any medical attention, because by the time she got to us she was in critical condition. Sadly, she didn't make it. We saw so many children like her.

It was a shock to even our most experienced surgeons. They had worked in trauma centres in big cities where they saw gunshot wounds and seriously injured people all the time. But here the patients came endlessly. In a single day, there were more trauma cases than a busy doctor would see at home in two years. There were many more deaths than any of us was used to. For Laura and me, it was nerve-racking to witness such darkness.

In 2020, our war against COVID-19 was different. For many people, combatting it meant staying in and enjoying the comforts of home. But there were very real consequences. I had a friend who was diagnosed with cancer. He got in most of his treatments before the pandemic struck, but the follow-up diagnostics were harder to come by. Some people would face the hardship of losing their jobs. Some people would get

With my wife, Laura, at the emergency field hospital near Mosul, Iraq, in 2017.

sick. And some would die. Without a doubt, it was a very grave situation, one that I felt ready to take on.

St. Paul's is an acute-care, teaching, and research hospital. It is home to many world-class medical and surgical programs, including heart and lung services, HIV/AIDS, mental health, emergency, critical care, kidney care, elder care, and numerous surgical specialties. The 4,000 of us who work here treat about 380,000 patients every year. It's a big place, with a lot of moving parts.

We knew COVID-19 was coming. The big question before us on that March day when the hospital's emergency committee met with all the department heads was: What do we have to change now to prepare? By then, the World Health Organization had declared a state of global emergency, and Canadian provinces and cities were on the brink of declaring states of emergency. While nothing would be resolved in a big meeting like that, by the time we wrapped up, every department had its marching orders. Everyone at St. Paul's felt it was time for action. The hospital shut down all nonessential health services—outpatient clinics and elective surgeries—and visiting was severely curtailed.

All the health-care staff had heard bits and pieces of information, and the coronavirus floated in the backs of our minds, but when the hospital instituted sweeping changes, that was when it suddenly became very real to us. We all said, "Oh, this is really happening. It's going to affect more than just people on the other side of the world. This is going to affect us and our families and our work."

Decisions had to be made within days but, strangely, despite being thrown into the deep end of my new job, I felt I had what it took to help make them. I became very involved in the logistics of how we were going to restructure the emergency department to anticipate the high volume of people coming in who were infected, or potentially infected, with COVID-19. What was the best way to treat them and also protect everybody in the department who would be in contact with them?

We knew COVID-19 was spread by droplets, either directly or indirectly. In that way, it was similar to the flu. Somebody coughs near your face and droplets get into your eyes or nose or mouth, or you touch a surface where the virus is resting and you get it on your hand and then you touch your face and get infected. The problem for us was that a lot of medical procedures we did routinely in Emergency could spread the virus. For example, a nebulizer turns a liquid into a vapor for patients to inhale, which helps a person with breathing problems (and we knew COVID-19 patients would often require help with breathing). But it can also diffuse the virus into the air. So that put our doctors and nurses, as well as other patients in the area, at high risk for exposure.

If we started to see our doctors and nurses get infected and not be able to come to work, then no matter how hard we tried and what policies we put in place, we weren't going to be able to provide the highest level of care. That's why we took infection prevention and control so seriously. It was just like setting up the security perimeters in Mosul.

At the outset of the pandemic, we were very worried about whether we had enough personal protective equipment (PPE). So in the name of conservation, we began reusing masks and gowns more frequently than we ever had before. We even started thinking about reusing masks more than once. That definitely raised the hairs on the backs of people's necks. Fortunately, it wasn't long before we were satisfied that we weren't going to run out of PPE and then we became even more careful. Normally we walked around in our scrubs. Now we made it mandatory to always wear a mask and eye protection. And whenever we provided bedside care, we donned full head-to-toe coverage that included a gown and a respirator mask.

We had our PPE, but what did our patients have to protect them? People still came into the hospital with other issues. They were still falling off ladders, breaking bones, having strokes. When someone came in with a heart attack or an overdose, we didn't want to save them from that but infect them with COVID-19 at the same time.

St. Paul's Hospital sees the vast majority of drug overdoses in Vancouver, almost ten times more than any other hospital. People come in high on crystal meth, agitated, combative, oftentimes spitting at security officers and medical personnel. We're really up close and personal with a lot of our patients.

We became highly suspicious of everybody who entered the hospital. We knew when someone had a drug overdose, but would we know if they also had COVID-19? The challenge was to provide care for this person without exposing everybody around them. If we were able to resuscitate the patient with the usual treatment, naloxone—the antidote for opioid overdose—that would be ideal. They would wake up and start breathing on their own again. But when they didn't respond to naloxone, we had to put in a breathing tube, which is considered an aerosol-generating medical procedure. If they had COVID-19, we were surely putting the virus into the air.

We were also accustomed to treating people with substance-induced psychosis. In other words, they weren't necessarily psychotic because they had a diagnosis of something like schizophrenia—though some did—but because the use of drugs made them psychotic. These patients required aggressive mental health treatment.

But once borders closed, the illegal shipments of fentanyl or carfentanil from the United States or China were limited. Drug prices went up on the street, which made people more desperate to get their fix. And drug suppliers began mixing more new substances into their supply than usual. That meant we didn't know what we were dealing with even more than usual.

In an emergency department, there is limited real estate. The distance between one person and the next is small, but we had to find a way to maintain a high level of care and not put everybody at risk. We needed more room. We decided to shut down our entire mental health ward and use that as extra space. Given that St. Paul's is located amid such a vulnerable population, it was definitely not an easy decision to make, but COVID-19 was deemed a bigger priority.

We also took space from our waiting area, which doesn't sound like a big deal, but it was. I remember being told about a woman who came in because she had a miscarriage. At the time, going by the book, her husband would not be allowed to stay by her side. But we were always asking ourselves just how strict we should be. In this case, we erred on the side of compassion and let him stay.

When I was involved with a patient who passed away in our department (from other causes, not COVID-19), we also strayed from the book. We took the deceased into a private room and allowed the family to come in and stay for as long as they liked. That was our normal practice, but we took extra precautions. Grieving by its very nature can be quite physical, so we gave everyone a mask, allowed them to hold the hand of their loved one, and asked them not to embrace each other if they could avoid it.

My eight-hour shifts stretched to nine or ten on most days. The first thing I did every morning was check in with as many of the night-shift doctors and nurses as I could. "Hey, how did it go last night? Did any big issues come up?"

Next I tried to deal with anything that was actionable. So, if it was a room that wasn't set up properly, or we didn't have enough of a certain medication, or a piece of equipment didn't work like it was supposed to—I tried to fix it. Then I could spend time with the bedside nurses, supporting them directly by helping them provide patient care, or indirectly by troubleshooting issues that came up because our department was running so differently from normal.

It was hard not to take work home. I found it difficult to leave any problems unresolved at the hospital. I couldn't just say, "I've clocked out. See you later." I answered emails in the evening and chatted with nurses on WhatsApp.

We were so worried about a wave of sick people coming to the hospital. Everyone desperately wanted to be prepared. We knew the next patient could very well be a member of our family. There was a sense of urgency I had never felt before, and a resurgence of pride in what we do.

It was inevitable, I suppose, that one of our staff would test positive. The first was a doctor. His symptoms weren't too serious, so he stayed home in isolation and recovered. I had worked with him and I had felt a little scratch in my throat, so I thought it would be wise to be tested. I was swabbed on a Monday and then went home to wait for the result. That was a tense time. The tests of health workers received priority analysis, so I had my result about fifteen hours later. It was negative, which was quite a relief. I went back to work that day.

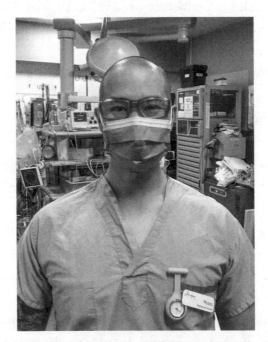

In the ER of St. Paul's Hospital in downtown
Vancouver during the COVID-19 pandemic.

My wife and I were very concerned about the safety of our son, Evan, who was almost two years old. Laura was also on the front lines, working in the intensive care unit at Vancouver General Hospital. She worked among critically ill patients, several of whom had tested positive for COVID-19. We knew that we were sources of possible infection for Evan, that he could become infected and, like most children, show no symptoms. But my parents helped us with childcare and they were in a high-risk demographic. I'm sure many families faced that childcare dilemma, but it was a special conundrum since both of us were health-care workers.

Even before the pandemic I always changed my clothes at the hospital before I came home. Now I became even more diligent about my routine. At the end of the day, I got out of my scrubs and put on my street clothes. When I arrived home I immediately undressed again, put all my clothes directly into the laundry, took a shower, then put on fresh clothes. Laura did the same thing.

At the hospital, I took on a new project—setting up an outdoor resuscitation zone. We erected a tent outside of the hospital where we could receive patients who had stopped breathing and needed a breathing tube. This was a high-risk procedure for exposure, but by bypassing the hospital's indoor resuscitation room, we could limit the number of people who came in contact with airborne droplets.

We did simulations and drills for a full week with doctors, nurses, and respiratory therapists. The goal was to provide the same standard of care despite all the precautions that we were taking, but it was very stressful for our team to have to throw on their full PPE suits, run outside with all their equipment while hoping they didn't forget something, and look after a really sick patient.

Some cases worked out well, but we soon concluded we were probably delaying patient care part of the time, so I helped renovate our indoor resuscitation room. We've now made it negative pressure. That means it has a ventilation system that allows air to flow into the isolation room but not escape (with any virus). There was a lot of clutter and things weren't set up very efficiently, so we also reconfigured the room to streamline our processes.

Once my work in the initial planning phase for the pandemic dropped off, I had the opportunity to spend more time in clinical practice at the bedside, providing direct patient care. Almost immediately I did CPR on a patient who came in with respiratory failure. The paramedics had found him overdosed, and we didn't know how long he had been unconscious. He didn't respond to any of the initial treatments or to our aggressive attempts to resuscitate him. It was just too late for him.

Whenever I witness a death, I take a moment to recognize that the body before me was a person. And they are no longer. It helps me process what happened, and I think it shows respect to the patient.

Normally, the medical team debriefed after a patient died. But now that had to wait. We had to shower right away and change all our clothes too. That had been drilled into us.

In the emergency department, you see people die more often than in other parts of the health-care system. Am I used to death? In a way, I am. But I'm always affected by it. Nursing has forced me to recognize mortality. We have a limited amount of time on this earth, but I believe each life is valued and sacred. I don't know much about each person's life before they come into my care, but I am part of their journey, sometimes at the end. I appreciate that that is a privilege.

We did lose patients to COVID-19, not in our emergency department but in the ICU after they'd come through Emergency. We wouldn't usually know the fate of a patient once they moved to another unit, but now we got updates because if a patient was confirmed positive we wanted to be sure that everybody who came in contact with them was aware.

Thankfully, British Columbia, whether through good planning or good luck, never really encountered a huge surge of patients. The fatigue we all felt was real, though, in part because we were bombarded with changes. The constant mental barrage of new emails telling us of another new policy raised anxiety and stress. For people who had long careers doing things in a certain way, it was very jarring to be told that everything they knew and everything they had been doing up to this point was not enough to save their patients and protect themselves. It made for a high-pressure workplace environment.

We worked hard to try to protect our mental health. At the best of times, we dealt with a lot of stressful things, such as abusive and violent behavior in the community, and that didn't change. If anything, we saw an uptick in violence-related injuries coming to Emergency—more stabbings, that kind of thing. People came in a lot edgier, and we often bore the brunt of it. But the usual ways our staff coped with the pressures of the job—things like going to the pub for a beer or to the gym—weren't accessible. So we started talking about how we could support each other more on the inside.

The importance of being there for one another is the big lesson we'll take away from this experience. I saw people break down every single day. Even as we tried to look after patients, there were tears. We had to keep each other's morale high. We had to realize that everybody was going through the same experiences and the same emotions. It wasn't about who was tougher or who was abler to handle this kind of stress. It was about seeing when someone was low and picking them up.

I've always wanted to help others—it's why I do this work and it's why I became a nurse. Each experience has given me the opportunity to make a difference. But being a clinical nurse leader during this crisis has taught me how important it is to invest in the people I work with. You can't just tell people what to do, you have to invest in your colleagues and trust them; otherwise we won't last at all. You have to empower them to do what they already do so very well.

When the pandemic started, I think most of us realized it would be difficult, but we would eventually go back to some kind of normal. Now I think we've come to understand that we'll never go back to what used to be. And that's not necessarily bad. COVID-19 has given us an opportunity to find better and more effective ways to do things, and in that way, the pandemic could be a catalyst for positive change.

But what I hope stays the same is the camaraderie and the surge of community support. That's going to be even more important at the other end of this.

Moses Li is a registered nurse in the emergency department of St. Paul's Hospital in Vancouver, where he provides medical care to an inner-city population as an emergency registered nurse. He has done volunteer humanitarian work in the Democratic Republic of the Congo, Thailand, the Philippines, Iraq, and Bangladesh. He lives in Vancouver with his wife, Laura, and their son, Evan.

NADINE CARON

Trust

*When I chose my path, there was not a single female
Indigenous general surgeon in Canada. That fact made my decision
different, even groundbreaking, but with it came sharp reminders
about the divide that still exists within our country.*

I remember exactly where I was when I decided I wanted to be a doctor. It was in a hospital in Jackson, Tennessee, thousands of kilometres away from my hometown of Kamloops, British Columbia.

It was all because of basketball. I was playing for the Simon Fraser University women's basketball team in British Columbia and we had played our way into one of the American university championships. We were amazing. One of the best teams not only in Canada but in North America. But even at twenty-one years of age, I knew I wasn't going to play basketball forever.

At the time, our team's corporate sponsor was the Hospital Corporation of America (HCA) and, coincidently, I had been looking into a possible career in the health-care system. So when one of their representatives, Jimmy Anderson, offered any of us a trip to Jackson, Tennessee, to visit one of their member hospitals, I thought about it and eventually said yes. Not long after, I found myself following a surgeon by the name of Dr. Tom Edwards to the operating room of that hospital in Jackson for an emergency surgery.

Just before we walked in the doors of the OR, he turned to me. "Have you ever seen a lot of blood?"

"Only during the odd injury on the basketball floor," I offered.

He quickly added, "Have you ever seen anyone die?"

"No," I answered, but that's a question, no matter the answer, that makes you pause about what might happen next. Still, I was intrigued. I wanted to go ahead with this new adventure.

The operation was for a ruptured aortic aneurysm. It was a critical surgery, one that doctors call a "Triple A," and it carried a high mortality rate, which explained the question about whether I'd ever seen anyone die. The operation lasted quite a few hours, and it was well into the night before it was over, but it was successful and, for me, time had raced by. The whole experience played in my mind as I went to the scrub room and washed off the blood. Dr. Edwards's warning had been right—there had been a lot of blood, and even as a witness I still got some on me too. But he had stayed so calm, so focused. I was absolutely enthralled by what I had witnessed. I reached for some paper towel to dry off. Then I stood there for a moment before reaching back to the towel dispenser. I took an extra strip, took my pen out, and wrote: "I *found* it. This is what I want to do."

I didn't just want to be a doctor; I wanted to be a surgeon.

But there's another important detail about that moment. I was a young woman, yes, but I was, and am, also Indigenous—Ojibway, to be precise. And that day when I chose my path, there was not a single female Indigenous general surgeon in Canada. That fact made my decision different, even groundbreaking, but with it came sharp reminders about the divide that still exists within our country.

*Here I am, number 25, with the Simon Fraser University women's
basketball team, holding up the District Championship title. Our win meant
that we were on our way to the NAIA National Tournament.*

I felt the pressure of being first from the beginning when I arrived
at university to study medicine. Being first carries a particular weight
in my family. My mother, Mabel, was the first person on her reserve
to graduate from a residential school, but I've never stopped learning
about the horrors that Indigenous children faced during that experience. The hard times, not being allowed to use their own language, and
the separation for months on end from family and friends. So I realized
that being first must have come with a heavy burden. I knew I was pi-
oneering a path for Indigenous women.

Every student in medical school feels the pressure to succeed, but for
me there were other pressures as well. On nights before major exams,
I asked myself, "If as the 'first,' I don't make it through, what are they

going to think of other First Nations people coming along, or even more generally, what are they going to think of other women?" The thought unsettled me. I worked hard, extremely hard, to keep my marks up. "Do I deserve to be here, or am I only here because I am First Nations?" This question rang in my head constantly, from the University of British Columbia to the University of California, San Francisco, to Harvard. I studied even harder, achieved marks as close to a hundred percent as possible, and earned awards, degrees, and fellowships at these schools, but that nagging thought never left me. Even today. What carried me through was realizing that the most I could do was my very best.

After I graduated from medical school, I went on to do my surgical training, which took me to different hospitals across the country. One day, I was sitting in the surgery lounge, a place for staff to take a break during what can be a very hectic pace, when a doctor came in who had just finished performing a long surgery. He was sweaty and drained from what he'd just been through, a feeling I was familiar with by then.

After he sat at our table, he said to no one in particular, "If I never operate on another Indian it will be too soon."

It wasn't the first time I'd heard a racist comment, but I wasn't expecting it from a doctor. It was hard to hear. It was awkward to sit there. I was angry and had an instantaneous gut reaction to strike back. My mom had always taught me not to do or say anything right away in such circumstances, but to count to ten first. It was good advice. I had used it often, but not this time.

I spoke out, firmly and directly. "If you don't want to operate on an Indian and get paid, then you certainly don't want to eat with an Indian for free."

And with that, I stood up, put the things on my tray, and walked to an empty table on the other side of the room. Slowly, one by one the other people who had been sitting with me also got up and moved over to join me. Finally, I looked over and saw that the offending surgeon was sitting alone.

Nothing more was said that day, and we all went on with our training for the weeks and months that followed. Eventually I went to another hospital as part of my training.

By 2005, I had been in residence in a lot of places—Victoria, Calgary, Vancouver, Kamloops, Edmonton, Boston, Memphis, and San Francisco, to name just some. I decided to begin my surgical practice at the hospital in Prince George, the largest city in northern BC, with one of the highest First Nations populations in the province. I saw a lot of different patients, and while I was Indigenous and incredibly proud of my heritage, unless I was wearing traditional clothing, such as a First Nations–styled scarf, most of my patients didn't notice my heritage, and if they did, they weren't fazed by it. In more than twenty years on the job, I've never had a non-Indigenous person show any pause with my treating them, though that hasn't always been the case with Indigenous patients.

One day, an elderly woman in her eighties walked into my office. She was First Nations, and she had come a distance to see me.

"What First Nation are you from?" I asked.

Here I am in the OR at the University Hospital of
Northern British Columbia in Prince George, BC. TIM SWANKY

She answered that it wasn't far from Prince George. She seemed nervous so I tried to calm her. "I'm Anishinaabe," I replied. "From the Sagamok First Nation."

She paused. And then she started to cry.

"I never thought I would ever, *ever*, see the day when I could come to talk to an Indian doctor. It's been eight decades." She wiped her eyes. "You've got to meet my granddaughters. You've got to come to my community. You have to tell them that *this is possible*."

It was an emotional moment. I teared up. I tear up even now when I think about it, because it captures the reality still faced by so many Indigenous women and girls.

After a minute or so, we talked about what brought her in. As I looked at the chart from the referring physician, I noticed all the blanks, all the standard procedures she'd never had. We proceeded to talk about her past and the fact that she'd rarely seen a doctor in her life. I explained mammograms—she'd never had one. I raised other procedures that were commonplace for non-Indigenous Canadians, but again she'd never experienced any.

That encounter taught me an early lesson, one I try to pass on to my colleagues in Prince George, Vancouver, and the other cities across the country where I'm often invited to lecture. As a relationship develops between a patient and a doctor, nurse, dentist, pharmacist, midwife, or any health-care professional, its success is based on trust. As doctors, we have an immense honour. People we've never met before come to us because they are worried or afraid about their health. And sometimes they are in pain. But we enter into this relationship as strangers, and we need to develop a level of trust with each other so that we can help them. In doing so, they can help us. Together we are a team and we both have to be in it, *all* in it.

It's not just the skill of how we use a scalpel; it's not just what we hear with the stethoscope; it's not just how we read the X-ray. It's putting all of that together and also being culturally aware so that anyone of any background feels comfortable coming to our offices, clinics, and hospitals, and knows they are going to be respected. That may sound obvious, but it's not. In fact, sometimes it's far from obvious because when it comes to Indigenous people in Canada, as physicians I think we fall short on trust, understanding, and respect, on creating a culturally safe environment.

Sometimes that's because of the fear many First Nations individuals have when they enter the health-care system—whether it be for a screening, treatment, or follow-up appointment—that they won't receive care that comes with an understanding of what they have been through.

Let me explain with an example from my family. My mother and I have a special relationship of honour and respect. Growing up, I loved nothing more than following her around and learning from her work. When my daughter, Aliah, was born, I knew I wanted to foster that same relationship. She's often close by my side, whether I'm in the lecture room, boardroom, or almost any room in a hospital. We are inseparable. And we talk about everything, just as my mother and I do, and I learn as much from Aliah as she learns from me.

When Aliah was four, we spent the summer preparing her for the fact that she would soon be going to kindergarten. We even went by the school she would be attending and saw the playground the kids would use. She was pumped.

But one day, when I was driving her to her daycare, I looked in the rearview mirror to check her in her booster seat and I saw tears rolling down her cheeks. I pulled over and parked.

"Aliah, what's going on? What's the matter?"

Aliah turned back and pointed toward a development we had just passed. It was under renovation. All the trees had been cut down, and only a partially constructed house was standing. It was a mess of broken windows, torn siding, and piles of dirt.

"Is that where I'm going to school?" she asked.

"No, Aliah, that's not the school. I showed you the school the other day, the one with the playground."

"Are you sure? Are you going to be allowed to see me?"

"Of course. Why would you say that?"

But she wasn't convinced. The questions kept coming.

"When you drop me off at school will you be allowed to pick me up? Will you still come when school is over every day?"

That was when it finally dawned on me what was happening. All the times my mom and I had talked about her experiences at a residential school, Aliah had been listening. And she had heard the stories reported on the radio while we were at home or driving in the car. She had consumed it all, and now, in the back seat of the car at the side of the road after passing that ugly mess just out the window, it was all coming back.

It was an eye-opener for me. I hadn't gone out of my way to teach her this part of Canada's history, a part of our family's history. I had wanted to shelter her from it, but suddenly I realized that I couldn't. And I shouldn't, because every Canadian needs to know our history—both good and bad. Even though Aliah was just four I should be able

My mother, Mabel, and my father, Zefferino, with Aliah in Kamloops.

to trust her to understand what she's hearing and seeing, just as my mother had understood what she had witnessed in real time. After all, it hadn't defeated her; she emerged as a powerful woman from that awful experience.

Nor should we in the health-care system shelter ourselves from these truths. Aliah was afraid of how she might be treated just from hearing these stories from the past. That should be enough, but imagine being my mother and actually experiencing it. When an Indigenous patient, no matter their age, no matter what they've been through, walks into a hospital, they should be treated with respect, not judgment or presumption.

Even at four years old, Aliah was teaching me.

This is where trust begins. Remember that doctor from my training days? Four years after that incident, I found myself working in a different hospital, and I noticed that he was there too. One day, during a slow moment in our area, he approached me and asked if we could talk. It had been so long since that day in training that I assumed he wanted to talk about our current work. But that wasn't what he wanted.

"I want to apologize," he began.

"For what?"

"Do you remember that day?" he asked.

"Sure I do," I replied.

"I want you to know I'm sorry."

"But what are you sorry for? Are you sorry for hurting my feelings?" I was testing him, testing his sincerity.

"Well, that's just it, Nadine. If I had apologized four years ago, I don't think you ever would have really accepted it because what I did was so much bigger than just the words I said. I've never stopped thinking about that day. Since then, whenever I see a patient who is Aboriginal, I catch myself. I think about what I said and just how wrong it was, everything about it— my assumptions, my biases, my stereotypes, and the racist way I thought."

I had to catch my breath. His apology was so transparent and honest.

I received an honorary PhD in science from Simon Fraser University in October 2019. Here I am speaking at the ceremony. COURTESY OF SFU

He was older than me. He was more experienced than me. He could have just let it go. But he didn't. He thought about what he had done, sat with it, and apologized. And the way he said sorry and the emotion he had left me with no doubt it was genuine. It was, in a word, courageous of him.

I accepted his words. I accepted his apology.

For a long time, I have thought about what my takeaway from that whole experience should be. This is what I've concluded: It's that his apology is the apology Indigenous people in Canada are waiting for from their government and from their fellow citizens. I don't know how we get that apology. I don't know what form it takes or who makes it and to whom. But I know it has to happen. It happened to me that day. It took four years, but it happened, and it will last my lifetime.

In 2008, Prime Minister Stephen Harper apologized in Parliament on behalf of the Canadian people. It was appreciated, but what I'm looking for is something that's somehow deeper, more personal, and therefore more meaningful—like that doctor.

When and if that kind of national apology comes, like my experience, it needs an equal and opposite reaction. Because it's not just the responsibility of people who have made mistakes to say they're sorry, to be remorseful. It's also the responsibility of those who have been hurt to be open to it, to accept it, and to move on together. For Indigenous people in Canada, if we point the finger with only a closed heart, we won't move anywhere. Reconciliation is a two-way street.

Today that kind of incident rarely happens to me, at least not directly. In the hospital, I'm protected by western measures of success. When you wear the white coat of a doctor, people don't say racist things to your face. When you have initials after your name, they can't say, "Oh, what stupid Indians." Or "Those First Nations, their graduation rate, they can't even get out of high school." But I still hear about similar situations. I still hear it because every day I have Indigenous patients come through my door and they share their stories with me. They don't wear white coats, and they may not have initials after their name. They hear the slurs. And they aren't protected.

It's easy to look at me and focus on the good I'm doing breaking down barriers and making a way for others to follow. And while I'm proud to be the first Indigenous female general surgeon in Canada, the distinction comes with another side, a darker side. Being first is a very lonely place to be because "first" also means "only." It's not right that we are placed there with the burden of responsibility of all on us when, in truth, the responsibility of being first also rests on our institutions.

I'm very thankful for what UBC did for me and is now doing for other Indigenous students, but I believe that they should only celebrate my being their first First Nations female medical school graduate if they also recognize the fact that they had never had such a graduate in the past. After all, it is one of the oldest schools in the country, and it took until 1997 for this distinction. And they are not the only ones. Many other universities and colleges need to acknowledge the decades-long gap. I appreciate that UBC, since my graduation, has taken steps in that direction. Our society needs to acknowledge its failures. Our country needs to accept responsibility.

Every day that I go into work, I'm reminded what an honour it is to be a doctor, especially a surgeon. It's an honour to develop a relationship with a patient. Whenever I am about to perform major surgery, I have a very special moment with the person who is placing their life in my care. Before I ask the anaesthetist to administer the drugs that will put the patient to sleep, I hold their hand and look into their eyes. Sometimes I see fear. Certainly a bit of anxiety, which is normal. But I also see something else. The thing I'm really looking for.

I see trust.

Nadine Caron is a general and endocrine surgeon at Prince George Regional Hospital, an associate professor in the department of surgery at the University of British Columbia's Faculty of Medicine, and an associate faculty member at Johns Hopkins Bloomberg School of Public Health. While completing her MD at UBC, she was recognized as the top-ranked student. She holds a master's in public health from Harvard University, a postgraduate fellowship at the University of California, San Francisco, and two honorary degrees. In 2014, she was appointed codirector of UBC's Centre for Excellence in Indigenous Health, and in 2016 she received the Dr. Thomas Dignan Indigenous Health Award from the Royal College of Physicians and Surgeons of Canada. She is a member of the Sagamok Anishnawbek First Nation. She lives with her husband, emergency medical doctor Patrick Turner, and their daughter, Aliah, in Prince George, BC.

PAT DANFORTH

Who I Am Now

Because of my disability, I became a whole new person.
One who could lift themselves from their chair to a toilet and back,
who could steer straight, who could dream of a future again.

All over my house, I have a lot of pictures and sculptures of mermaids because I think we share a connection. Neither of us can walk on dry land, but we both have adapted to our circumstances.

Everybody remembers their twenty-first birthday. It's a milestone that signals adulthood, and for me, a young woman living in Calgary in 1970, that was even truer because I was finally of legal voting and drinking age. Needless to say, my birthday was a big deal, though, as it turns out, not for those reasons.

I had two invitations for my birthday: dinner out in Calgary or a baseball game in rural Alberta. Thinking I should do something different to mark my special day, I chose the baseball game.

It was a beautiful Sunday in May, and we three girls piled into the front seat of the car, a shiny, white convertible. One friend drove, another sat in the middle, and I was happily by the passenger door. Of course, back then, there were no seatbelts.

We were driving along a gravel road, chatting up a storm, not a care in the world, not another vehicle in sight, when suddenly we began to spin out of control. As we went around and around, I bumped up against the door handle. The door sprang open, and I flew out. Everything happened so fast. I remember hitting the ground hard, then bouncing and rolling. The next thing I knew I was in a ditch.

I don't know how much time passed after that, but I vaguely recall people floating around me, including a woman who assured me that an ambulance was on the way. I tried to move my left arm, but when I couldn't, I thought, "It must be broken." Then I tried to sit up. I couldn't do that either.

"How are my friends?" I asked, hoping they were all right. Fortunately, they were. The driver had some bruises on her thighs, and the girl in the middle didn't have a scratch.

We were about three hours from Calgary, near the town of Taber, when we'd had the accident. The ambulance took me to the Taber hospital, and then I was transferred to the intensive care unit at Foothills Hospital in Calgary. There I was completely immobilized: I was put into a special bed that rotated to turn me upside down from time to time so I wouldn't develop bedsores.

I knew my back was broken, but oddly that prospect wasn't nearly as scary as it should have been. I thought everything broken could be fixed. After all, this wasn't the first time I had seriously hurt myself.

I grew up with my two sisters and brother on the Canadian navy base in Esquimalt, BC, near Victoria. My dad was a navy man, and in 1953, when I was four, he had just come back from the Korean War. I thought the navy would take us to all sorts of places around the world, but we were really settled on the west coast and, to my disappointment, the navy never sent us anywhere.

One late summer day, my mother was busy doing laundry. We had a wringer washing machine, which was state of the art for that time. It had

Here I am at two and a half years old on the porch
of our house on the navy base in BC.

a tub that cleaned the clothes and at the top was a wringer—two rollers that squeezed the water out of each piece of clothing as they were passed through. Basically, what the spin cycle of a modern washing machine does, so there was a good deal of pressure between the rollers.

After my mother had wrung out the clothes, she went outside to the clothesline. Meanwhile, I decided to help by washing up with a face-cloth. When I was done, I started to put it through the wringer. At first, I pushed it toward the rollers with my left hand, but it didn't go through, so I put the cloth in my right hand and tried again. That's when my hand got caught between the rollers.

I pulled furiously to get my hand out. When I finally succeeded, my index finger and the tops of the rest of my fingers were in the washing machine.

The next few hours are a little fuzzy in my memory. Fortunately, our house on the base was pretty much right across from the RCMP detachment. My mother carried me there, and the police drove me to the hospital. I remember sitting in the back of the police car and being bothered by the loud siren. "Could you turn that off?" I asked. "I don't like that noise."

I was very lucky that Dr. Gordon Grant was at the hospital. He specialized in hand reconstruction. While there was nothing he could do to save the index finger, he did save the rest of my fingers to the first knuckle. The fact that he didn't amputate my whole hand became very important later on after my car accident.

As I got older and my hand grew, I was in and out of the hospital for skin grafting. I was there so often that the nurses extended a real privilege to me and let me see the new babies in the nursery. For two weeks every summer, I went in for surgery and came out with a cast that I would have to keep dry for the rest of my holidays, which meant I had to swim with my right arm out of the water. My mother used to laugh and say that she could always tell it was me in the water—I was the kid with her arm straight up in the air.

She was good at seeing the humour of the situation. The truth was that my hospital bills were taking a financial toll on my parents. There was no Medicare at the time, and we were far from wealthy.

One of my earliest memories is when my dad first came back from Korea and found out that my mother had been buying food on credit. She just didn't have enough money to do it any other way, but my dad was angry. "You should never use credit to pay for food," he said. That stayed with me, and to this day I never have.

By the time I graduated from high school, my hand surgeries were over, but my family still didn't have a lot of money.

My parents told me, "We can't afford to send you to university."

None of my siblings had been able to go to university either, but I was disappointed. I wanted to become a kindergarten teacher. One of my favourite memories was when I was learning how to tie my shoes in kindergarten. I couldn't use the fingers on one hand, but my teacher worked with me until I mastered the task, and I wanted to be like her.

I couldn't find ongoing work in BC, so I decided to move to Calgary, where I could share an apartment with my sister Janice, who already lived there. I got a job as a data clerk processing computer punch cards.

And that's what I was doing when I turned twenty-one, when I made that fateful decision to go to a baseball game.

The first family member to see me in the ICU at Foothills Hospital was my sister Janice. I still don't know how she found out about the accident, but my immediate concern was that she didn't tell our parents. "Don't tell Mother and Dad," I implored her. "They'll just be angry and upset." In order to calm me down, she agreed, but of course she'd already told them, and they arrived soon after, not angry at all. They were half expecting I would be dead, so they were just happy I was still alive.

I had broken my left shoulder as well as that shoulder blade. I couldn't use my left arm at all, but it was nothing they couldn't fix. More concerning was my back. I had broken a lot of vertebrae. The good news was that my spinal cord wasn't damaged above lumbar 1, meaning I had lost most of the function in my hips and legs, but I was okay above that. My back needed to be fused. I hadn't had any feeling in my legs since my accident.

I needed the surgery, but I developed pneumonia, so everything was delayed for two weeks while I recovered. But even after all the surgery, I still had no feeling in my legs and only partial sensation at hip level. I persisted in believing that I'd be walking again once my back healed, until finally a doctor told me, "You're paralyzed. At best you could walk with braces and crutches." He said it just like that. I didn't believe him.

What followed was nine long months of recovery, first in the hospital and then in the rehab centre. I was in pain most of the time and on a lot of medication for that, including Valium, which was prescribed to quiet the muscle spasms that often accompany spinal cord injuries.

After the first few months of rehab, my left arm had healed enough that I could try using a wheelchair. I remembered a friend of my parents, Helen Austin, who had polio as a child. She had six kids whom I used to play with at her house. For as long as I had known her, Helen had a wheelchair, which I always thought was completely normal. When the staff helped me into my wheelchair, Helen's image was in my head, and I was confident I was going to be okay because she was okay.

When a representative from the wheelchair company came into my room with the chair, it was a simple manual chair. I was thankful that, years earlier, my doctor had saved the fingers of my right hand. Without them, I wouldn't have been able to steer.

That's not to say it was easy that first day. The hospital hallways were so wide, and I was ping-ponging from one wall to the other wall. I just could not go straight.

The rep watched me and said, "That chair is too big. I'm going to bring you one that will fit you." Sure enough, she came back with a smaller chair, and after that I could navigate much more easily.

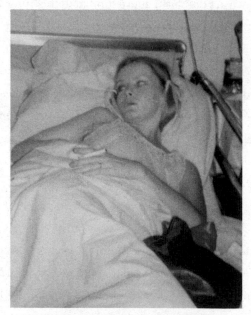

About five months after my accident, in rehab
at Calgary General Hospital.

But there was more to life in a wheelchair than just steering. I had to learn how to move from my wheelchair to a toilet and back again. I would practice going into a washroom that had only standard, narrow cubicles because I knew that was what the real world looked like—there weren't as many wheelchair-accessible bathrooms as there are now. It was hard. At first, I didn't have the strength to lift myself from my chair, and so I spent a lot of my time building up my muscles.

I was learning to do everything differently, and nothing was easy or direct. And mentally, I was struggling to adjust to my new reality—life in a wheelchair—in part because the pain medication made me feel numb all the time. I didn't know who I was anymore, and the drugs weren't helping. Eventually, I told the doctors I wanted to stop taking them. They agreed, and very soon the fog I was under began to lift. I realized I would never be the old me again.

Because of my disability, I became a whole new person. One who could lift themselves from their chair to a toilet and back, who could steer straight, who could dream of a future again.

Now when I meet people who have a new spinal cord injury, I tell them, "For the first two years you won't know who you are, but then you will learn about the new version of you."

I knew who I was, but the medical team often seemed to treat me as a case and not as a person. My physiatrist (a doctor in rehab medicine) used to tell me what I could and couldn't do anymore. I remember I could flex a muscle in my left thigh. It didn't do any practical good, but I could do it. One day, I showed the doctor, and his reaction was, "You can't do that."

"But I am doing it," I replied.

"No, you're not. It's a spasm."

"No, it's not. Tell me to do it and I'll do it on command."

But he was insistent. "You can't do that with the level of your injury. You cannot do that."

"What do you know?" I thought.

After that, I decided to do some research on my own and find out as much as I could about paraplegia. There was a library at the rehab centre, and I read a lot of books about people like me. In one, there was a line about a paraplegic woman who had given birth. "Well," I thought, "if you can give birth, you can get pregnant, which I certainly want to do one day, but I don't want to do it just yet."

When I asked the doctor about birth control, he said, "I don't answer those questions. You should go see your general practitioner." So I did.

The summer I left rehab, I went to a camp for people with disabilities in Bragg Creek, just outside Calgary, and there I met Dan. He was one of the counselors, and we ended up dating and eventually getting married.

Just a few years earlier, university hadn't been an option for me, but with the help of what was then called Vocational Rehabilitation for Disabled Persons, a program for people with disabilities that covered the cost of going to university—including tuition, books, and living expenses—I could afford to go to school. I chose to pursue a degree in education at the University of Calgary. Maybe I would become a kindergarten teacher after all.

It was there that I learned a simple lesson that would forever give my life a sense of purpose: Somebody has to be an advocate.

When I went to university, it became apparent very quickly that there were barriers for students with disabilities. There was a small group of us on campus, and we banded together to advocate for changes that would make the school more accessible. For example, the university had one wheelchair-accessible washroom, but it was only for men because apparently only men use wheelchairs or the washroom. I had to laugh at stuff like that or else I'd cry. But we, as disabled people, made our voices heard, and we saw change.

Before my accident, if I wanted to get around, I either walked everywhere or took the bus. After, I had to use a private company that had a vehicle with a wheelchair ramp. They'd take me anywhere I wanted to go, but a one-way trip cost $5. That's about $35 in today's money and it was way more than I could afford. My insurance paid $120 a month and my rent was $85. I had to rely on other people to take me places. Dan made sure I got where I needed to go, but it always pissed me off that I couldn't get on the bloody bus.

I encountered barriers all the time. Whenever that happened, I knew I had a choice: I could do nothing, or I could see what I could do to remove the barrier. I never chose to do nothing. I started to talk to other people with disabilities in Calgary and a small action group in Edmonton about the need for greater access to public services. We formed the Alberta Action Group of the Handicapped, now called Voice of Albertans with Disabilities. I served on the board. I was young, and when you're young you can do anything. Dan was very supportive, and he understood how important it was for me to have independence.

Eventually, I did learn how to drive a car—with hand controls instead of pedals. Even before my accident, I had never learned to drive a car, so fortunately I didn't have to unlearn anything, and driving with hand controls came very easily to me. Sometimes I tell able-bodied people, "I don't know what you do with your feet."

Learning to drive wasn't nearly as difficult as getting into the car in the first place. I had to figure out how to move my body into the passenger seat, fold my wheelchair, tuck it into the back seat, close the door, then slide across to the driver's seat. But I became more proficient with practice. I earned my license and got a car, and after that I didn't have to rely on Dan or anyone else to take me to my advocacy meetings.

In 1974, I had a year left at university when my life changed in another big way. I was pregnant and due to give birth in September. Sometimes people with paraplegia can't feel when they're going into labour, so as a precaution, I was put into the hospital in late August, despite me saying I would know when I was in labour. Dan had just gotten a teaching job in Grande Prairie, so he headed out there, intending to race back to Calgary, a seven-hour drive, at the first sign that I would be giving birth. It was a good plan, but our son, Carl, didn't cooperate. He arrived in the world a couple of hours before Dan arrived at the hospital.

When Carl was two or three weeks old, we joined Dan in Grande Prairie, and I soon continued my advocacy work. I met a woman who was legally blind, and we commiserated on what we needed to change in the city. We knew that two people fighting alone wouldn't get very far, and we looked for who else had disabilities to enlist them in the cause. Grande Prairie is a small city, so we went to the phone book and called each and every number. When someone answered, we simply asked, "Is there anyone in your household with a disability?"

By the end of the phone book, we had a list of about one hundred individuals, which told us that there was a population out there that needed changes. As a group, we attended a couple of city council meetings. The meeting room wasn't accessible, so Dan had to pick me up and carry me up the stairs, but at least they could see that people with disabilities were a part of the community.

We fought for things that would be important for the future. For example, Grande Prairie didn't yet have a bus system, but we got the city to agree that if it ever got a bus system it would be wheelchair accessible. We wanted to ensure that accessibility was integrated from the beginning.

After two years, I was offered an advocacy job in Edmonton. Dan agreed that I should take it, so I never saw the fruits of our labour in Grand Prairie; but today the city has a transit system and every bus is wheelchair accessible.

In Edmonton we found an apartment—though Dan had to build a ramp so I could get into the building—and I began my work. My job was as an information officer with the Alberta Committee Action Group of People with Disabilities, which researched and wrote reports for the government recommending changes in society. For example, integrating accessibility into building codes, including people with disabilities in human rights legislation, and making it government policy to pay for assisted technology like wheelchairs. I would go down to the legislative building and knock on the doors of elected members to make sure they read our report. Sometimes, I would give them a quick summary of what we were asking for. In other words, it was my job to convince people to enact our changes. I found that most people were willing to listen if I had the right approach and didn't waste their time with other things.

The Alberta attorney general Neil Crawford once said to me, "Pat, every time I see you, you're always friendly and you always stick to what you came to talk about."

I took that as a compliment.

We had some important victories in Alberta. When the province adopted the national building code as their provincial code, we made sure they included the optional provisions for accessibility. The code was rudimentary compared to what we now have, but it provided minimal accessibility and established the principle going forward.

Our next success was addressing the need for equipment for people with disabilities. Saskatchewan had a program for people with a disability to get a wheelchair, crutches, or other mobility aids, and there were similar programs outside of Canada as well. We cited these examples from other jurisdictions—which was important because politicians can be reluctant to try things that have never been done before—and we were able to get that government program in Alberta. It still exists today.

As does a program called Assured Income for the Severely Handicapped. Poverty often goes hand in hand with a disability because many people with disabilities are not able to work full time, and they've often been denied the opportunity to acquire the necessary skills to get a good job. Even for those of us with an education, the unemployment rate is much higher than it is among able-bodied people with the same amount of schooling. Moving from a charity model to more of a social justice model takes a long time, but we fought and secured funding beyond basic social assistance. Since then, the program has been expanded. Success builds on success, and now almost every province has similar disability assistance programs.

Despite these strides forward, I could never be fooled into believing everything was fine. I had regular and hurtful reminders that I wasn't like everybody else.

In 1977, I went to the airport to fly to Grande Prairie, where I had interviews lined up for some staff jobs with the committee. It was a 45-minute flight from Edmonton that I had taken many times before, but when I went to board this time, I was pulled aside and told I couldn't fly.

"Why not?" I asked.

"You don't have anybody with you to take care of you," said the person from Canadian Pacific Airlines.

I laughed. "Are you kidding? I have flown using a wheelchair for seven or eight years. Mostly alone. I've never had any problems."

In front of everybody else in the boarding area, they asked me a string of personal questions.

"What happens if you have to use the washroom?"

"It's a forty-five-minute flight," I replied. "I'll be fine without using the washroom."

And on it went. I had never been more embarrassed. They even asked, "What happens if the plane crashes?"

"I would probably die," I said, exasperated. "Like everybody else." They didn't like that answer.

This stalemate continued until the airline said that I could fly only if the pilot said so. I spoke to him, and he agreed it was fine. The flight was, of course, uneventful. When I got off I reminded them that I would be back the next day to fly home.

But when I returned to the airport, I went through the same rigmarole. This time it ended with one of their staff flying with me. I couldn't believe it. I had no recourse under the law at the time. The airline could simply refuse to put a person like me on an airplane if they thought I would be a burden. I was shocked and horrified that this not only happened, but happened to me, somebody who knew my rights as a disabled person.

Earlier that year, Canada had passed the Canadian Human Rights Act. While it prohibited discrimination based on physical disability, it was only in federally regulated employment. I was being denied transportation, a public service, and that too became an ongoing issue.

The mid-1970s was a pivotal time in the development of our voice, and I was proudly part of the birth of the Coalition of Provincial Organizations of the Handicapped, now known as the Council of Canadians with Disabilities. We are a social justice organization of people with all kinds of disabilities that advocates for an inclusive and accessible Canada, where people with disabilities have full realization of their human rights, as described in the UN Convention on the Rights of Persons with Disabilities (CRPD). The CRPD came about in 2006, in part, because people with disabilities spent decades increasing our understanding of human rights—for example, expanding the definition of disability to include persons with mental disabilities.

By the mid-1980s, it was clear to me and to others in my circle that women with disabilities needed a greater voice to fight for their needs. Disabled women tend to be raped and exploited sexually more than other women. Unemployment is higher. Poverty rates are higher. A drunk and abusive father can sometimes be considered a better parent than a disabled mother. Women are generally undervalued in society, and for women with disabilities it's worse, and worse still if they're also Indigenous or gay.

There was no shortage of problems to address. Together with a group of women, we founded the DisAbled Women's Network (DAWN) to combat these problems. As a woman with a disability myself, this was an issue that was near and dear to my heart.

Around this time, my eyes were opened to another harsh truth that many people with disabilities face when it comes to their own medical care.

I heard of a young boy with a significant intellectual disability whose parents had given him to the care of the province of BC. His name was Stephen Dawson, and he had a shunt in his head to drain excessive fluid from his brain; it had become clogged and needed to be replaced. This is a relatively routine procedure for anybody with a shunt, but Stephen's parents suddenly reentered the picture and said they didn't want the shunt replaced. It meant Stephen would die. The B.C. Association for the Mentally Retarded (now Inclusion BC) went to bat for Stephen, arguing that it was wrong to deny him a life-saving procedure just because he had a disability. Thankfully, the judge agreed.

That was the first time I learned that something could go wrong with me and my life could be in the hands of others who could make decisions for me without necessarily knowing all the facts. It was sobering to realize that if you live with a disability, there's a higher chance you will die, not because it's your choice but because somebody else has decided for you. I talked to Dan about my future and made it clear that I did not want my life taken because somebody thought it would be best for me.

That wasn't the case for twelve-year-old Tracy Latimer from Wilkie, Saskatchewan. Born with cerebral palsy, Tracy lived with severe physical and intellectual disabilities and had undergone many operations. In 1993, she was scheduled for another surgery, but two weeks before the surgery, her father, Robert Latimer, killed her. Robert had the sympathy of a great number of Canadians. Even my father told me, "I can see why he did what he did." I thought my dad just didn't understand that his own daughter could be in that precarious position.

For me, this was murder. And anyone who said otherwise had a misguided perception of people with disabilities. Robert Latimer was convicted of murder, but there were allegations of jury tampering. When I heard that a second trial had been ordered, I took some vacation time and attended as a private citizen. I thought it was important for people—disabled or not—to see someone in a wheelchair. I wanted to be a physical reminder that no one can change the rules because somebody lives with a disability.

It was one of the most important and hardest things I've ever done in my life. As I sat through the trial, I heard about all of Tracy's surgeries. I'd had many of those same operations, but they were just part of who I was. Tracy and I both used wheelchairs, but she had an intellectual disability and was not able to speak for herself. I couldn't help but think that if I had had different parents, things could've ended badly for me.

It kept coming up at the trial that Tracy had Harrington rods implanted in her back for stability, and the rods were always spoken of as if they were torturous medical devices. But I had had them in my back while I healed after the car accident. I knew that what everyone thought was horrific wasn't.

I was sitting next to a reporter, so I leaned over and whispered, "I've had those in my back. It's not a big deal."

He was quite surprised. His normal and my normal were two different things. That was the point I was trying to make. If we look at the world through an ableist lens, we see less value in the life of a disabled person, and suddenly, murder becomes excusable. Regardless of what you think of someone's quality of life, our criminal code says that if you murder somebody, you murder somebody. In the end, the jury saw it the same way, and Robert Latimer was convicted of second-degree murder.

These incidents drove home just how important protection for people with disabilities under the law was. A few years before the Latimer case, I had begun working for the Saskatchewan human rights commission. Initially I was their intake officer, determining whether or not a complainant had enough evidence to move forward. When someone's rights have been violated, they have to substantiate their case and show that it's covered under the law.

I learned that not everything has to be elevated to a government body. Sometimes reasonable people, acting reasonably, can work things out. Eventually I moved from hearing complaints to working with employers and school districts to develop equity programs. It was the kind of work that led to incremental change—slower than I hoped, but it was still change, and that was rewarding for me. I knew the world was not going to be transformed all at once.

It was during this time that I ended up filing a human rights complaint of my own, though not in Saskatchewan.

I took Carl, who was then sixteen, to a Rod Stewart concert at the stadium in Ottawa. When I bought the tickets, I made sure that I would be sitting next to him. It shouldn't have been a big deal. They had wheelchair spaces.

When we arrived at the stadium, the ticket taker said, "You sit there with your wheelchair, and your son sits over there."

"No, no," I said. "I want to sit with my son."

"Sorry, but that's not the way we do it," he told us. "People in wheelchairs go over there, and whoever you came with sits there."

So we were separated. I guess I still enjoyed the concert, but it wasn't the experience it should have been. I wanted to be able to take it all in with my son, feel the exact same vibrations from the music, talk to him while it was happening. Instead, I was surrounded by strangers.

I knew that couldn't have happened in Saskatchewan, where, under human rights law, it had been determined that an accompanying person should be able to sit beside you, not in a separate area.

After I filed a complaint with the human rights commission in Ontario, we negotiated a settlement which included an agreement by the city of Ottawa and the National Capital Commission that any new facilities would be accessible. I felt very good that this solution would benefit others in the future.

At the end of the day, it shouldn't be a battle between the abled and

*With my sister Janice, in 1991, along
the inner harbour in Victoria.*

the disabled. Or between a person with one type of disability and a person with another type of disability—which sometimes happens. We're all a part of the community. The goal is to design our world so that anybody can move about. We don't want you to notice an accessible entrance. It's just an entrance. As we've made progress, cities and towns have understood that when they build or renovate, accessibility features are just a routine part of the budget. That's what a caring society does.

But the truth is that we're always dealing with preconceptions of what people with disabilities can do. Too many people still see my wheelchair before they see me, and they make assumptions. For example, I often take my older sister shopping for food. Others frequently say to me, "It's so nice that your sister takes you to get groceries." We always laugh and my sister corrects them and tells them it's the reverse.

Fifty years ago, my life completely changed in an instant. With my diagnosis, I became a different person. I found strength that I never knew I had. I went places and accomplished things that I never thought I would. Do I sometimes miss my legs? Yes. Do I get frustrated when I can't do certain things? Yes. But like a mermaid, I've adapted. And over the years, I've stopped thinking about who I might have been and realized who I am.

I'm an advocate, and I'm never going to stop working for disabled Canadians. Because we're not fighting for our privileges; we're fighting for our rights.

Pat Danforth has been advocating for people with a disability for fifty years. A founder of the DisAbled Women's Network, she has also worked for the Saskatchewan Human Rights Commission, the Canadian Labour Congress, and a number of advocacy organizations. She has volunteered for many groups, including the Canadian Union of Public Employees, the Disability Alliance BC, and the Council of Canadians with Disabilities. She lives in Saanich, BC.

LEVON JOHNSON
Deeds, Not Words

*Little has been written about our missions,
and I can assure you that no blockbuster movies have been made
about us. But now in the pages that follow, that's going to change a bit,
because I've been given some freedom to talk. . . . This is a
story of how Canadian troops held Taliban leaders accountable
for how they targeted our own in southern Afghanistan.*

"Congratulations. You are going to be a professional killer."
Those words, or something like them, have been barked out by tough-talking basic-training leaders to thousands of young recruits who enter the Canadian Armed Forces over the years. Just in case you really hadn't thought about what your career choice meant, those words, no matter what field you wound up in, were a stark reminder of what your role could potentially be.

Of course, most new recruits never get to be in that kind of situation. They'll never fire a shot in combat. They'll never hear one either. Regardless, we are all trained to make the decision extremely carefully to pull the trigger.

The first time I was called on to make that choice was during my first tour in Afghanistan. It was a horrifying experience.

Keeping watch in a Kandahar village. COURTESY OF JTF2

We were in a close-quarters house-to-house battle with the Taliban when suddenly an enemy fighter was in front of me, pointing his weapon at me. But before he could pull the trigger, I shot him and he fell back. In my mind, this unfolded over a matter of minutes, but in reality it happened in fractions of seconds. As he hit the ground, I realized that there were two young kids crumpled behind him. They were covered in blood. My heart dropped in my chest. Had they been hit by my shot?

I thought I was going to throw up. And then, everything changed. Both kids opened their eyes, got up, and scurried away. In that moment, I became human again. "Oh, man, this is real life," I whispered.

I couldn't dwell on what had just happened because the skirmish continued around me. I had to push those feelings aside and let my training take over as the enemy became the target again. But when the battle was over, those emotions did return. This is the way it always goes. I've learned that the way to deal with them is to talk about them with my colleagues. We all try very hard not to leave anything bundled up inside.

In the months and years that followed Canada's decision to enter the war in Afghanistan, Canadians learned that their soldiers were being killed as a result of roadside bombs, or, as they're called, IEDs (improvised explosive devices). And by the time Canada abandoned its combat role in Afghanistan, 159 Canadians had been killed. Most of them, 98, were killed not in an active firefight but instead were blown apart in their vehicles by mines hidden in the dirt of Afghan roads. If this had been a conventional battle, where both sides faced each other head-on, the coalition forces of which Canada was a part would have won quickly and relatively easily. We were better trained, better equipped, and, bottom line, better fighters. But it wasn't conventional, and a lot of Canadians paid the ultimate price as a result.

I know. I was there. I was one of those who witnessed the flag-draped coffins loaded onto the big transport planes at the Kandahar airport for the long, lonely, solemn flight back to Canada. I read the stories about the grieving families and friends back home who were trying to come to grips with the loss of their loved ones so far away. I heard about how thousands of ordinary Canadians lined the highways to honour their soldiers who were returning home in a box instead of to a parade.

In 2008, I was a Warrant Officer in Joint Task Force 2, a highly secret special operations branch of the CAF. You may have heard of the US SEAL teams and the British SAS forces—specially trained operational units that are designed to take on the most dangerous missions behind enemy lines. The most famous mission was the capture and killing of Osama bin Laden by US SEAL Team Six. They flew into Pakistan on specially built, super-quiet, never-before-used-in-operations helicopters. Upon landing, they broke into the house where bin Laden was hiding, killed his bodyguards, executed the Al Qaeda leader, and then slipped out without a single American hurt. It was a remarkable mission and worthy of the articles, books, and movies that have been made about it.

Canada's JTF2 never had a target as universally famous as bin Laden, but we too have had serious bad guys in our sights. And, not surprisingly, we think we're just as good at carrying out our capture or kill missions as anyone else. That's what we call them: capture or kill. Many of these missions involve combat, and the kill option comes into play quite often. You won't see any news conferences explaining our actions—we rarely talk about them ourselves. Little has been written about our missions, and I can assure you that no blockbuster movies have been made about us.

But now in the pages that follow, that's going to change a bit, because I've been given some freedom to talk. *Some* freedom. Certain names, including my own, and certain operational details have either been changed or left out to protect those involved. We do worry about retaliation against our families or friends, and that worry governs what we can say. But what is here will give you a sense of one of our special ops missions, a mission that was designed to counter those members of the Taliban who were directly behind some of the deadly roadside bombings that claimed so many Canadian lives. This is a story of how Canadian troops held Taliban leaders accountable for how they targeted our own in southern Afghanistan. This operation was about payback.

In the fall of 2008, our intelligence people got wind of a meeting of the Taliban's top bomb makers, the men trained to make the IEDs that were killing our fellow soldiers. They called their meetings shuras, and this was going to be a big one. Our intelligence indicated that these guys were planning a whole new, next-level IED campaign focused on Canadians on the roads and in the villages in and around Kandahar. They wanted to up their game by causing even more human carnage. The shura was to be held in a remote compound in the countryside that night, and our team was designated to pull a capture or kill on the four key bomb makers in attendance. Ironically perhaps, we were also designated, and had been for some time, to end our latest Afghanistan tour and head back to Canada *the next day*. So this was going to be quite the "end of tour" get-together.

By this time, we had completed many missions in our five-month tour of duty. Most nights had involved raids in the city of Kandahar or just on the outskirts. Our intelligence people would obtain the whereabouts of a target, and then we'd be moved in and let loose. We were doing capture or kill missions so often, and they had been so successful, that they called us the Kandahar Swat. We were pretty confident that we could handle anything the Taliban threw at us, and it was easy to become complacent with overconfidence. That was dangerous and we knew it.

But this last night was a whole new challenge. For starters, the mission wouldn't be in Kandahar, it would be well out in the countryside, hours from our base. This would be no pushover. In the past, our leader had been pretty subdued about the direction he gave us, but not now. When we gathered for the final on-base briefing the difference was clear.

"Okay, boys, we're going into the bees' nest. There are hundreds of Taliban fighters in the region."

That was the clear warning that this was going to be a major fight, that if something was ever going to go bad, this was the night it could. So we got our game faces on in a hurry. We were still confident of what we had to do, but we put any *over*confidence aside. I remember thinking that this was the way my coach used to get us ready for a big hockey game.

In the last hour before we leave on a major mission, certain traditions are always carried out, and tonight was no different. Some of the guys listened to heavy music, some guys topped up on power drinks like Red Bull, and some guys played video games. Then, and this may sound dark, we got together in our different units and had someone take our picture. It's been a tradition for special forces teams that dates back to the Second World War. You can probably guess why. We wanted something of the team together in case one of us, or more, didn't come back.

I told you it was dark.

There were challenges ahead for sure, but there were also things on our side. Number one: the element of surprise. The target was deep in the desert, but if we did our jobs right, they wouldn't see or hear us coming. They wouldn't see us because it was a moonless night and it was very dark, which was a problem for the enemy but not for us. We all had special night vision equipment; they had candles. For us, our equipment made night look like day. As we prepared to board helicopters for the initial stage of the journey into battle, I felt good knowing that we owned the night.

I walked across the tarmac, the first test of my natural senses. No problem. I could smell the fuel in the air and the helicopter exhaust wafting by as the engines warmed up.

When we boarded the transport choppers, we got some bad news. The helicopter gunship that was going to escort us and give us air cover at the target had been reassigned to another operation. That caused consternation among some of the commanders. The conversation was whether they should call the op off. The verdict was no. The decision was "let's get the job done."

As we buckled into our seats, there was a certain irony to the chopper we'd climbed aboard. Canada had to lease transport choppers for the Afghan conflict because our existing ones weren't built for this type of operation and buying new ones would have taken too long for delivery. There's no Hertz or Avis for military choppers, so that left us leasing Russia's frontline helicopter, the Mi-17. Russia was not our natural ally, and they were the same guys who had lost the last Afghan war. The Mi-17 was ugly, rough, and uncomfortable but, damn, the pilots swore by them as perfect for this kind of operation. Still, it was no fun to be in them when landing in a dust cloud—as we were about to do.

The pilots dropped the Mi-17s from about 50 feet (about 15 metres). The chopper hit the ground and then rolled forward all in one motion. It was like a crash landing, far from flying business class on Air Canada! Seconds later, the back ramp swung down, and we exited like a herd of cattle. When the last guy stepped off the chopper, it lifted off in a cloud of dust and disappeared.

On one of many night raids. COURTESY OF JTF2

We all dropped to one knee, weapons at the ready, unsure of what to expect. It was a perfect spot for an ambush, but none unfolded, so we focused on getting to the location of the shura. While we'd arrived unnoticed, we were farther away from the target than we'd planned. According to the GPS, we were short of our planned landing area by at least two kilometres, which was still another ten kilometres from the shura. We were going to have to hike two and a half hours through the desert, avoiding nomad tribes and small villages, all of which could also be doubling as forward listening posts for the bomb makers. Fortunately, we could see them but they couldn't see us.

We started walking, and when I say "walk," it's a walk where you have a big load, but you also have to be ready to spring into lethal action at any point. We each carried about sixty-five pounds of gear. We try to divide the weight up equally; each guy is tasked differently with gear—one focuses on medical gear, one on comms equipment, and so on. In my case, I carried a ladder and a whole bunch of charges to blow holes in the mud walls when we got to the compound, and the weight of everything was about seventy-five pounds. It was hard slogging.

After hiking twelve to fourteen kilometres, we could see the target buildings that housed the enemy. So far, we had gone undetected. The only way the Taliban could be warned was if their counterparts in the villages we had passed through signalled them with flares. They had no electronics. We'd seen this in past ops—their friends would spend the night on house roofs taking turns as lookouts, and if they saw or heard anything suspicious they'd fire off flares. Primitive, almost like an old Western movie and smoke signals, but it worked and had messed up a few previous missions. But not this time. No flares.

Our special operations colleagues (CSOR) set up key points to encircle the compound. Their job wasn't about what would happen inside, but rather to make sure nothing bad would come from the outside.

We were ready for what we'd come to do. Kill or capture. It was the middle of the night—the darkest hour—the perfect time to strike. Silently we got ready to make our move.

People ask me whether it's at this moment that I get nervous. To be honest, no one has time to get nervous. The movie had started. I was in it. The action was already underway. The next few minutes would determine the outcome, and there was really no time, no desire, and quite frankly no ability to think about anything other than the mission at hand. There was time to be nervous the night before in those moments before sleep hits, and there might be time to be nervous when it was all over and I relived the moments of great tension, but not now.

And, then, a shot. One of our sharpshooters took out a Taliban lookout who had noticed us. It barely broke the silence. I say that because all our weapons have suppressors attached. Silencers. They certainly muffle the sound, but they don't kill it, and within minutes a full-scale gun-fight was underway. The Taliban may have been asleep, but their fighters quickly hit the ground running.

We might have been better fighters, but that didn't mean the battle was a walk in the park. Far from it. The Taliban were dedicated to their cause, and they kept coming. Every time we thought we'd crushed them, there was another group ready to engage. But some were farmers, just off the fields with an AK-47 and the most basic of training. They didn't know that an AK-47 has serious blowback, which means that as it fires the barrel rises up slightly. As a result, the shots were over our heads. Meanwhile, we were in the proper firing position, shooting from the shoulder with precise results. Other members of the enemy were behind mud walls holding their guns over the top with a "spray and pray" firing pattern. It didn't work. Their fighters were inexperienced, a fact the Taliban commanders had accepted, which was why their main strategy was IEDs. They knew that gunfights meant dead fighters.

That was what was unfolding on this night in the Afghan desert, but the battle was going to last at least two hours. We had four teams of com-mandos with between four and six men on each team. To capture or kill, we had to, as we say, "clean out" the compound, which had about twenty rooms in it. Each team had its own section to deal with.

As my team entered our area, two Taliban guards popped their heads up above a mud wall to our right. They started firing and lobbed something in our direction. My buddy beside me started yelling, and it sounded like: "Rah, rah, rah."

"What the hell is he talking about?" I thought, but I focused on the area where the two Taliban were.

Suddenly, just behind me, a huge explosion blew out part of the wall on that side. Two things happen when there's an explosion like that. First, fragmentation. Small pieces of steel fly everywhere, but in this case they were mostly absorbed by the mud wall. But the wall couldn't absorb the sound and the concussion that goes with it. My auditory system kind of shut down, but my mind was still working, and that was when I realized what my buddy had actually been yelling: "RPG, RPG, RPG."

Rocket-propelled grenade. Believe it or not, it was a comical moment and actually forced both of us to snap back into reality. Within seconds we had neutralized the two Taliban guys. Killed them. There would be no RPGs from them anymore.

But the fight was far from over.

The next room contained a much different challenge. It was, in fact, a room within a room. One fighter, one of the bomb makers as it turned out, was barricaded inside a smaller, walled-off area, further protected by sandbags and carpets piled on top of each other. He had a machine gun and, it appeared, a lot of ammunition. Going inside that room to get him seemed like certain death.

It was time for a different kind of fighter.

It was time for Angus, a highly trained member of a small American special forces team that was working with us on this mission.

Angus was a Belgian Malinois, a breed of Shepherd, slightly smaller than a German Shepherd, picked for his lack of shyness but also for his ability to be aggressive when the situation called for it. He'd been trained to show no fear, not to be distracted by unsure footing, dark spaces, or loud noises like gunfire or explosions. Angus and his handler had been with us for some time, sleeping and eating with us so that he got used to our individual scents. He knew us, and in the heat of battle he wouldn't confuse any of us for the enemy.

So we sent Angus in, and he did as he was trained. He attacked. But the Taliban fighter was not surrendering to an attacking dog even though Angus managed some serious bites. In return he was shot, a number of times. But not enough to drop him. Angus limped out of the room.

His handler tried to treat him, but Angus wanted another go and managed to get back in for a second attack.

Same result and more shots.

And then a third attempt. It would be the last one. Angus died on the floor of that room. So, moments later, did the Taliban bomb maker when we rushed in and took him out.

None of us who fought that night will ever forget Angus. He was incredibly loyal and brave and saved us from injury, even death.

The battle was not over, and our focus was on ensuring it ended the right way. We started clearing the compound room by room. The frontline members engaged the Taliban who were hiding behind, and firing from, beds and tables and makeshift couches. Typically, I want to be in the front to lead the charge, but that night I was on rear security, about ten metres behind the front guys. Still, I was busy, very busy. There were a lot of enemy coming at us from behind, and I started neutralizing them with everything I had. Gunfire and grenades. At one point I was beside a doorway as two Taliban came at me from the other side. I tossed a grenade at them. As it exploded, taking them out of the action, I felt an intense heat all along the side of my body. When you're hit, you sometimes don't know just how bad it is because the body shuts the pain down if it's really severe. But you do feel the heat, and I sure did in that moment.

"Oh, no, I just blew myself up," I thought.

In reality, the heat from the explosion had slipped through a crack in the mud wall. The heat passed. But something else did happen.

When I'd thrown the grenade I hadn't realized that one of our snipers was on the roof directly above the enemy fighters. The explosion tossed him about four feet into the air, throwing him off the roof. Miraculously, he was unhurt. Somehow we even managed a smile as we acknowledged each other.

An integral part of our mission, a highly trained Belgian Malinois.
ASSOCIATED PRESS/KRISTY WIGGLESWORTH

Everything was happening very quickly. It had been less than ten minutes since that first shot and my mind was racing, focused on what was ahead, but never forgetting the danger from behind.

This is what I was trained to do. Imagine a really confusing, dark compound with all these doorways and entrances and holes. And then imagine there are fighters coming at you from what feels like every angle. It feels like chaos, but we know what to do. We look for the best route through the maze in an orchestrated and planned manner. Some of this is automatic for us because this is our job. When we are not in Afghanistan or Iraq or wherever the generals send us, we are at home training. Every day. It's intense. So, in a sense that night in the desert was, as hard as this is to say, just another day at the office. I'm not trying to sound like a hero here. It's just our job. To be able to do this precisely, effectively, as a team and with as little emotion as possible.

Pockets of gunfire were coming from rooms we hadn't yet taken. As we cleared each room, the specialized teams came in. First the explosives technicians to make sure there were no IEDs in the room, followed quickly by the medics to handle the wounded no matter which side they were on. Then the linguists to deal with translation barriers.

But up ahead our guys were still engaging. I was at the front of my team now, moving ahead, while my buddies were facing in the other direction about ten metres behind me dealing with some of the enemy who'd given up as we moved through the compound. I was advancing slowly, careful not to become isolated and alone.

Then I saw a shadow carrying what to me appeared to be the unmistakable outline of an AK-47. He hadn't seen me, so I had the advantage. But I didn't like being, in effect, cut off from my team. We deal with the unexpected better when we're together.

All of a sudden, a shot whizzed past me. While I was assessing the situation he must have noticed me, smelled me, heard me breathing. Something. Whatever it was, he fired a shot in my direction. It missed. My flurry of shots in return didn't.

I turned to see the guys on my team. The closest to me was in the process of cuffing a prisoner, but he was looking up at me. "Hey, thanks, buddy, that was close."

He thought the Taliban fighter had been shooting at him because the shot he'd fired that missed me kept on going and just missed him.

"No problem, got your back," I replied as if it had all been planned that way. We moved on, no further comment needed.

When I think back at this moment now, it feels like it unfolded over minutes, but it was actually seconds. And our whole exchange in the middle of a serious and lengthy gunfight was so matter of fact. It was almost like, "Hey, thanks for saving me that parking spot at Timmies!"

Finally, the fighting was over and, with the enemy silenced, the cleanup began. We piled up all their weapons and their munitions, and anything that could later be used against us, and then the explosives guys came by and blew them up. The medics looked after the wounded. The prisoners were taken into custody.

There had been casualties. For us, only a few were wounded. Everyone was alive. The Taliban were not so fortunate. Quite a few were wounded and quite a few were dead, including three of the bomb makers. The fourth was taken alive and would be interrogated in the hopes of discovering information about those still out there killing Canadian troops.

But we did have one fatality. Angus. He died on the battlefield. There would be no flag-draped coffin driven down the Highway of Heroes for Angus, but his fellow American team members lived true to their unofficial motto of "never leave a man behind" and they didn't leave Angus behind either. They wrapped him in a body bag, and together we carried him across the desert to the helicopters. I remember that walk very well. We carried Angus as if he were on a stretcher with one man at either end. At one end was his handler, who was clearly overcome by what had happened. He never let go. We Canadians took turns holding the other end. The walk was a silent tribute. On the helicopter, it was a slow, quiet, early-morning flight across the Afghan desert back to base. From there, the process of decompression began. But it takes a while to move on from a night like that.

There's a scene in the movie *The Hurt Locker* where an expert member of a US forces bomb disposal unit in Iraq returns home after a particularly harrowing tour. He finds himself one day in a supermarket walking along the row of cereals. There are so many different types and he can't decide. The irony is obvious and I know the feeling—when you are overseas at war, you make split-second decisions, decisions that can affect many lives including your own. But back home, picking a cereal is just too much.

I think about that every time I go home. I'm married to an incredible woman and we have a wonderful family. I take my kids to school like other parents. I go shopping with them on the weekends. I cherish every moment with them. They've grown accustomed to their dad leaving without warning in the middle of the night, to waking up in the morning and not even being allowed to know where I am, what I'm doing, or how long I'll be gone.

This has been my life for almost twenty years, and it's missions like the one I've described that make it worth it. What we were able to do on that night did, in effect, settle a score. Those bomb makers had killed a lot of Canadians, some of them my friends. Nothing will bring them back, but on that night we reminded everyone that we won't forget them.

It was important work. But I know it won't last forever. I also know who will make that determination. When my wife looks at me and says, "Enough," it will be enough.

Levon Johnson is a pseudonym for a Warrant Officer in Joint Task Force 2, a special operations force of the Canadian Armed Forces that protects Canadian national interests and combats terrorism and threats to Canadians at home and abroad. He has taken part in a dozen special ops missions in hot spots around the world, including three tours in Afghanistan.

FRANCES WRIGHT
Fighting for Equality

All of us build Canada: men and women, old and young, new Canadians and always Canadians. We all have something to contribute.

I was meant to be a Canadian! If I had not come to Canada when I was six, I know I would have come when I turned eighteen. My entire life I have been preoccupied with equality, especially for women, and it has been in Canada that I've seen great strides toward a better future for us all. I'm forever grateful Canada opened her arms to me.

I was born in South Africa in 1947, but my mother, Irma Toth, hailed from the flattest prairie province, Saskatchewan. When the world was on the cusp of its second world war, she joined the Royal Canadian Air Force Women's Division as a secretary and was stationed in London, England, where she met my father, Frank Wright. He was from South Africa. During the war, he was captured in North Africa and put into a POW camp. He managed to escape but was recaptured and taken to another POW camp in Italy, which was much worse. By the time he was liberated, he was in pretty bad shape and was shipped off to London to recover in a hospital there. That's where he met a nurse who quite liked him and invited him over for tea after he was discharged. That nurse was my mother's roommate, and when Frank met Irma, sparks flew!

Before long, Frank had to return to South Africa, and he wrote Irma saying, "I'd like to marry you." Irma wasn't sure about marriage, but she agreed to go to South Africa, instead of home to Canada, and get to know Frank better. Within a couple of months, Frank and Irma were married in a double ceremony with my father's sister and her new husband.

That's when I came into the picture. I grew up with my younger sister and brother in East London, a little town on the southeast coast of South Africa. It was an enchanting landscape for a little girl. From our backyard I watched giraffes, zebras, elephants, and wildebeest go by.

As a child, I didn't understand what was happening politically in South Africa. It wasn't until I was a teenager that I learned what apartheid was and the devastating effects those almost fifty years of racial segregation—a policy steeped in racism—had on nonwhite South Africans.

My only memory of apartheid was my nanny, a Black woman. Each of us children had one. Because of segregation, they lived in a mud hut at the back of our property. My parents treated our nannies kindly and spoke to them as valued employees, not as faceless underlings.

I remember my mother doing some of her own housework and other women in the neighborhood saying that was terrible. They said she should be in charge of running the house and leave the actual chores to the nannies.

After about seven years, my mother, with a critical eye on social justice, had had enough and was homesick. She wanted to return to Canada, and my father agreed to the adventure.

The problem was that the South African government discouraged whites from emigrating, so we told everyone we were going on a vacation. The next thing I knew I was boarding a boat with my parents and siblings headed for England. I was six years old. I remember standing by the rail and watching South Africa disappear. I've never gone back.

When we landed in England, my parents sent a cable to my father's family telling them the truth—that we were headed to Canada to live. The South African government intercepted all international communication, so when they learned that we weren't coming back, they seized our property and bank accounts.

Originally, we planned on settling in Hamilton, Ontario, where most of my mother's family was then living. But for some reason my father didn't like it there, and so my mother proudly suggested Regina. The very night we arrived, white stuff came down from the sky. I had never seen or even read about snow. I thought it was ice cream on the lawn. We kids got down on our hands and knees and ate it. The next day, I filled several mason jars with snow and planned to send them to my friends in South Africa, but the snow melted in the refrigerator.

November 1953. Two months after leaving sunny, lush South Africa,
Les, Kay, and I were enjoying the snow in Calgary, Alberta.

Several weeks later, we moved to Calgary, which was booming at the time. I loved the city, though not everything was perfect. At school, a couple of boys said I wasn't a real Canadian and called me a DP. About 150,000 so-called displaced persons had come to Canada after the Second World War, so the expression was common in the 1950s. All I wanted to do was blend in, but my South African accent got in the way. When I called my sweater a jersey, the boys would razz me, and I made a concerted attempt to use the new terms and lose my accent.

Other than a few hiccups early on, I found Canada to be a wonderful, welcoming place full of opportunity, and when I turned eighteen, my mother encouraged me to become a citizen. Even though she was Canadian, the law at the time said that only children born overseas to a Canadian father were considered citizens. It was only later that I realized how wrong that law was.

When I passed my citizenship test and appeared before the citizenship judge, a stern man in his late sixties, he asked me if I was ready to pledge my loyalty to Her Majesty, Queen Elizabeth.

I smiled at him. "I'm here to pledge my loyalty to Canada."

"No," he replied. "The way the system works here is you have to pledge your loyalty to Her Majesty the Queen."

I had nothing against the queen—and I understood that Canada was a constitutional monarchy—but I wasn't interested in being loyal to her, and so the judge told me to leave.

A year later, I capitulated. I didn't see any hope that the system would change (and indeed it hasn't to this day). That second time, in front of the same judge, I said, "Okay, I'll pledge my loyalty to the queen but I want you to understand that my pledge is really to Canada."

He wasn't interested in debating the issue. He raced through the pledge, and I crossed my ankles and my fingers as I said the words that made me a Canadian.

By the end of high school, I was beginning to see injustices around me. Several of my neighbours and kids at school didn't have loving, safe families, and I knew that one of the ways to help them was as a social worker. So I applied to the University of Calgary to study psychology and sociology—there was no Faculty of Social Work then—with plans to pick up a few courses later on to qualify as a social worker. To my delight, I was accepted and even got a few scholarships.

When I finished my BA, I told my parents I was going to move to Ottawa. On a trip home from Expo '67, a girlfriend and I had explored our capital. We saw the Parliament buildings and walked along Sparks Street and the Rideau Canal. I loved the city immediately. There was something about the buildings, the people, the gorgeous trees. It just said to me, "This is a city you need to be in."

My parents were surprised at my decision, but they had friends there I could stay with until I found an apartment of my own, so off I went! I had a hard time getting a job in counseling, but I could type, and I ended up working for a temporary placement service that sent me all over the city, including onto Parliament Hill. Even though it was temp work, that job taught me how much of Ottawa operated.

At one point, I worked for the Ministry of Indian Affairs, which was led by Jean Chrétien. In 1969, he had proposed a piece of legislation that called for the abolishment of the Indian Act, and a commission was travelling across Canada to hear what Canadians thought of his idea. It was my job to transcribe the testimonies. The quality of the audiotapes was terrible. Even worse were some of the remarks made by a few of the commissioners and those who testified. I would type everything out, putting exclamation marks in red pen beside the things I considered appalling, in particular the disparaging comments to the Indigenous people who had come to tell their stories.

After a while, I was called into Mr. Chrétien's office and I had a chat with his assistant, who said, "Thanks. Keep your red pen busy pointing these things out."

My work with the government piqued my interest in the intersection of politics and journalism, so I enrolled in a one-year Honours

Journalism program at Carleton University, but the school rejected me. However, by then I had become pretty feisty, so I wrote to the director of the School of Journalism with three questions: How many women do you have in the program? How many of your students are from Alberta? How many of your students have experience working on Parliament Hill?

A few days later the director of the school called me. "We have one woman from Alberta," he said. "But she's the only student from Alberta and one of only seven women in the program. We don't have anybody who has experience working on Parliament Hill. So, okay, you're in."

Carleton was a fabulous experience. We read about poverty and injustice and then we talked about how the issues applied to our lives and to our communities. What were the solutions to problems? What could we do to move the solutions forward? It was riveting stuff and got me thinking about life in a broader sense. I'll forever be grateful to the journalism faculty for waking up my mind.

In 1972, I returned to Calgary just as a federal election campaign was about to start, and my mother, who had been a Liberal Party supporter since her days as a teenager in Saskatchewan, had a friend, Mary Guichon, who needed a campaign manager. Even though I had no experience, I was hired. Of course a Liberal in Alberta had almost no chance of winning, but even in a losing campaign, which it was, I learned a lot about leadership, teamwork, and messaging—skills that would become very important throughout my life.

After that, I put politics aside for a while. I was in need of an intellectual challenge and tried my hand at being a stockbroker. As it turned out, I had a knack for researching companies and investing money. The work was eye-opening, not just on a professional level but as a woman.

Almost everyone at my firm was a man, and there was one guy who thought nothing of nibbling my ear and reaching over my shoulder to touch my breast. I kept saying, "Stop it." But it didn't stop him.

One day, he and his friends were gathered in the office and he called me over and put his arms around me and started to touch my breast. I had had enough. I grabbed his crotch in front of all his buddies and said, "Don't ever do that again." He went red and started shrieking and calling me names. Then he marched into the general manager's office and insisted I be fired.

The boss was pretty easygoing and tried to smooth things over. "I'm sure it was all a mistake," he said. And that was that. It was never spoken of again, but the man with the wandering hands kept his distance.

In 1974, the Liberal budget changed how energy companies were going to pay their federal taxes—that is, federal taxes were to be paid on revenues prior to the deduction of provincial royalties. The day after the announcement, I went into work to find fifty or sixty angry men waiting for me. Since I was a known member of the Liberal Party, they yelled and screamed at me that this was going to be the end of Calgary, the province, and the energy industry. They swore, shook their fists in front of my face, and shoved me up against the wall. I went home with bruises on my back and on my arms. Oddly, the experience didn't scare me; instead, it made me determined to defend Liberal policies even more publicly. I decided to see if I could run in the forthcoming election.

Senator Earl Hastings was the chair of the Liberal campaign in Calgary. My call to him started off well. He knew and respected my parents and listened as I told him a bit about myself. But then he said, "I'm not interested in having you as a candidate. You're female and a feminist. I won't sign your papers."

I wondered how I could get around the senator. During my time on Parliament Hill, I had met a number of people, one of them being Mary MacDonald, who worked as Prime Minister Pierre Trudeau's executive secretary. I called her.

"What would you think about me running as a candidate in Calgary Centre?" I asked.

"I think that would be terrific."

In the garden of 24 Sussex Avenue, Ottawa, Ontario, in July 1974.
Prime Minister Pierre Elliott Trudeau and I are having one of our discussions about
women's rights and Western Canadian alienation and what needed to be done.
Trudeau was always respectful and curious and kept asking me: "Why do you
feel so strongly about this issue? What if this changed? Then what?" PMO

"Would you mind asking around? And asking Mr. Trudeau if he thinks I'm good enough?" Mr. Trudeau and I had chatted several times when I worked on the Hill.

A couple of days later, Mary called and said everyone was on board. I circled back to Hastings and explained I had the go-ahead, but still he refused to sign my nomination papers. Now I was miffed. I called Mary again.

"Don't worry about it," she said coolly. "I'll just go down to Liberal headquarters, pick up the papers, and have Mr. Trudeau sign them."

And so she did!

When Hastings found out, he was furious and wouldn't cooperate with my campaign. He wouldn't even tell me when the prime minister was coming to Calgary to campaign. Fortunately, Mary filled me in from

Ottawa, and the prime minister was very kind to me, always making sure I was standing near him when he was in the city.

I felt we had a message that was important about building Canada, but when I knocked on doors, I met people who were angry about the new metric system, bilingualism, and the potential decline of the oil industry. They crumpled up our campaign literature, swore at me, slammed doors, and chased me off their property.

I wasn't deluded enough to think I had a chance of winning, yet on election night, when I lost by almost 14,000 votes, I had done better than any other Calgary Liberal candidate. But I still felt a stab of disappointment. Once again, I found myself looking around for something fulfilling to do that would help people.

In 1977, a new opportunity in politics presented itself. Alderman Ross Alger was running again for mayor of Calgary. He'd lost once before, so he and his organizers decided that this time they needed a more diverse campaign. They asked me to cochair and then manage the campaign because I wasn't male, old, or Conservative, but I didn't know anything about mayoral politics, so I said thanks but no. They kept asking, and eventually I gave in and Alger promised, "If I get elected, I'll make you my executive assistant at City Hall."

Three or four days before the election, he grew distant, canceling meetings and avoiding conversations with me. On election night we won, but the next day he took me aside, saying, "If I hire you as my executive assistant, I'm told the Conservative provincial government will not look kindly upon the city of Calgary."

And so I was left behind. After the lengths they had gone to bring me into the campaign, it was a stinging betrayal.

Three years later, Alger ran for reelection and lost. That's when he apologized to me. "If I had brought you on staff as I had planned, I would have been reelected. The diversity and intelligence you brought to my campaign made the difference."

But I didn't walk away from politics, not even after I ran as a federal Liberal candidate for a second time in 1979, endured a death threat, and lost by about 10,000 votes (but again got a bigger percentage of the vote than any other Liberal in Calgary).

I'm glad I stuck with politics because politics brought someone special into my life. By the 1980 federal election, I was managing the Liberal campaign in Calgary Centre. One dark and stormy night, a very handsome man walked through the door of the campaign office. His name was Richard Pootmans. He was from Ottawa, had worked in the oil fields, and had just graduated from Carleton with an honours BA. Now he was looking for a permanent job in the oil patch. Richard did everything I asked him to do and he did it very well with great charm. He and my mother quickly became good friends too. And that's how I met the man who would become my dear husband. We're now into our fourth decade together, which included a ten-year adventure running six Ports International clothing stores. (Incidentally, I finally experienced electoral success when Richard was elected twice to Calgary's city council!)

In 1991, the provincial Liberal leader Laurence Decore asked me to be a candidate in the next election. I said no twice, but when he asked a third time I said I'd do it if at least a quarter of the party's candidates were women and we ran some workshops for them to make them better campaigners. Laurence agreed. We came close to winning the election, but it was former Liberal Ralph Klein, now the Progressive Conservative leader, who won. After I lost the 1993 campaign by fewer than 2,000 votes, I decided to find a different way, outside politics, to contribute to Canada and push for the things I believed in.

Two years later, I went to lunch with a few women, one of whom was my good friend Nancy Millar. Nancy was writing a book that would tell the story of women in Canadian history through their gravestones. I looked through her initial research about amazing women who had stood up for women's rights; established libraries, hospitals, and schools; and been great contributors to their communities, but had none of these achievements acknowledged on their gravestones.

I turned to Nancy. "What about the Famous Five?"

"No," she said. "There isn't much more than MOTHER or LOVED AND REMEMBERED on their gravestones."

I had learned about the Famous Five women only about ten years earlier when my mother, as a member of the local Council of Women, had a hand in persuading the province of Alberta to declare the Calgary house where Nellie McClung had lived a heritage site. At the time, I couldn't even name all the women, but it didn't take much digging to realize they were Canada's democratic champions. They were largely responsible for women having the right to vote, serve as elected officials, and become senators. "Wow!" I thought. "These women are incredible! Such fabulous role models!"

Nellie McClung was a journalist who led the fight for female suffrage when Manitoba became the first province to allow women to vote; she was also elected as a Liberal member of the legislative assembly in Edmonton. Emily Murphy fought for a woman to share ownership of matrimonial property, and later became the first female magistrate in the British Empire. Louise McKinney was the first woman elected to a legislature in the British Empire when she was sworn into the legislative assembly of Alberta in 1917 as an independent. Henrietta Muir Edwards helped found the Victorian Order of Nurses and the prototype of the Canadian YWCA. Irene Parlby became the first female cabinet minister in Alberta as a United Farmers of Alberta member and helped establish travelling medical clinics and libraries.

They were notable as individuals, and even more formidable as a group. In 1928, the Supreme Court of Canada had unanimously decided that, under section 24 of the British North America Act, women were not "persons" and therefore, like criminals, idiots, and children, weren't fit to be appointed to the Senate. The Famous Five were very disappointed and persuaded the federal government to appeal the dreadful decision to the Judicial Committee of the Privy Council in Britain, which in those days was really our Supreme Court. In perhaps the most logical verdict in the history of any court, the Privy Council wrote, "To those who ask why the word [persons] should include females, the obvious answer is, why should it not?" That was October 18, 1929—the day that women became political equals in our country.

The Famous Five weren't perfect women—they had their flaws and some misguided beliefs—but through their suffrage victories and now this decision, they engineered a transfer of power in Canada without a single person being injured or killed. Men, who had been the deciders, were going to share their power with women, and this they have done without any lingering hostilities. It remains a powerful and magnificent chapter in Canada's history.

Sixty-six years later, Nancy and I decided that we should do something to commemorate the Famous Five before the end of the twentieth century. The target we set was October 18, 1999, the seventieth anniversary of the Persons Case. Our mutual friend, Maria Eriksen, joined us. Maria and I had worked on several initiatives resulting in losing battles to get the elected members of Calgary's city council to call themselves councillors instead of aldermen, and to adopt policies of gender equity and pay equity.

I wrote a business plan and became the CEO of the Famous 5 Foundation, and Maria became the chair. She wanted a university conference and a big dinner celebration. Nancy wanted a school curriculum guide so young people would understand what these extraordinary Canadians achieved. We agreed on those projects, but for me it wasn't enough. One of the ways our society honours its heroes is by naming something after them: a building, a bridge, or a street. "Or," I thought, "putting up a statue."

In Calgary, there wasn't a single statue honouring an identifiable woman. I phoned friends across Canada to ask what was in their town or city, and I went to libraries looking for information. I concluded that three women had statues in Canada—Queen Elizabeth, Queen Victoria, and Mary, mother of Jesus.

We decided to build a monument in Calgary to the Famous Five, even though we had no experience with anything of this scale. In fact, I persuaded the group that because this was a national story, we should have a second statue on Parliament Hill. I did some research, calculated some costs, and told the foundation, "We need a million dollars."

There were just five of us at that point, and we sat there looking at each other.

"Who here has raised a million dollars?" Maria asked.

No hands went up.

"Who here has raised half a million dollars?"

"A hundred thousand dollars?"

"Fifty thousand dollars?"

At fifteen thousand dollars, I put my hand up because one of my election campaigns had raised that much. That was enough to make me the chief fundraiser. We had big plans, and three and a half years until the seventieth anniversary of the Persons Case. All we needed now was a million dollars.

We started with some fundraising lunches and began taking in small donations. Five dollars, fifty dollars, a hundred dollars. I wrote a thank-you note by hand to each contributor. How many notes would I have to write before we had a million dollars? On a piece of paper, I wrote 200,000 donations of $5; therefore, I'd have to write 200,000 thank-you notes. Suddenly, I saw a different possibility—five donations of $200,000. The foundation agreed—it had to be five women, donating $200,000 each.

I drew up a list of potential angels. A woman would have to have a net worth of approximately $5 million, be involved in the community, and know about the Famous Five—or at least be willing to speak honestly about their beliefs, good and bad.

The first woman I approached was Ann McCaig. I didn't know her personally, but I knew she had exceeded her fundraising goal for the University of Calgary and had a sterling reputation. I arranged to meet with her to share our idea.

The night before, Richard asked me, "What are you going to say to her?"

"I'm going to say we want to do these monuments in Calgary and Ottawa and ask her to give me two hundred thousand dollars over three years."

Richard thought it would be a good idea to role play. "I'll be her, and you be you."

We practiced and practiced until I had the pitch tightly structured. Then Richard (as Ann) said, "So, Frances, what would you like me to do?"

"I would like you to . . . I would like you to give us . . ." It was hard to spit the whole thing out. How could I possibly ask for that kind of money from a woman I was meeting for the very first time? What nerve! "I would like you to please give us two hundred thousand dollars over three years."

He made me say that line over and over again until it became muscle memory.

The next day, Maria and I met with Ann and quickly discovered what a wonderful person she was. We chatted amiably about the project until Ann said, "So, Frances, what would you like me to do?"

"Ann, I would like you to please give us two hundred thousand dollars over three years." My voice was strong and clear, but my mind and heart were racing!

"Well," Ann replied. "I love the project. I think I would like to be involved, but may I have a day or so to think about it?"

"By all means, Ann."

Two days later she called me. "Yes," she said. "I'd like to do it but I'd like my two daughters involved as well. I'd like Roxanne and Jane to learn how to be good philanthropists, so we'd like each of us to give a portion of the two hundred thousand dollars."

That wasn't exactly what I wanted to hear. "Ann, I'm sorry, but that's not possible. We want to have just five women involved, to mirror the Famous Five. But let me check with my board, just in case."

Ann must have been surprised that someone was saying no to her generous gift, but she graciously told me to let her know what the board said.

We had a meeting a day or two later, and I told the foundation what I had done. No one screamed, but they said, "That was absolutely the wrong response, Frances. Go back to Ann and say, 'Sorry. Yes, of course, your daughters are welcome. Thank you very much for your generous donation.'"

They were right, and I quickly phoned Ann. "I'm really sorry. I made a mistake. You and your daughters are welcome to be donors with you. The board thinks it'll be a good way to tell the story of the contributions mothers and daughters have made to building Canada."

So Ann McCaig became our first important major donor.

The second donation was made by the family of Lena Ann Hanen in recognition of her life and contributions to religious harmony across Western Canada as she built a chain of women's clothing stores, the Betty Shops.

Soon after, Richard came home from an investment seminar in Banff and told me he had met a financier from Toronto named Kiki Delaney. "She is an extraordinary professional and she's a feminist, so I think you should talk to her."

I did just that, and this very impressive woman agreed, making her donation to inspire women's financial independence.

We were getting closer to our goal, so we started talking with the City of Calgary about giving us a spot for the statue on Olympic Plaza, a beautiful space that had been built in the heart of our downtown for the 1988 Olympics.

As for Parliament Hill, an interview in the *Ottawa Citizen* resulted in the formation of the Famous 5 Ottawa chapter, a wonderful group of thirty women led by the talented Isabel Metcalfe and Janice Liebe. I had already met with the leading politicians, but I also had a list of key civil servants I knew we had to get involved. Isabel and I started with the most senior civil servant, the Clerk of the Privy Council, Jocelyne Bourgon, who was cautiously supportive. Liberal MP Jean Augustine, the first African Canadian woman elected to Parliament, agreed to present a special resolution to allow the statue on the Hill. Deborah Grey, the first Reform Party MP, actually had a picture of Nellie McClung on her office wall. When she told me Nellie was her hero, I lit up. How fantastic that a key member of the official opposition supported us!

It would take unanimous consent to move the project forward, and I had discovered that Parliament Hill had guidelines for statues: only monarchs, deceased prime ministers, and Fathers of Confederation were allowed. I knew the Famous Five couldn't be Mothers of Confederation since they hadn't been part of 1867. Instead, in every meeting with a politician, an aide, or a bureaucrat, I argued that they were Mothers of *the* Confederation who had helped to build Canada. I also challenged parliamentarians and others to identify which Canadian prime minister had increased democracy as much as these women had. The silence was deafening.

When Jean Augustine presented her special resolution, the first naysayer was an independent MP, John Nunziata, whom I had forgotten to contact. He voted no, and the resolution died. He told reporters that he was a lawyer and a learned man, but he knew nothing about the Famous Five so there was no way he'd support such a statue on the Hill. But when it came time for the second vote, he stayed away from the House of Commons. I later learned that his mother had phoned him and said, "The Famous Five are my heroes, and I'm very disappointed that you don't know who they are. If you want to come for Christmas dinner, support them."

Another opponent, Garry Breitkreuz, a Reform MP from Saskatchewan, thought he had succeeded in stopping the resolution from coming to a vote the second time the House was asked leave to consider it. He shouted no and left the chamber. That's when Marlene Catterall, a

Liberal MP from Ottawa, politely challenged the Speaker with a procedural argument. The Speaker then allowed the vote, and the special resolution was passed unanimously. However, we couldn't celebrate just yet. Next up was the Senate.

Again there was stiff opposition. Our champions were Senators Joyce Fairbairn (Liberal) and Marjory LeBreton (Conservative). After two deferrals, the final unanimous resolution passed on December 18, 1997, thanks to the unexpected but greatly appreciated intervention of Senator Gérald Beaudoin, former dean of law at the University of Ottawa. And it was Henrietta Edwards's one hundred forty-eighth birthday!

All this was happening as I continued to look for two more major donors.

I reached out to newly appointed senator Vivienne Poy. Because she was a senator, her donation would have obvious symbolic significance. She had had a successful career in fashion design, manufacturing, wholesale, and retail, and was doing her PhD in feminist history. With enthusiasm, we welcomed her as our fourth donor and recognized the role Asian Canadian women had played in the building of Canada.

We still needed one more donor. I invited several women from Quebec and Atlantic Canada as well as two Indigenous women to participate, but they all declined.

Then a friend asked me, "Have you considered Heather Reisman?" Heather had just started Indigo Books. She lived in Toronto but had been raised in Montreal, which was important because she had links to Quebeckers. When I met with Heather, she immediately agreed to donate $200,000, for which we were very grateful. Her contribution was to support women being politically active.

We had our million dollars! We were all so busy pushing our plan ahead, we didn't think about having a celebration. There just wasn't time. . . .

Once Ottawa agreed that the Famous Five could live on Parliament Hill, it took darn ol' Calgary another seven months to agree to accept them too. Meanwhile, design work was well underway. We had pored over portfolios from about fifty sculptors and asked fifteen to prepare a proposal. Then a sculptor called from Edmonton. "I know I just missed the deadline," she said. "But I would love to be part of this project."

We had selected eight male and seven female sculptors, so I thought an eighth woman was a good idea. Her name was Barbara Paterson. And wouldn't you know it, she won!

Her design brought these champions to life by showing the five women celebrating their legal victory. Nellie McClung held a newspaper aloft with some of the actual headlines that were printed across Canada when the Persons Case was decided. The statue included an empty chair, which would allow visitors to sit with the women—a touch of interactivity before that word became ubiquitous.

October 18, 1999, was the seventieth anniversary of the Persons Case. In Calgary's Olympic Plaza, there was just a light breeze and the temperature was a comfortable 11 degrees Celsius. Four thousand people, including many schoolkids, stood shoulder to shoulder as a crane lifted a huge piece of fabric to reveal the monument honouring Canada's Famous Five. It was absolutely thrilling! Thrilling! Thrilling! CBC Newsworld broadcast the ceremony live across the country, and I was standing next to their anchor, Kathleen Petty, telling the country about these five remarkable women who had had their setbacks and had made mistakes, but who had contributed so significantly to improving life in Canada. Since then, many people have told me how inspired and uplifted they feel when seeing the monument. There's pride in their voices when they say, "I brought my daughter" or "I brought my granddaughter."

Volunteers had done almost all the work in Calgary, but in Ottawa, the government had to approve nearly everything, and we had several bargaining sessions on where the statue would go. I walked around Parliament Hill over and over again. Finally, late one snowy night, I saw an open space not too far from the Senate side of the centre block. Near the

On October 18, 2015, the eighty-sixth anniversary of the Persons Case,
the Famous 5 Foundation launched the Women Belong campaign. Here I am
speaking at Olympic Plaza in Calgary in the centre of the Famous 5 statue. On the left
behind the seated women is Emily Murphy, and on the right is Nellie McClung,
holding the newspaper aloft next to Irene Parlby. FAMOUS 5 FOUNDATION

statues of John A. Macdonald, who excluded women in the British North America Act, William Lyon Mackenzie, who had supported the Famous Five's quest, and Queen Elizabeth II, who represented the Privy Council in our story, was a lovely, lonely patch of grass. Bingo!

Public Works thought the location was too busy. "Wouldn't you like a quieter location where people can contemplate the contributions of the Famous Five?" they said.

"No," we replied. "We love the busyness, the prominence. We want people to walk by it every day."

With the support of Sheila Copps, the minister of Canadian Heritage, we carried the day, and on October 18, 2000, a year after the Calgary statue was unveiled, I presented the monument to the minister of Public Works, Alfonso Gagliano, who accepted it on behalf of the Government of Canada. Thousands of people listened to speeches and watched Governor General Adrienne Clarkson and Prime Minister Jean Chrétien cut the ribbon. They were inspired by a theatrical enactment honouring the Famous Five played by five marvelous Canadian actresses. It was an absolutely wonderful day! All the hard work and the exhausting hours had been worth it.

We—and by then there were hundreds of people involved—had come a long way in a very short time, but I knew that only a small proportion of Canadians would ever see the statues in either Calgary or Ottawa. I kept asking myself, "What do all Canadians share?" The answer was our anthem, our flag, and our money.

The Bank of Canada issues a new series of bills every ten years or so to defeat counterfeiters, and luckily for us, it was choosing designs for a future series, so I went to see a man at the bank. When I asked if they would consider putting the Famous Five on the new five-dollar bill, he looked at me as if I had asked about desecrating the flag.

"No, no. Definitely not interested. Canadians like to have animals on their money, things like elk and buffalo."

However, when the Bank brought a mock-up of a bill with an elk on it for approval by a subcommittee of the cabinet, Herb Gray, the deputy prime minister, asked, "Isn't there a suggestion that we honour Canadians and their achievements?"

"Yes, but Canadians like to have animals and scenery on their money."

Sheila Copps piped up. "How do you know that? Have you done a survey?"

"No," said the man from the bank.

Well, it turns out that 96 percent of Canadians said they'd rather see people and their achievements on their money, not large animals.

The Bank offered us the fifty-dollar bill. The five would have been better because it's used more, especially by young people, but the number 5 was on a 50, and the prime minister during the Persons Case, William Lyon Mackenzie King, was on the front of the bill, so it was a good fit. On October 18, 2004, the seventy-fifth anniversary, the Bank of Canada unveiled the bill in Calgary. It was the first time an identifiable Canadian woman other than the queen appeared on our currency. It circulated for barely eight years, until another government decided to replace it with an Arctic research icebreaker. The Famous Five deserved more time, but at the very least, they could have put another woman on the banknote.

After that, my mind returned to something Professor Elizabeth Donaldson from the University of Calgary had said to me years earlier during one of our fundraising luncheons. She complained that we were singing a sexist national anthem, pointing to the line "True patriot love in all thy *sons* command."

"Where are the women?" she asked.

She wasn't the only one asking.

In partnership with the Girl Guides of Canada, I had toured the country with a scale model of the Famous Five monument. At each ceremony we opened with "O Canada" and then one of the girls would speak. A number of times at the end of the day, the father of the Girl Guide would pull me aside.

"Frances," he'd say. "I'm really in a quandary right now. I've just seen how beautifully my daughter speaks in public, how passionate she is about important issues, and how much she wants to be involved. But we also sang an anthem that excludes her. I have a son whom I love, but I love my daughter equally. We have to do something."

Now was the time for that something. Discussions ensued with linguists and songwriters who agreed that the best replacement would be "True patriot love in all *of us* command." On July 30, 2001, Jeanne d'Arc Sharp and I started a petition campaign. I went on numerous radio hotline programs too. Some callers agreed with our idea, but many others were extremely hostile. I got hate mail too. How dare I suggest a change to the anthem?

Opponents often said that their father and grandfather fought and died for the current anthem, but the truth was that "O Canada" wasn't our anthem until 1980, long after our major wars. When I spoke to the Canadian Legion, they said they weren't necessarily opposed to the change, but maybe it would be easier in ten or fifteen years when many of these veterans had passed on.

It would, indeed, take years and years. In 2003, thanks to Senator Poy, we got a resolution through a Senate committee to change the two words, but we couldn't crack the House of Commons.

Over the ensuing years, Mauril Bélanger, an opposition Liberal MP from Ottawa, agreed to put a private member's bill forward, but it was defeated twice. After the 2015 election, Mauril was reelected and campaigned to become Speaker of the House, but he withdrew when he was diagnosed with ALS. Apparently, Prime Minister Justin Trudeau asked him if there was any particular piece of legislation that he would like to see achieved in the near future. He chose restoring "O Canada" to its original inclusiveness. On June 15, 2017, just two months before he died, he was successful. The new version of the anthem was sung with gusto at Mauril's funeral.

Unfortunately, despite passage of the bill in the House and the success of Senator Poy's resolution in committee, Conservative senators refused to consider the bill on the floor of the Senate for nearly two years. Senator Nancy Ruth had been a big supporter when she was in office, and thanks to the Liberal and independent senators, including Senator Frances Lankin, who followed in Nancy's footsteps, the bill was passed on January 30, 2019.

I believe so strongly that all of us build Canada: men and women, old and young, new Canadians and always Canadians. We all have something to contribute. Canada empowers all of us to follow our dreams. It is such a truly extraordinary country, so sing out proudly, "True patriot love, in all of us command!" And then do something to help build Canada.

Frances Wright is a tireless ambassador for grassroots and social justice. In 1996, she coestablished the Famous 5 Foundation, an organization devoted to recognizing women as nation builders. More recently, she helped launch the Canadian Centre for Male Survivors of Child Sexual Abuse when she discovered that one in six Canadian men have been sexually abused before the age of eighteen. Her awards and honours include a Governor General's Award, the Rotary Integrity Award, and the Alberta Order of Excellence. She lives in Calgary, Alberta, with her dear husband, and is bringing women together to develop grand plans for the ninety-fifth anniversary of the Persons Case in 2024.

MATT DEVLIN
From the Heart

*As the Raptors went deeper in the playoffs, something
else happened that was quintessentially Canadian. Something that
says how this country, often rife with regional differences, can
also be united with an inspiring common goal. Canadians from coast
to coast to coast suddenly got really into basketball.*

Robin Roberts Stadium in Springfield, Illinois, is a slice of American history. Situated right in the heartland of the United States, the stadium, with some modernization over the years, has been home to various minor league baseball teams since 1928, making it one of the oldest stadiums in the country.

While Canada is my home, it's places like Roberts Stadium where my journey to becoming a Canadian really began. And it's a lesson about the moments in our lives that prepare us for something bigger than ourselves.

Roberts is the kind of place where the crack of a bat brings back memories of another era. For starters, it's got real grass—no artificial turf for Springfield. Three hundred and twenty feet down the lines, four hundred and fifteen feet to deep centre. Its very name heralds a local hero—Robin Roberts, a pitcher who went to school in the Depression years just down the road at Lanphier High, before heading out of town on the legendary highway, Route 66, to join the big leagues. Roberts was so good at throwing the fastball that after a solid major league career, he made it to the Hall of Fame. Springfield celebrates that with his name stretched over the stadium's entrance. It's not a big place, only holds fifty-two hundred fans. But they're smart, they know their baseball, so if you're going to talk baseball in Springfield you better know what you're talking about.

And that's why I found myself sitting in the stands at Roberts Stadium in the summer of 1992.

I had graduated from Boston College in 1990 with a communications degree specializing in marketing. My dream was to do play-by-play sportscasting, but it had been a struggle catching on somewhere, and in the meantime I was grabbing work where I could, which included selling clothes in a menswear store in Houston, Texas. The truth was I had very little experience, but I was hoping that would change. I had just been hired to be the number two play-by-play guy in the broadcast team of the Springfield Cardinals. Number One called the games, but Number Two didn't even get to the booth during the game—instead I was kind of a "gofer." Go for coffee, go for the lineup sheets, go for the broom to sweep the floor. If there was a "go for" task, I was the one sent. Until the day, having grown increasingly frustrated, I asked Number One if I would ever get a chance to do a game.

"When you show me you can," he replied. "When you show *yourself* you can!"

"How will I ever do that?"

He was quick with the answer. He told me that during the next game, when my chores were done, I should go sit in the stands with a tape recorder and start talking.

So I did. I got an old cassette tape recorder and a plug-in microphone and went and sat in the stands. I pushed the record button and just started talking.

"Fred Johnston is up to bat for the Cards, batting left and struggling at the plate."

I searched my notes for something else to say while I waited for the pitcher to engage. There were as many "ums" and "ahs" as there were facts.

"Here comes the pitch. Swing and a miss."

Around me fans were turning their heads, confused and a bit stunned. Some laughed. To be honest, quite a few laughed. They certainly thought I was a bit odd, but I stuck with it for a while until I'd filled up most of a half-hour cassette. Then I went home to listen.

Number One had been right. Listening told me the truth. It was brutal. No excitement. No emotion. Too many clichés and predictable comments. Too many pauses at times, not enough pauses at other times. This was going to need work. And practice. And guidance. But I was determined to make it work. It was my life's dream.

In many ways, climbing up through the ranks of different sports, I've never stopped trying to be better. And most often the key to getting better is guidance, a kind of unofficial mentorship.

I can remember once going to watch a game with the parent club, the St. Louis Cardinals of the National League. This was the real deal, and it was exciting. At batting practice, I saw the famed St. Louis play-by-play broadcaster Jack Buck as he stood behind the practice batting cage watching the players taking swings. And listening. Listening to the stories the players and coaches told about the game. He'd store them in his remarkable baseball mind and pull them out to fill time on air later.

I screwed up my courage and walked over to the famous Mr. Buck.

"Sir, my name is Matt Devlin, and I do play-by-play for the Springfield Cardinals. I was wondering if there might be a chance to sit quietly in your booth and watch and listen to you doing your work?"

It was pretty presumptuous of me, and I expected the odds were high I was going to be told to buzz off. But I was wrong.

"Absolutely," he replied.

I spent an afternoon getting a master class in the art of the call. I was in awe, almost spellbound. But that day and others that followed taught me a lot about sports play-by-play broadcasting, not how to copy but how to learn from one of the greats about developing my own style. How to research, how to make notes on the game sheet that I could go to at a moment's notice, and most importantly how to ad-lib in a way that wasn't tedious but that helped the audience feel they were right there in the stadium with me. Bottom line—how to speak from the heart.

It was all heady stuff for a kid from Nashville, Tennessee, who had decided that broadcasting was the job for him when a local TV reporter came to speak to his class. Nashville seemed to groom good broadcasters—that reporter was John Seigenthaler, who later became a backup to Tom Brokaw at NBC. And guess what local TV weatherman was about to make a name for himself as a top game-show host? Pat Sajak, best known for a little show called *Wheel of Fortune*.

So I was convinced that Matt Devlin could reach for the sky too.

But it would be a long and winding road through many cities and many sports: Abilene, Texas; Springfield, Illinois; Palm Springs, California; Memphis, Tennessee; Charlotte, North Carolina, to name just a few. Baseball, basketball, football, tennis, Olympic wrestling . . . I've broadcast them all.

Understanding the rhythm of a game is really important. Every sport has a different rhythm. In hockey and basketball, the puck and the ball move constantly and you stay with the movement. In baseball, there's a lot of downtime, and then suddenly you're dealing with serious action—when a ground ball is hit sharply deep into the corner, everyone starts moving—and you have to be on top of it all. Then there's football, which someone once said to me is a continuing series of five seconds of chaos followed by twenty-five seconds of fill. They all presented their own challenges, but as I got older I knew I was going to have to make a choice about what sport to build my career on.

*A photo from earlier in my career, when I was calling the wrestling
for NBC during the 2008 Beijing Olympics.*

By the early 2000s, it was clear to me that the answer to that question
was basketball. I loved the game, and I loved that I got to broadcast right
on the floor, directly behind or beside the teams. All the other sports had
their broadcasters up in the air—doing their play-by-play from the booths
on the upper levels to give them the whole view of the big playing surface.
Basketball didn't have that issue. And in 2008, I got the opportunity of a
lifetime when Chuck Swirsky, the longtime play-by-play broadcaster for
the Toronto Raptors, left for the Chicago Bulls. Now Chuck loved Toronto and Toronto loved him, but when an opening came up for the same
job with his beloved Bulls, he couldn't say no and neither could the Bulls.

I'd been to Toronto a few times broadcasting games between the Raptors and first the Memphis Grizzlies, then the Charlotte Bobcats, for both
of whom I did play-by-play. I loved Toronto, the city and its people, and

I was convinced the Raptors were a team on the upswing. I got myself in contention for the job along with two or three others who were equally interested and flew to Toronto for an interview session with the Raptor brass. I felt I'd put my best case forward, but I didn't hear anything for a few days. However, a few weeks later, they called me to say the job was mine.

I was ecstatic but knew full well it was going to be a challenge.

Chuck had been an institution in Toronto, and replacing him was not going to be easy. I knew I had to work at earning the audience, and part of that was developing my own style to fit the Raptor audience and part of that was having my own, for the lack of a better word, gimmicks. For me, it was about involving as much of the city of Toronto as possible in every game. I found the answer in the way I described a successful three-point shot. Whenever a Raptor made one, I'd include a local reference.

"Lowry from Scarborough, bucket and book it."

"Ibaka drains it from Mississauga."

"Powell from Pickering."

I was living the dream, and my whole family loved it.

The longer we stayed in Canada, the more we realized just how much we loved it. All of us: my wife, Erin, and our three sons, Jack, Ian, and Luke. When there were opportunities to leave Canada for good broadcast jobs in the US, I said no because our family realized *this* had become home. I had travelled all over for my job, but I'd never lived in one place as long as I've lived in Canada. And by 2018, I thought that one of the greatest gifts Erin and I could give the boys would be to become citizens of Canada. So we applied for citizenship and began a year-long process of classes and tests which ironically would culminate in the middle of the greatest playoff run the Toronto Raptors had ever made.

Which brings me to May 12, 2019, and the moment that proved to me and to basketball fans across Canada that this was not going to be what past springs had been—another year when the Toronto Raptors couldn't dig down and move up in the playoffs.

It was Game 7 of round two of the playoffs. The Raptors had never gone further than this. With the clock running out, and the game tied, there was a distinct possibility that history was about to repeat itself.

There were five seconds left in the game against their longtime rivals, the Philadelphia 76ers. A timeout was in effect. The Raptors would have the ball when the timeout ended. I knew that, barring a catastrophe, the worst that could happen was the game would go to overtime. The best that could happen would be a buzzer-beater, a last-second, all-or-nothing shot by the Raptors that would go in. Then we would be on to the next round of the playoffs—but that had never happened in the history of playoff Game 7s in the NBA.

In my mind, I ran through my last-minute checklist. Time, score, timeouts remaining, which team had a foul to give or not give. My job was simple, all my training had told me—follow the ball, don't take your eyes off it. And then suddenly the ball was in play and in the hands of the most dynamic player to ever wear a Raptors uniform.

"Kawhi up top . . . looks at the clock . . . turns the corner . . ."

Kawhi Leonard was circling near the Philadelphia basket, his head down, determined to go to his favourite spot. With one second left, from deep in the baseline corner he was in the air releasing a jumper that sailed high over the 76ers' star centre Joel Embiid's outstretched hands.

"Kawhi for the winner!"

Everyone following on television, on radio, everyone watching in the arena, including me, felt like what followed was unfolding in slow motion.

"It's hanging in the air . . ."

The ball had reached the top of its arc toward the net and then, agonizingly for those watching, began its fall toward the basket.

From a distance, it looked like it would fall short.

It did fall *just* short.

It hit the rim.

And, then, magic.

Bounce, bounce, bounce, bounce—swish.

"Kawhi Leonard . . . with the game winner! The ball suspended in the air!"

And then a quick reference to how a jinx had been broken—a similar shot against the same team in a same Game 7 of a same round two in 2001 had not fallen, and had broken so many hearts, seemingly setting a pattern that other Raptor teams would never break. But not anymore.

"And some eighteen years later, the Raptors get this shot to go in!"

I didn't need to say any more. Everyone knew what I meant.

There was pandemonium around me. Raptor players and fans were screaming, hugging, celebrating in disbelief. The 76er players were stunned, their faces frozen in the moment. It was one of those times I'd learned back in those Jack Buck days that my job was quite simple—just stop talking and let the moment breathe. Everyone around me, no matter their emotion, was speaking from the heart.

I had never seen anything like it. It was one of the greatest moments that I've witnessed from a play-calling standpoint. I've seen those last few seconds played back hundreds and hundreds of times. Like a lot of my fellow Canadians, I can't take my eyes off it even though I knew it all firsthand—I had witnessed it all, I had been right there, just metres from Leonard when the ball left his fingers. But I don't think I'll ever tire of watching it again.

My fellow Canadians.

I smile looking at those words. They were something that before the playoffs I'd never been able to say. But a few weeks after what's become known as "the Shot," on the day after the first game of the *final* round of the playoffs, Erin, Jack, Ian, Luke, and I stood before a citizenship court judge and swore our allegiance to Canada with one hundred and four others representing twenty-eight different countries. Standing there, I thought about the impact that moment had, not only on me but on all the others in the room who felt like me that they were doing this for a better life. It was incredibly moving and powerful.

*Me, Jack, Erin, Ian, and Luke proudly waving our flags as newly minted
Canadians after our citizenship ceremony.*

As the Raptors went deeper in the playoffs, something else happened
that was quintessentially Canadian. Something that says how this country, often ripe with regional differences, can also be united with an inspiring common goal. Canadians from coast to coast to coast suddenly
got really into basketball. In a hockey country, in the middle of the Stanley Cup playoffs, people were talking . . . hoops. It even changed my
play-calling style.

No more focus just on Toronto. This was Canada's team now.

So there I was saying:

"Siakam hits it from Saskatoon."

And "VanVleet banks it in from Vancouver."

But this may have been my all-time favourite:

"Lowry nails it from Pond Inlet."

I'm told that one had people jumping in the streets of the tiny
Nunavut town.

*Holding the Larry O'Brien trophy after the
Toronto Raptors won the NBA championship.*

Well, they weren't alone. Things kept going right for the Raptors
and their storybook run in the playoffs, and people were in the streets
in big cities and small towns across the country the night the Raptors
convincingly won the final playoff round against the defending champion
Golden State Warriors. I was sitting in Oakland calling the game but
was watching my monitors with pride as fans poured out into the streets
across Canada to celebrate a historic victory.

But that night's celebrations were nothing compared with what happened a few days later at the official welcome home in Toronto, when
hundreds of thousands gathered and roared in and around City Hall
square. The crowds had formed to celebrate the newly crowned champions, and I was in the middle of the incredible atmosphere.

I witnessed the first time the Larry O'Brien trophy would leave the
United States for Canada. The Larry O'Brien trophy, you say? Okay, so

the name doesn't quite have the ring of history that the Stanley Cup carries in Canada, but our neighbours to the south love their former NBA commissioners just as much as we love our former governors general!

It was hard to beat the excitement in the air, but what happened next did. I was about to make the "call" of my life.

The crowd that day was huge. It's estimated that one to three million people lined the parade route that wound its way through downtown Toronto to the last stop: Nathan Phillips Square at Toronto City Hall. It was a gorgeous day, hot but not sweltering, with a clear blue sky. The fans had been amazingly patient waiting for their heroes to arrive.

Finally, hours later than many had expected, the Raptor players were there and up on the stage in front of the crowd. First there were the politicians, including Prime Minister Justin Trudeau, along with the team owners. I guess that was a necessary touch but they did look a little awkward, perhaps knowing full well they were not who the crowd was there to see. Then the players took their place on the stage, dressed casually and thoroughly enjoying the moment and the thunderous adulation it generated.

I was the emcee, and it was an easy job. Introduce the players and the officials with their prepared speeches. And that's exactly the way it went—until it didn't. It was during owner Larry Tannenbaum's remarks that I first realized something wasn't quite right. I was wearing a small earpiece receiving instructions about the lineup of the stage show when suddenly the person talking to me changed her tone. She said there was an emergency and we had to stop the speech. Then she repeated herself. I could see her across the other side of the stage, so I quickly raced behind those on stage to where she was standing.

I told her that I had to know what the emergency was because if I was to interrupt the speech, what I said would depend on what was going on. Earlier, someone had fainted in the crowd and the crowd was asked to make room for medical staff to get in. Was it another situation like that? Would I need to clear a section of fans? Would I need to ask for a pathway to be opened up for emergency workers? The person who had signaled me in my earpiece didn't know the answers so she handed me a walkie-talkie to speak with security. They were very clear, very precise, and wasted no time.

"There's a gunman at the intersection of Queen and Bay Streets."

That was only about a hundred metres away from where I was standing. They told me nothing else, but suddenly everything was very different. I moved rapidly toward the podium. Only seconds had passed.

As I moved toward Mr. Tannenbaum, I repeated to myself these key thoughts: "Words are powerful; your tone is extremely important."

I took the microphone from Larry, put my hand on his back, and whispered, "I'm sorry, I need to interrupt." He knew I would only do that in an emergency, and he stepped back immediately.

I leaned into the microphone and talked from the heart. "We're here to celebrate, which we will. This is about love, it's about rejoicing. But I want everybody to just take a moment, please stay strong, stay together. There is an emergency. It *is* being dealt with."

I talked for about a minute or so, repeating those key elements. My hope was to keep people calm, engaged, and in one place, and let them know that the situation was being handled. I deliberately never used the word "gun." No one told me not to, I just knew that if I did mention a gun, it could easily create a situation much worse than what was already happening. It could cause panic and a human stampede. I could tell from my position that in and around the Bay and Queen corner there was already movement, and the last thing we needed was for it to intensify and spread across the whole square.

I signaled to Mr. Tannenbaum that it was now okay to finish his remarks, and he did without commenting on my interruption. As I backed away from the podium, I looked at the array of players and politicians and officials perched on their stools on the stage. Not one had moved, not even the prime minister. Justin Trudeau, casual in jeans and a T-shirt, was sitting beside the giant seven-foot Raptor forward Marc Gasol, and neither of them had budged. If any of them, and especially the PM, had suddenly moved, or been moved, off the stage after my remarks, that would have led, I'm sure, to chaos. But that didn't happen. They, like the crowd, had been calmed.

The whole episode lasted just minutes, and then the crowd and all those on stage were singing Freddie Mercury and Queen's "We Are the Champions" with heartfelt joy. We learned later that four people had been shot, but their injuries were not life-threatening, and three suspects were arrested within hours.

A lot of people have since credited me with preventing a disaster that day. That's very kind, but let's be serious. It was the people of Toronto who didn't let a disaster happen. The Toronto police moved quickly with arrests; emergency medical staff looked after those who had been shot; and people like the prime minister didn't race for cover knowing full well that too could have caused panic.

On stage in Nathan Phillips Square leading the crowd in "We Are the Champions."

When I got home that night I was drained. Emotionally, physically, and mentally. It had been an exhausting few weeks with every twist imaginable. Becoming a Canadian, watching a championship run, and witnessing a city stand tall in the face of danger.

Since then, I've thought about that day many times and how I handled things. And I smile.

It takes me back to sitting in the baseball stands in Springfield. Standing behind the batting cage with Jack Buck. Sitting in the radio booth listening to great broadcasters like Tom Cheek and Jerry Howarth. All those moments and many more that helped teach me the art of ad-libbing in broadcasting, and now in real life too.

When you're a play-by-play announcer, you're living in the moment as you call a game, no matter what that game is. You may do prep work, but once the ball goes up in the air, once the puck is dropped, once the football is kicked, once the baseball is thrown, all you can do is react and respond to what is happening right in front of you. So I don't remember everything that I said on stage that day other than that I remained true to those nuggets of wisdom I was taught so many years ago—live in the moment, be true to what you're witnessing, and, always, speak from the heart.

Bucket and book it.

Matt Devlin was born in Syracuse, New York. Nicknamed Matty D, he is the current play-by-play TV announcer for the Toronto Raptors. In his long-running career, he has called NBA games for the Memphis Grizzlies and the Charlotte Bobcats and has covered a variety of other sporting events, including MLB, NFL, and Olympic broadcasts. In 2011, he hosted the pregame and postgame shows for the Toronto Maple Leafs on Leafs TV. A proud Canadian, he lives with his wife and kids in Toronto.

JANICE EISENHAUER

Canadian Women for Women in Afghanistan

I asked myself: What is my role in bringing human rights to someone half a world away? Where do I fit? How can I help? What can I do?

"**B**OOM!" The bang reverberated through our little apartment. At first, I thought a barbecue had exploded, which in retrospect was completely ridiculous because I wasn't at home in Calgary. I was with my friend Carolyn Reicher, more than 10,000 kilometres away in Kabul, the capital of Afghanistan.

It was a bomb, of course.

The cleaning woman, Golperi, who happened to be in the apartment with us, took my hand and put it on her heart. It was beating like a drum—she was so scared. I ran to the balcony with Carolyn and we swung open the doors, but there was nothing to see. The explosion had been on the other side of the district.

That moment has stayed with me. Because of the sheltered life I led in Canada, a loud bang did not immediately make me think a bomb had detonated. But to an Afghan, it was more than obvious, even a regular occurrence.

For six years I had been working to support Afghan women as they strived to improve their lives. But this was the first time I had visited the

*Carolyn and I with our friend Golperi, on our first trip
to Afghanistan in 2004. I'm on the far right.*

country and experienced what Afghanistan's women went through each day. I only got a fleeting, mild taste of what their lives were like, but my eyes had been opened. My heart had been broken.

I didn't grow up with any special knowledge of, or ties to, Afghanistan. Like many Canadians, for most of my early life I couldn't find Afghanistan on a map. So what led me to this moment in 2004? Let me tell you.

When I was growing up, my dad was a big influence on the person I became. I was only ten when my mother died of cancer, and after that he made a commitment that I and my two older brothers would have the best life possible under the circumstances. He provided stability, and I could always trust him to do what he believed was the right thing.

Perhaps because of that, I've always had a bit of an independent streak. At seventeen, I decided I was ready to be on my own and moved into an apartment with a friend. A few months later, I finished high school. My brothers were in university, but I wanted to earn money to pay the rent, so I went to work instead.

I found a job at a bank. This was the 1970s, before computers, so I recorded mortgage payments by hand onto sheets of paper fourteen inches long. Page after page. I was good with numbers, and I began to make my way up the ladder. By the time I was twenty-eight years old, I was in charge of a mortgage portfolio worth over $11 million. It was a good job and great people, but not at all fulfilling.

I felt like I was on a treadmill, moving furiously but going no-where. I had married my childhood sweetheart but then divorced. I was taking university courses part-time, but I kept coming up against a wall. I wanted to be engaged in something that mattered. The more I thought about it, the more I realized what excited me. It was cul-ture. It was women's issues. It was trying to understand how the world worked, physically, socially, and politically.

I had been contributing to a pension plan at the bank, and I decided to withdraw the money, quit my job, and travel for a year. A friend said to me, "You know you're supposed to use that money when you retire." But that seemed so far off.

That year of travel was everything I hoped it would be. China, Japan, New Zealand, Australia, Singapore, Malaysia, and through South America as well. The trip made me even more curious about culture and people and renewed my interest in university. When I dis-covered the University of Calgary's program of development studies, I was awakened to world issues. For the first time, I felt like I could understand and learn and move forward.

Then one assignment changed my life.

We had to identify a critical world issue and devise a plan to do some-thing about it. That night I went home and began leafing through a magazine called *Homemakers*. It's no longer around, but back then the pub-lication was filled mostly with recipes, health advice, and child-rearing tips. Except this 1997 issue had something special: a story by Sally Armstrong about Afghan women's lives under the Taliban. That article introduced me—and the world, really—to the Taliban. It was groundbreaking journalism, describing the appalling human rights violations against women in Afghanistan. Girls couldn't get an education. Women weren't allowed to have a job or get medical help. On the street they were forced to wear burkas to cover themselves from head to toe, and women were basically locked up under the Taliban regime. Their lives had been stolen. While I didn't know the complex history of the country or its people, I knew that what Sally was describing was an abomination.

I brought the article to school the next day and showed it to a classmate, Carolyn Reicher. We decided our project would focus on the women of Afghanistan. Now, understand this was an academic exercise. The assignment was hypothetical. What would we do in the real world, if we could?

We brainstormed how to raise awareness in Canada. One idea was to organize a Sally Armstrong speaking tour of the country. Another was to bring an Afghan woman to Canada to describe her lived experience. Another was to apply for a Canadian government development aid grant. The more we theorized, the more we kept saying to each other, "I wish this was a real project. The world needs to know what's going on in Afghanistan."

So we made it real. Together, Carolyn and I founded the nonprofit organization Canadian Women for Women in Afghanistan (CW4WAfghan). The truth is we can't always rely on government and international agencies to do everything. Each of us has to take some individual responsibility.

It was all well-intentioned, but we didn't know how to help Afghan women. We didn't even know an Afghan woman. I heard there was a young Afghan woman working as a hairdresser in my local area in Calgary, and I practically stalked her trying to talk to her. I desperately wanted to understand what was going on in Afghanistan. At university, we were learning that so much can go wrong with development efforts overseas and we wanted to avoid becoming just another money-wasting failure.

We researched everything we could about Afghanistan. Looking back, it frustrates me how slow a process it was, but there was so much we didn't understand. We took it for granted that, in Canada, women had rights, so we initially thought that the treatment of women was about religion or culture. But then we began to realize this oppression of women is clearly all about basic human rights.

I asked myself: What is my role in bringing human rights to someone half a world away? Where do I fit? How can I help? What can I do?

Around this same time, my son, Daniel, was ready to start school. My spouse, Richard, and I were assessing our options—public schools and private schools. These were all the normal things parents do to provide what's best for their children, but it was impossible not to see how privileged we were in Canada, debating these things while in Afghanistan every school door was closed to girls. Women in Afghanistan wanted to give their children the same opportunities we do, but they had no ability to do that. I felt for them woman-to-woman and couldn't understand how we could let this poverty and horrific violence continue when we have all this freedom for our children.

Carolyn and I knew we couldn't do anything without money, so we wrote letters to nine groups that we knew had some connection to helping Afghans. Would they be willing to give us a grant? Eight of them didn't even bother to say no. They completely ignored us. But Rights and Democracy, which was created by Parliament to support the universal values of human rights, took a chance on us. In 1999 they gave us a $9,000 grant and promised to consider another grant the following year if we spent the money wisely.

It wasn't a lot of money, but it was an important start for CW4WAfghan. Real money meant real responsibility. We weren't on the sidelines any longer; we were on the field of play. We began drafting a mission statement to establish solid goals and objectives and what we were going to do to accomplish them.

We were determined that our money would actually get to the women in Afghanistan we were trying to help, not be frittered away in red tape.

We decided not to funnel cash through any of the large development agencies and instead came up with a model to direct funds to local Afghan female-managed organizations in Afghanistan that were working directly in their communities with women and children. They were the ones with the expertise in what was needed and we had to listen and learn from them.

It wasn't easy to find these Afghan partners. We started with the *Homemakers* article, reaching out to any name that was mentioned. One name was Dr. Sima Samar, a doctor who had fled to Pakistan because the Taliban had arrested her husband. From there she established the Shuhada Organization, dedicated to providing Afghan women and girls with health care. It was exactly what we were looking for.

We also found the Afghan Women's Resource Center, which was running clandestine schools in Pakistan's refugee camps, and we provided a small grant to them to help pay their rent so they could continue to run their programs.

Another name in the magazine article was Deborah Ellis, who was a little-known author back then. She was deeply concerned with human rights and wanted to help the women of Afghanistan, so Carolyn and I flew to Toronto to meet her. We sat at a picnic table on a university campus, and it took no time to realize we shared common goals. We brainstormed about what we should do, and she said, "Well, let's ask Afghan women." And that became our mantra. Listen to the voices of Afghan women.

"I'm not a fundraiser," Deb told me. "I can't bring people together, and I can't organize, but I can write. I'm going to Afghanistan. I'm going to find out what's happening. And I'm going to document the stories of women there and make sure their voices are heard."

Deb did go to Afghanistan, and she wrote the story of a young girl named Parvana who cut her hair and dressed like a boy so she could work to support her family. The novel was called *The Breadwinner*. Deb had received a $3,000 advance from her publisher, and she wanted to give it to us. "You can do more with this money than I could," she said. "I'd like to donate the advance and any future royalties from this book to you."

That was huge for us. Back then, even $30 was a big donation. Deb's generosity was inspiring and empowering because there was so much we wanted to do that was impossible without money.

Then the world turned upside down.

The morning of September 11, 2001, I was in Calgary having breakfast, getting ready for the day ahead. I turned on the television and saw the carnage unfolding at the World Trade Center in New York. As the day went on, I began hearing the experts speculate that the attack may have originated with terrorists in Afghanistan. I had a terrible feeling in the pit of my stomach to hear Afghanistan mentioned that way. I knew the women there, our colleagues and friends, were now going to be characterized as part of the evil Other.

In fact, one of those women sent me an email that day. "We understand something horrible has happened in North America," it began. "Are you okay?"

Imagine that. With everything they dealt with every day, they were reaching out to ask if we were okay!

Before 9/11 we had expended lots of time and energy explaining to people what the heck was going on in Afghanistan and why they should fund us. After 9/11 the world's attention turned to Afghanistan, and in many ways we became more effective because we could access funding more readily. We could also work directly in the country rather than in refugee camps in Pakistan.

Teachers around the world were scrambling for material to explain Afghanistan to their students. Deb's book, *The Breadwinner*, had just hit the bookstores and it took off. The royalties began to pump in much quicker and much larger than we could ever imagine. Today it adds up to about $2 million.

A few years ago, I went for a walk with Deb one day when she was in Calgary. "Do you realize," I asked her, "how much money you've sent our way? Are you still okay with that?"

"You can do a lot more with that money than I ever could. This is how I can make a difference, through the work that you are doing."

In 2011, Deb travelled with me to Afghanistan to see the impact of her support and meet our Afghan staff, project partners, teachers, and students. She interviewed women and girls at every opportunity. When she returned to Canada she wrote another book, *Kids of Kabul*, and once again donated all the royalties to CW4WAfghan. Ask any charity how hard it is to get sustainable funding like this that you can rely on year after year. We can't thank Deb enough.

After the initial fighting in Afghanistan, the Taliban was ousted from power and we brought Dr. Samar to Canada to raise awareness about the reality for women in Afghanistan in speaking engagements across the country. She was in Edmonton when she got a phone call informing her that she had been appointed deputy prime minister in the new Afghan government. We had her staying at a modest bed-and-breakfast, and that night two big RCMP guys sat outside her bedroom door. Things were definitely changing.

But not as fast as some would have you believe. In 2002, President George W. Bush invited Dr. Samar to watch his State of the Union address from the visitors' gallery of the House of Representatives. He proudly introduced her. "Today women are free, and are part of Afghanistan's new government," he said.

I was angry at that. Yes, here was one Afghan woman who had rights. But there was still an enormous amount of work to be done to make sure other Afghan women had their rights. He had no understanding of what a long process that is and the volatile journey ahead.

The more we listened to Afghan women, the more we tried to respond to their specific needs. Can we help in health care? Can we help

Deb Ellis having a laugh with some of the girls in 2011.

in leadership and the political realm? But we realized that we were trying to do too much. We needed to zero in on one thing where we could be most effective. Afghan women were telling us, "If we gradually are able to get our education and are able to participate in society, we can affect change." We listened. We focused on education because it is the basic human right underpinning everything that Afghan women are trying to achieve for themselves and their families.

Meanwhile, here at home, we weren't so alone anymore. Canadians were trying to find ways to help women in Afghanistan. I began getting messages from people about starting local chapters of CW4WAfghan. One of the first was from Lauryn Oates in Vancouver. She said her mother knew someone who knew the journalist Sally Armstrong, and Lauryn wanted to bring her to Vancouver to do some fundraising. And she did! I asked Lauryn to ask Sally to come to Calgary on her way home to Ontario. And she did that too!

When I went to pick up Sally at the airport, she immediately started talking to me about Lauryn. "Do you know that she's just sixteen years old?"

I gulped, thinking I had really screwed up, letting a teenager take care of our local chapter and hosting an important person like Sally Armstrong. "No, I didn't know that."

"Do you know she has green hair?"

My voice got quieter. "No, I didn't know that either."

"And she's fantastic!" Sally said.

With that kind of new energy, CW4WAfghan moved forward. Over the last twenty years, Lauryn has been an integral part of the success of the organization, volunteering and working as programs director. Currently, Dr. Lauryn Oates is our new executive director, taking over my role as we work toward our CW4WAfghan succession planning. I couldn't be more thrilled to have her at the helm!

Throughout these past decades, we have learned to honour the baby steps in addition to the milestones in our growth. I often use those words "baby steps" because we had to move cautiously and at times

Lauryn Oates introducing Sally Armstrong (left) at a CW4WAfghan event in Oakville in 2011. I'm next to Sally.

more slowly than we'd prefer. Change takes patience. And we had to be confident that every dollar we raised here in Canada was having a real and positive impact in Afghanistan. We found ways to make sure that the programs we designed and implemented were meeting our goals and that the Afghan staff running the programs were dedicated, trustworthy, and reliable. It took a lot of relationship building and understanding over many years to cement these ties between us and the people in Afghanistan, but those baby steps have given us a strong foundation for our work.

That brings me back to 2004, when Carolyn and I went to Afghanistan for the first time. I've already told you about the bombing we witnessed. Thankfully, we saw much more.

During our trip, we went to an orphanage we were supporting. It was a life-changing moment. The kids had been prepared for our arrival so there they were, smiling, at the front door. Carolyn responded in one way, and I responded in another. She had tears in her eyes, hugging everyone in sight, but I had hardened my heart. I didn't want to get emotionally attached to them because I felt guilty. Of course I was glad we were helping these children, but there were millions of kids around Afghanistan whom we couldn't help.

As the afternoon went on and we talked with our partners about how we could be more effective, my heart opened up. I started to see those kids as individuals, and I was able to honour the little ones in front of me and not beat myself up about the other millions. And Carolyn started to toughen up a little bit. "There's only thirty here," she said to me as we packed up to leave. "There are a lot more we have to help."

It was an important learning experience for both of us. We continually look for effective ways to help at the systemic level through, for example, teacher training to reach more women and children, but we also stayed the course with those kids. One of them, just five years old when we first met her, is now going to university in Europe.

Another time, we spent the day with an Afghan woman who was running one of the projects that we funded. At the end of our visit, as we all got ready to leave, she put on a burka. In my head, this powerful, strong, intelligent Afghan woman suddenly became a victim. We agreed to share a taxi to drop her off at her home on the way back to our apartment, and she made us stop several blocks from her house because she was afraid to be seen getting out of a car with North Americans. There were a lot of reminders on our trip that the journey to equality for Afghan women was long, bumpy, and uncertain.

As long as our troops were in Afghanistan, Canadians seemed prepared to join us on that journey. People could see our soldiers and diplomats doing important work. There was genuine pride in Canada's role. But we all felt the pain whenever a Canadian was killed there. And we shared the pain when our Afghan colleagues and friends were killed. Each loss wounded our nations.

One death had a personal effect on me. In 2009, *Calgary Herald* reporter Michelle Lang sat in my living room, talking to me to gather background information before she went off to cover the war. A few months later, while riding in an armoured military vehicle, she was killed when a roadside bomb exploded. She was just thirty-four years old, a young, vibrant woman who took a huge risk to help Canadians understand why Afghanistan was important. She was a bright light I still miss. Even today, I can't believe it ever happened. But the sad truth is that this type of tragedy happens every day to women and children in Afghanistan.

Afghanistan has become such a deep part of my life and thousands and thousands of other Canadian lives. In recent years, however, the world's attention has shifted away from the country. Now it's a little more difficult to engage average Canadians. But the reality is that life goes on for Afghans. I speak to Afghan women often who are terrified of what the future holds. They are particularly afraid that the Taliban, a group that continues to show it is capable of grotesque cruelty, will regain power. Women tell me that unless they are full and equal members of Afghanistan's society, it will never be a healthy and peaceful country.

Afghans tend to be pretty cynical and skeptical (or I'm overly optimistic), and who can blame them? They've seen so many well-meaning people come and go. Afghan women, though, are determined. They tell me, "We know what we want and we're going to get it. We will never go back to the oppressive life under the Taliban! We have made too many gains and they are very fragile."

I believe that Canadians can help, and because we *can* help, we *must* help. Universal human rights are everyone's responsibility. We will have a role as long as there are Afghan women wanting our support.

As I grew up in Calgary, a little aimlessly at first, I never thought I would have the tools and knowledge to make a difference in a foreign

Education is the first step in helping Afghan women. Here is one of the village literacy classes in 2016.

land. If you had told me when we started CW4WAfghan that we would raise more than $10 million, I would have told you that was impossible. But it wasn't. Through our organization, we've trained 10,000 teachers, put libraries and science labs in more than 250 schools, run literacy classes where more than 3,000 women have learned to read and write, built one school, refurbished another, and run a school and lunch program for 400 girls. That's for starters.

After twenty years, the community of people working for change has become my family, a family that stretches from coast to coast here in Canada, and across a vast distance of time and space with people half a world away in Afghanistan.

Editor's note:

In the spring of 2021, US president Joe Biden decided that all American troops would be withdrawn from Afghanistan. Even before that could be accomplished, the Taliban took over the entire country, meeting almost no resistance from the Afghan army. The new Taliban government says women's rights will be respected "within the framework of Islamic law." Janice Eisenhauer is among those who find no comfort in those words.

Back in 1996, some Afghans cheered the arrival of the Taliban and were hopeful that all the killing that took place during the country's civil war would finally stop, that these little-known Talib fighters would bring stability and peace. But as one Afghan woman said, "Jail is peaceful. But we need our basic rights: freedom of association, access to food, health care, and education."

In 2021, as the Taliban swept through the country headed for the capital, Kabul, they once again systematically murdered civilians, sexually enslaved women and girls, and committed unspeakable atrocities. We heard of edicts demanding that families hand over girls aged fifteen and up and widows under the age of forty-five to be married to Taliban fighters; of the girls' schools, libraries, and homes burned down; of the women forbidden from leaving home, and from working. We read reports of enforced dress codes, beatings, and floggings, even executions of ethnic minorities.

Then Kabul fell and Afghanistan was surrendered to the terrorists; the insurgents who had committed these terrible atrocities are now the government, with Afghans at their mercy.

I shared tears with close friends and staff here in Canada, both Afghans and non-Afghans who worked their entire lives to bring basic human rights to women and girls in Afghanistan. They struggled around the clock to keep their families, and our colleagues and beneficiaries, safe in Afghanistan. Everything was brought so close to home for me when I heard that my friend's five siblings, four of whom were single women—one in a wheelchair—and her brother, who is in his mid-twenties and the same age as my son, made a terrifying trip through Taliban-controlled areas to another city to try to find safe passage out of the country. Had they been a day later, they would not have made it out, but, thanks to my friend urging them on over her cell phone late into the night, monitoring and sharing what she was learning about the Taliban's movements, they made it out of the country.

I'm grateful that many people have yet again reached out to ask, "What can I do to help?" The first thing I tell them is to ask their elected government representatives what they will do in response to the human rights and humanitarian crisis in Afghanistan. Because we must not give up on Afghanistan. If this was your mother, daughter, sister, or best friend in Afghanistan, would you look the other way? Or would you stand together with them in their fight for basic rights? The world can do so much better than it is doing. We must remember the millions of people left behind, people who cling to their hopes and dreams for a better future.

In my heart I know that the work we have done over twenty years has emboldened the women of Afghanistan in the fight for their human rights, and as they strive to live their lives with dignity and respect. But I confess that I struggle to cling to hope. The pathway ahead seems so dark, frightening, and uncertain. I try to draw on the lessons I learned while working with so many Canadians and Afghans over these decades. I've seen through the struggles of Afghan women how resilience and resolve are born of pure hope. They've shown me how hope is not a passive thing you can give or take, but something real and embedded in our individual actions. In her book *Hope in the Dark*, the American historian Rebecca Solnit suggests that we wield hope like an ax when she writes "hope is an ax you break down doors with in an emergency."

We must all help to wield that hope like an axe and become a powerful surge together. Whatever we can do, we must do. We will not stop, nor walk away from the fight for the rights of Afghan women. CW4WA's mission is more relevant now than ever. We stand in solidarity with Afghan women and girls.

Janice Eisenhauer cofounded Canadian Women for Women in Afghanistan in 1998. She is senior board advisor, having recently retired after two decades as volunteer executive director where she managed the day-to-day activities of the national office. She works closely with the CW4WAfghan leadership team, including volunteer members, the board of directors, and executive and Afghan staff in Kabul. Janice has received numerous awards for her humanitarian work, including the Alberta Centennial Medal, the Queen Elizabeth II Diamond Jubilee Medal, the Calgary Rotary Integrity Award, the Soroptimist International Make a Difference for Women Award, the World University Service of Canada Lewis Perinbam Award, the City of Calgary's Signature Award for bringing international acclaim to the city, and an honorary doctor of laws degree (2016) from the University of Calgary. A member of the Alberta Order of Excellence, she lives in Calgary, Alberta.

SUSAN ROSE

Equality and Justice for All

*Every child wants to belong. Every child wants to
fit in and feel a sense of "I'm welcome here. People like me here."
Once you have that feeling, you can follow your passions
and realize your potential. But the only way we're going to live in
a society where we value and respect differences, where people
stop judging and thinking in terms of "us and them," is to
teach our children that's what we want.*

When I was twenty-two years old, I was engaged to be married. Max and I had been going out for four years, and now I was just a few months away from promising "till death do us part." The problem was, I was in the closet.

It was my mother who gave my head a shake. In her Newfoundland voice, she said to me, "Myself and your father are really concerned."

"Mom, don't you love Max?"

"Well, myself and your father do, but we don't think you do. I see you with your friend Gaye. You light up when she comes into the room. I don't see that with Max."

*At ten years old with my mother in 1968. From
an early age, she accepted me the way I was.*

She was right, but I wasn't about to admit it. This was the late 1970s
and in small-town Corner Brook, Newfoundland, no less. Forget gay
marriage—any homosexual act was illegal in Canada. Far away in the
Northwest Territories, the courts were about to sentence a man to an
indefinite prison sentence as a "dangerous sex offender" because he
had consensual sex with other men.

My mother was way ahead of her time, but still I argued with her
that I wasn't a lesbian even though Gaye *was* my girlfriend. Intimate
girlfriend. Our plan was for both of us to marry men but continue our
relationship. We'd have children and everybody would be happy and
we could still be involved with each other. It was bizarre, but there was
no other way back then.

When I thought about where I wanted to be for emotional and spiritual growth, it wasn't with Max. I was more comfortable with another

woman. My mother's words sealed it for me. Max was very hurt when I broke it off. He landed on his feet, though. He moved to Halifax, got married, and had two kids. I still see him every now and then.

As I grew up, my mother always handled my "differences" with wisdom and gentle kindness. She didn't overreact when I was put outside on my first day of kindergarten because I was hyperactive. I also had a learning disability—undiagnosed at the time—that made me a terrible speller. In every class, the teacher would put up a chart to show which students did best on spelling tests. My name was never there. My mother convinced me that "it was a small mind that only knew one way to spell a word."

My father loved and adored me for who I was too. I was a "tomboy." I didn't like dolls so my parents bought me play guns, trains, and dump trucks. But my grandmother would insist on buying me pretty dresses and ignore me when I said I didn't want to wear them. She'd just put a dress over my head, then I'd run outside and roll in the mud.

My mother allowed me to be who I needed to be. She let me get my hair cut at the barbershop instead of the beauty salon. She fought with the school to let me wear jeans every day instead of a skirt or dress. I was very lucky because my mother protected me. She made me feel that the world was wrong and not me. My mother was my saviour. I don't know where I would be if it weren't for her.

Even as a little girl, I was attracted to my girlfriends. I just wasn't interested in boys at all. From a young age, I knew I was different, but I also knew I couldn't say anything about it. A lot of gay people who grew up in that time didn't talk about it because we didn't even have the words to describe ourselves. The only word we knew was "homosexual," and that was associated with pedophiles, monsters, and child molesters. That wasn't me. I knew two homosexual men in Corner Brook, but they were ostracized and made fun of. I remember thinking, "Am I like them? Oh my God!"

I had been raised in a churchgoing family. I sat there on many Sundays, barely hanging on, knowing the Holy Spirit didn't want anything to do with me. It terrified me, and I became very depressed and cried a lot.

One January night when I was in grade nine, I bought a pack of razor blades from the store. The store owner, a friend of my parents, called my mom and said, "Bertha, something strange just happened. Susan bought a pack of razor blades."

My mom knew I was really struggling, and she immediately rounded up some people to look for me. My dad and my uncle found me in the woods behind our house. I had cut my wrists and arms and face. They called an ambulance to bring me to the hospital. Despite what I had done, I knew I didn't want to die.

I was admitted to Waterford, a hospital for the mentally ill, but my mother pulled me out of there before they administered shock therapy. Then I spent seven months at the Janeway Children's Hospital. When I finally came home, I wrote to The Johns Hopkins Hospital in the United States to get information on homosexuality. I was always careful to check the mailbox before my mom or dad saw anything Johns Hopkins sent to me, not that they would have been angry or shocked. One day a package did arrive. I hurried into my bedroom, closed the door, and began reading about this mysterious thing called homosexuality. Nonjudgmental, factual information. And, oh my God, it was welcome. I began to understand and put into words who I was.

My mom spent the next two or three years frightened to death every time I went into the washroom, but she had nothing to worry about. Though my parents never ever talked about me being gay, I somehow got the message that even if I was gay, it was okay. They loved me.

By then I knew that Mom and Dad weren't my biological parents, that they had adopted me when I was almost three months old. The day I found out is still firmly lodged in my memory.

I was eleven years old, walking with a group of girlfriends past a restaurant that had thrown out a bag of rotten potatoes. We girls got into a little potato fight. I threw a potato and hit a girl named Pauline in the head. She got angry and said, "You're adopted anyhow. You don't have a real mother and father."

She went off crying, and I ran home and confronted my mother. "Pauline just said I was adopted. What does she mean?"

My mother dropped the broom she had in her hand, went right to the phone, and called Pauline's mother. Her end of the conversation was very angry. I stood there thinking, "What is going on?"

Mom hung up the phone, turned to me, and told me that my mother had died when I was born. She and Dad went to the hospital and picked me out of all the children there. I was very special, she continued, and they loved me dearly.

I ran away to do some thinking. When I came back, I had a good talk with my parents, and things settled down again.

I can't remember when I found out that Mom hadn't told me the truth, that my biological mother was actually alive. I guess the lie had come naturally to her when she was suddenly facing an eleven-year-old wanting answers. There was no book back then on how to handle that situation. I do remember that at some point my parents agreed that I could try to find my biological mother once I finished university.

When I graduated from Memorial University, I went to the provincial department of social services and began looking for my biological mother. For three months, they interviewed me and Mom. We didn't want my dad involved because he was old-school and my search was painful to him. Social services made contact with my biological mother, and she agreed to have a phone conversation with me.

Around the same time, a dear childhood friend of mine came down from Cape Breton to St. John's to spend the week with me. I was very excited to tell her all about the chat I would soon be having with my biological mother, but then social services decided to stop the whole thing because my adoptive father wasn't part of the process. "My God," I thought, "will I have to wait 'til Dad dies to find out who my biological mother is?"

My friend left, but before she returned to Cape Breton she flew to Corner Brook, where we had grown up, to visit her family. When her aunt picked her up at the airport, she was bubbling up with news.

"I've got something to tell you. You're not going to believe this," her aunt said. "I have a daughter."

My friend put two and two together and immediately realized the daughter was me.

That's how I discovered my biological mother. The funny thing was, I actually knew her. She had had me when she was just eighteen, so she wasn't much older than me, and we had played sports together. And I knew she was gay.

She wasn't out, though. She was married and had nine children, and her husband knew the truth. I once had a long conversation with him. "Why are you with her?" I asked.

"I love her. She's the mother of my children. I'm okay with it," he told me. He stayed with her until he died. Their story was mind-blowing to me. But I was coming to realize that being gay meant different things to different people.

After I called off my marriage, I went back to university for an education degree and started teaching in 1985. I dated women, but I didn't live an openly gay life.

In 1969, same-sex acts had been decriminalized and Newfoundland enacted a human rights code, but neither protected people from discrimination based on sexual orientation. There were gay pride parades, which I would go to, but I would wear a paper bag over my head with two holes cut out for my eyes. I went to gay clubs in St. John's, and there was many a Saturday night when I'd be happily dancing until the police raided the place. There was nothing illegal in what we were doing; they just enjoyed feeling us up a little bit, tossing us into the paddy wagon, making fun of us before letting us go. I learned to be very quiet, but the whole time I was scared. Since almost everyone was hiding their sexual orientation, we couldn't complain in public about the treatment.

At work, being in the closet was very stressful. There were many uncomfortable days in the staff room when I'd hear the other teachers talking about gay people. One guy used to say, "If my kid ever dated a gay person, I would kill him." I always stood my ground, talking about respecting and understanding people, but I didn't want to give away my secret, so I didn't make it personal.

One day in the staff room, I mentioned that I was taking care of a friend of mine who was dying of AIDS. A male colleague jumped up out of his chair. "My God," he shouted. "What are you doing? You shouldn't be in this building." He made the assumption that I was a lesbian and that I was passing along the AIDS virus to everyone I met.

I hadn't come out, but after that, two teachers would call me "dyke" as I walked down the corridor. I knew there were other gay and lesbian teachers at school, but none of them stood up for me or for themselves because none of them were out. Everybody was afraid to be seen as gay. My teachers' union never helped me. The school board never helped. When I complained to the minister of education about what was happening to me as a lesbian, he told me that if I made an issue of my treatment he would fire me.

The easiest thing to do was to stay in the closet and transfer to another school, which I did. I went to a junior high school; it was the largest in the province, with 950 students. I ran the chess club and I also coached grade nine girls' volleyball.

The kids were curious about me. "Miss, are you married? Miss, do you have a boyfriend? Miss, why don't we know anything about you?"

I'd tell them, "I don't talk about my personal life, and that's the end of it."

One night, I was out at a gay club and turned around to come face-to-face with one of my volleyball players, who immediately began to cry.

"Oh, miss," she sobbed. "I thought you were. Please don't tell anyone I am."

I was gobsmacked. She was just thirteen years old. She couldn't be in the club. She was scared.

I remember there was a male student in the school who came from a very religious family and he often tried to talk to me. I was sure he was gay, but I was reluctant to be specific with him because I could never be myself. He committed suicide. I was heartbroken and scared for these kids who had nowhere to turn. So many years had passed since my own suicide attempt, but it seemed that nothing had changed.

With my dad in 1985, the year I began teaching. I was not out, though my dad knew and supported me.

In 1988, when the Newfoundland Human Rights Commission fought to broaden the discrimination laws to protect gay and lesbian people, some politicians said they'd as soon throw the whole human rights code away rather than add protection for gays. In 1990, the justice minister said protecting gays would protect pedophiles. How's that for a progressive view?

It took until 1997 for the province to prohibit discrimination on the basis of sexual orientation. For me, that changed everything. I could come out without fear of losing my job.

My partner at the time was also a teacher. A CBC reporter found out about us through the grapevine, came to our house, and asked, "Are you two women willing to talk about being teachers and being in a relationship?" We said we were.

I knew the time was right to stop hiding. I was tired of being invisible. Invisibility goes hand in hand with helplessness. I wanted to exist. I wanted to speak out about the hatred and homophobia that I was experiencing as a teacher. I wanted the students to see that I was okay. I had a good life. I had a good family, friends, a partner, and a house with a white picket fence. I wanted the kids to see me succeeding. So I came out in living colour on that night's TV news. It felt damned good.

The next morning, I drove to school, got out of my car, and started walking into the building. The grade nine boys' basketball team surrounded me and chanted, "Dyke. Dyke. Dyke." The phys ed teacher was a very good friend of mine so I went to her right away and told her what happened. At lunchtime she called all the boys into the gym and asked them to apologize to me.

"Why should we do that?" some of them wondered.

"It's this simple. Ms. Rose is a dear friend of mine. How dare you insult her? If this were a Black woman would you have chanted the N-word?"

They got the message that their behaviour was unacceptable.

The school principal was unhappy too, but not with the boys. With me. He called me into his office. "Why did you do that?" he asked.

"Why did I do what?"

"You plastered your personal life all over the news."

I was flabbergasted. "You have three big pictures of your wife and children in this office. That's advertising your life. Most teachers in this building have family pictures on their desks. I don't have a picture of my partner on my desk. So don't you ever call me into this office again with that kind of question."

I lost some gay and lesbian friends that day. They felt that I made their lives uncomfortable because they were "known associates" of mine. Too many people were still judging people based on whom they slept with, instead of on the content of their character.

That first day after I came out wasn't an aberration. Teaching at that school became so stressful I decided to transfer again and teach younger kids, but that didn't go as smoothly as I hoped.

In my grade four class, I had a student who told me, "My grandfather said you shouldn't be teaching. He saw you on TV." I was deeply saddened. The other kids in the class adored me, and so did this little girl. But I thought it best that she be removed from my class.

The principal was not supportive. He was closeted, married, and filled with internalized homophobia. (Eventually, he did come out and left his wife.) When I went to him with a problem, he would say, "You brought it on yourself, so you deal with it. If someone calls you a dyke, I don't care. You did put your bedroom on the blackboard, didn't you?"

"I thought there was a whole lot more to me than sex," I told him. "That part of my life is just as boring as everybody else's."

No one protected me. Not my union or my principal. The department of education decided I had made my own bed. I never thought it would get as bad as it did.

I had teachers say to me, "You probably shouldn't be teaching grade four and five kids. Maybe you'd be okay in junior high, but I wouldn't want my kid in your class." These were well-educated, supposedly enlightened teachers, who thought I was going to somehow infect young children with gayness. Some of my "colleagues" thought they had the right to embarrass and humiliate me. No one was telling them they didn't. I could never win, and it damaged me.

By 2006, I'd had enough. After so many years as a teacher, I just couldn't fight the system any longer. Once I left my job, I felt broken.

I went into about a year of depression until I got a call from Planned Parenthood. They wanted me to develop a workshop on what it meant to be gay or lesbian for Planned Parenthood to give high school teachers. That ignited me. I became passionate about something again, got back into life.

Then in 2009, I traveled around the province with the director of Planned Parenthood and talked to teachers, high school students, and principals about how hard it was for gay students. I always found it interesting to arrive at a school where a guidance counselor met us at the door with a smile and reassuring words. "Welcome, but we don't have any queer kids in this community." How eloquently that spoke to the pain of invisibility.

That same year I was asked to join the board of directors of Egale Canada. Egale works to improve the lives of lesbian, gay, bisexual, transgender, queer or questioning, intersex, two-spirit people by informing public policy and promoting human rights and inclusion through research, education, awareness, and legal advocacy. I thought I could use Egale to wrestle with the education system and create safe, inclusive spaces for kids in school. But we were nearly bankrupt. Gay marriage had just become legal in Canada, and most people declared victory and went home. They felt Egale wasn't needed anymore. They were very wrong.

Thankfully, Egale has been able to get back on its feet, and it's done enormous good. Our *If You Can Play, You Can Play* project has made it a bit easier for gay athletes to be out, though it's still tough, especially for professional athletes. We've worked with police departments on how to handle homophobic violence and with numerous businesses and government agencies on policies of inclusion.

Of course, I have focused on schools. We've done surveys with distressing results. Gay kids are the most vulnerable in the school system today. About 65 percent of LGBTQ+ students say they feel unsafe in school. They report verbal, physical, and sexual harassment. It's hard to find a gay kid who has never heard a homophobic comment from a student or teacher.

I've become the LGBTQ+ guru for anybody and everything in education. I've met with thousands of principals, teachers, students, and families and helped them cope, helped them exist, and helped them deal with different situations that have come up. My phone rings at all hours of the day and night. Here's a typical case.

"Hello," the voice at the other end begins. "Are you Sue Rose?"

"Yes."

"I'm Jim in Lewisporte. I'm not in school anymore. I can't take it."

"Are you out to your parents?" I ask.

"No."

"Is there a teacher that you can talk to?"

"No."

When I get two nos, that's dangerous. I know LGBTQ+ allies all over the island, so I start calling around, trying to get some connection for that kid. Oftentimes, I drive to the kid and spend some time getting to know him or her.

Sometimes it's the parent of a gay child who calls me. I remember a mother (who was also a teacher) from Rocky Harbour who told me that her grade eight daughter had just come out. She said, "I can't believe what's happening. My daughter was well liked. Now she's come out as a lesbian, everyone's calling her 'dyke' and they're vandalizing her locker."

In fact, her daughter wasn't a lesbian. She was trans, and before long

Natalie was Nate. I drove down to Rocky Harbour to meet him. He was very depressed. "No one wants to hang around with me anymore," he told me. I took the story to the director of education and said, "We have an issue at this school board."

What happened? Did the department read the riot act to the board and insist that it make its school safe for this boy? No. The department chose, after much negotiation, to pay to have him stay with another family about two hours away so he could go to a school in a different district. The next year, the ministry arranged for his mother to transfer to a job at the same board and paid to move the family as well.

I can get calls from kids at six in the morning. People have suggested I tell them to call the Kids Help Phone. When I do, the caller usually asks, "Will I get to speak to someone who's gay?"

"No," I say. "But the person will be trained to deal with you."

"I want to talk to someone like you, someone who's like me."

When I hear that, I can't hang up.

A kid once called me to say he had made a terrible mistake coming out to his family. He was seventeen years old, tall, and handsome. Everyone always teased him about how he'd have his pick of girlfriends. When he told his family he was gay, his father was apoplectic. He had to move out of his home and go live with an aunt in another community.

"I thought it was going to be fine," he told me. "My whole family loves to watch Ellen on TV. They have no problem with her being gay."

I'm just trying to be a resource for kids who have nothing. I'm trying to be a resource for teachers too. Some want to help kids by saying something positive in their classes about being gay, and I advise them on how to deal with the aftermath when parents come into the school angry at them because they're saying being gay is okay.

I was once talking to the president of the Newfoundland and Labrador Teachers' Association. "Sue," he started to explain. "You know that even as the union president I still teach. I see what's going on in school. My kid has gay friends. Things just aren't so bad."

I gave him the names of three students at his school. "Do you know where they're living?"

"No."

"They've been kicked out of their homes because they came out to their parents as gay. The department of education has put them in an apartment in downtown St. John's, and now all of them have started to sell their bodies."

"My God."

"You're a teacher at that school, and you're the president of the union, and you don't know that's happened."

"I get your point," he replied.

After that, he and I started to work with the Newfoundland and Labrador Psychological Association to try to improve things. One of the psychologists once sent me a note expressing her exasperation.

"Sue, I don't know how to help the kids anymore. I don't know how to stop the prayer meetings trying to save their souls. I don't know how to persuade my colleagues to change their behaviour. They're good people, good Christians, who say I can't expect them to tell a kid that being gay is okay. Sue, we just have to admit that students can't stay in such a toxic environment."

There's not one province in Canada with a mandatory LGBTQ+ requirement in the curriculum. Not one. It's in the curriculum, but unless it's required, we're never going to be able to make the classroom a consistently safe place for everyone because teachers get to pick and choose. Some are willing to run with the work, but others say they're not comfortable with it. Unless it comes from the top down, we're never going to get anywhere. Gays make up about 10 percent of the population, but where is the curriculum that represents our community, our culture, who we are?

Every child wants to belong. Every child wants to fit in and feel a sense of "I'm welcome here. People like me here." Once you have that feeling, you can follow your passions and realize your potential. But the only way we're going to live in a society where we value and respect differences, where people stop judging and thinking in terms of "us and them," is to teach our children that's what we want. Teach them through the same education system that teaches them everything else.

We are two decades into the twenty-first century, and yet we see a video from a high school in Carbonear where a gay student is relentlessly bullied. He just throws up his hands and says, "I'm not a person to fight. I don't like fighting." His mother says that off-camera the bullies told her son to "drink bleach" and "go choke and die." She complained to the principal and she says he called it "teenage drama."

The school board tells the media that it takes bullying seriously, that it "will not tolerate abuse and/or discrimination of any kind," but it does tolerate it. I talked to the student, and he told me the abuse started in kindergarten.

"What do you mean?" I asked.

"In kindergarten my mom and dad were called into the school because the little boys didn't want to play with me. They were beating me up. The school told my parents I had to start hanging around with the girls."

Thirteen years later, the boy has moved to Alberta. "I no longer felt safe in the school," he said.

Sometimes I think I'm just spinning my wheels. It seems the more I do, the more I see what needs to be done. There's no doubt it gets tiring.

You'd think I'm so far out of the closet that everyone would know I'm gay, and they wouldn't say hurtful things to me. I'm popular enough where I live to have been elected to town council. But I run into people all the time who tell me, "I really like you, but your lifestyle drives me nuts. I can't accept that, but I really like you." That's an everyday thing. I just walk away from things like that.

The year after I came out, my aunt and uncle came for a visit from British Columbia. They had dinner with me and my partner, and for some reason my uncle started talking about the gay people he saw in Vancouver and how he'd like to kill them.

I was dumbfounded. "You do know I'm a lesbian and this is my partner, right?"

He got angry, and we kicked him out. The next thing we knew, my grandmother was calling to find out what went down. Things like that happen all the time.

I was flying back home from Mexico a few years ago, sitting beside my partner, in business class no less. We had a man say to us, "Can you stop holding hands?"

This time I was ticked. "Can you please read your book and mind your own business?"

It was a couple of tense hours after that. The flight attendants warned him a few times, but he kept spouting off about how we shouldn't be allowed in the same cabin as him. It takes a bit of your soul away every time you have to go through something like that. Every episode drains you of energy. Is this going to be confrontational? Should I just go back into hiding and let it go?

My parents saved me, which makes me one of the lucky ones. So many people like me continue to struggle with poverty, homelessness, violence, hate crimes, and access to health care and employment. That's the future for our young people unless we can stamp out the mindless bigotry once and for all.

I'm very proud about the things that have been accomplished in Canada and in Newfoundland to improve life for LGBTQ+ kids. But the only long-term strategy that will work involves the education system. Our education system is the most important institution in our society. We mold and shape the hearts and minds of our youth, the people who will be tomorrow's leaders. Every child must see them-

In 2020, I received the Order of Newfoundland and Labrador for my advocacy work. From left to right: (front row) Howard Foote, Lieutenant Governor Judy Foote, me, and Premier Dwight Ball; (second row) my cousin Jocelyn Rose and Ann Shortall, my former partner who I came out with on CBC in 1998; (third row) my friend Katherine Burgess, my cousin Chesley Rose, and my friend Dan Goodyear.

selves and their families in the curriculum. It's no more than that. We have the right to marry, yet we can't talk about being gay in our primary and elementary schools.

I was a teacher. I know how hard teaching can be. I know how many responsibilities a teacher has. For me, though, one responsibility rises above all the others. And that's to create a safe and respectful environment for children to blossom and bloom. All children.

Susan Rose is a former schoolteacher. In 1991, she developed the Newfoundland Amazon Network, a free call-in service that operated as a support group for lesbians living in the province. In 2010, she was Pride Citizen of the year in her province. From 2012 to 2014, she assisted the provincial Department of Education and Early Childhood Development in providing a province-wide LGBTQ+ training initiative for the K–12 school system. An active member of Egale Canada and the Canada Human Rights Trust, she won the Newfoundland and Labrador Human Rights Commission's Human Rights Award in 2017 and the Memorial University Alumni award for Outstanding Community Service in 2019. In 2020, she was made a member of the Order of Newfoundland and Labrador. She lives in Broad Cove, Newfoundland and Labrador.

RABBI REUVEN BULKA
A Day to Remember

*The lasting feeling I got from that first ceremony was
that I had been blessed with a chance to meet authentic Canadian
heroes face-to-face, and I hoped I had let them know their
country would never forget what they did.*

November 11 is often quite cold in Ottawa, and November 11, 1991, was no exception. By about 9:30 that morning the temperature had managed to struggle just above the freezing point when I parked my car and began walking toward the National War Memorial. Hundreds of people were already in the area. It was Remembrance Day, and for the first time, as the honorary chaplain of the Dominion Command of the Royal Canadian Legion, I would be delivering the benediction at the national service of remembrance.

The governor general would be there, along with the prime minister, the minister of defence, the chief of the defence staff, and just about every ambassador and high commissioner in town. And of course more than a million people would be watching on television from coast to coast to coast.

None of that worried me, though. I had spoken in public more than a thousand times. What made me nervous as I stepped onto Confederation

Square where the National War Memorial has stood since its unveiling in 1939 was the audience. That's when I saw the veterans. For many of them, huddled in coats and under blankets, being at the ceremony is an act of courage in itself. I imagined how this day transported them back to when they had fought in weather conditions that had been even worse. I said hello to some of them, gaining an appreciation, even then, of their bravery. There were tears in their eyes as they were reminded of the friends they had lost. It was very inspiring.

I stood at one side of the memorial as the dignitaries arrived, then the choir sang "O Canada." Eleven o'clock approached and the bugler played the unmistakable notes of "The Last Post," followed by a minute of silence, a piper's lament, and the bugler again with "The Rouse." I became increasingly anxious as the chaplain general of the armed forces spoke, the laying of wreaths went on, and my time slot moved closer.

Then someone signaled to me. I honestly can't tell you how much my knees were knocking as I moved to the lectern. I wondered if my words could possibly rise to the occasion. Could they do justice to the veterans braving the elements to remember their fallen comrades?

But maybe I'd been born for just this moment. You see, my birthday is June 6, 1944—D-Day, the day the Second World War Allies landed in Normandy and started the drive to liberate Europe from Nazi occupation, a monumental chapter of history that I would come to recognize years later. While my birth wasn't the most important event of the day, maybe it was a portent of the relationship that was unfolding with the military on this cold Remembrance Day in Ottawa in 1991.

* * *

In 1944, my parents lived in London, England, but they were very worried about the ongoing war and applied for visas to go to the United States. This was not their first move. Before the war began, both of them had fled Eastern Europe. My father, Jacob, had come from Germany to England in the mid-1930s when his father saw the storm clouds gathering and sent him away. At the time, my father was just fifteen years old, but he was forced to leave his family behind. When the war ended, he learned that his parents and his brother had been murdered. No one is sure when or where. My grandfather was a book publisher and he may have been killed in Warsaw when he was there on business, but it's impossible to be certain.

My mother, Ida, made it out of Stettin (Szczecin), Poland, to England on a *kindertransport*, a series of trains that took Jewish children away from the nightmare of persecution. She got out on the very last transport before war broke out in September 1939. She was seventeen years old and, like my father, she was forced to leave her entire family behind. Her parents did not survive the Holocaust either, but her brother, Max, survived Auschwitz and Buchenwald. He was brutally tortured, and the fact that he came out alive is truly a miracle.

When I was growing up, my parents never talked about any of this with me or my siblings, Rivka and Yitzchok. Never. These were childhood traumas they just did not share, and we understood we could ask our parents about anything, but not this. It was only years later, when I was a teenager and my cousin Judy, who survived seven different concentration camps including Auschwitz, started telling me about her own history, that I discovered this part of my family's history. I know now that Holocaust survivors sometimes felt the things that had happened to them in the concentration camps were so unspeakable that they doubted people would believe them. That is why they did not say anything. It makes me wonder if my parents, who spent the war in relative safety in England, felt that the scars they carried did not qualify as survival, so they refused to talk to their children about any of it.

But I'm getting ahead of the story.

My mother and father, with me and my sister, Rivka, in England.

In 1948, when I was four, my parents' visas finally came through. The bureaucracy had taken hold of their application, so permission to come to America wasn't granted until after the war was over. Though there was no longer an urgent reason to leave England, my parents also felt like they had nothing to stay for. My father tried his hand at business, but that did not work out well.

In hindsight, I suspect that they were mentally committed to emigrating and wanted to make a fresh start. They moved to Providence, Rhode Island, where they stayed for just a year, and then to New York City. I was quite young, so I obviously had no say in the matter.

When I was seven or eight years old, we were living in Queens, and my father, who was working as a teacher of religion, saw a job opening for a rabbi at Khal Adath Yeshurun, a synagogue in the Bronx. It was a job every rabbi wanted. At least fifty men applied because it was an exciting opportunity. People told my father he was wasting his time putting in his application. They said that he had no chance of getting it because there would be so many more experienced rabbis up for the job.

The synagogue looked through the list of applicants, whittling it down based on résumés, and somehow my father survived the first cut. He was actually in the running! We did not know how many others were left in the competition, but now our house was alive with conversations about "What if?" and "Do you think it can really happen?" We did not want to get too hopeful because we knew it was still a long shot, but we allowed ourselves to dream.

Well, he got it. I remember the euphoria in the house when my father came home and told my mother that Rabbi Jacob Bulka was the new rabbi at the synagogue in the Bronx. My mother went wild with excitement and let out a primal scream of joy. "You're kidding me. It can't be true."

But it was.

My father's salary was, shall we say, modest, but we felt like we had fallen into the lap of luxury. We never lacked for anything because my parents scraped and scrounged to make sure we had what we needed. For me the big thrill was to be able to go to a Yankees baseball game every few years and sit in the bleachers, where the tickets cost 75 cents each. We were even able to buy our first car—something my parents never thought we'd be able to afford. It was a dilapidated pink Ford Mercury. It wasn't the colour they would have chosen, but colour was not a priority. My parents were just so happy to have it they did not even care that it was pink. My father took driving seriously. When he was behind the wheel he insisted that everyone in the car be one hundred percent silent so he could concentrate on the road. No arguments in the back seat from me, Rivka, or Yitzchok. We were okay with that because riding in a car was such a novelty to us. I sat happily, looking out the window. I felt like a young person today must feel when they get a new iPhone—on top of the world.

The apartment we moved into was very small but no one complained, even though it often held more than just our family. Members of the congregation dropped in all the time, which meant there was always plenty of food in the house. My mother's philosophy was that anyone who came through our door had to eat. No visit was complete without some potato kugel or coffee or cake.

My mother was completely devoted to my father's career. She understood he would be leaving home before sunrise every morning to get to the synagogue for morning prayers, and she sometimes would not see him again until close to midnight, after he had spent the day taking the subway all over the city to visit congregants in hospitals, talking with a bride and groom about an upcoming wedding, or consoling family members after a loved one passed away. She often sat down with him to share dinner many hours after we kids went to sleep.

The best part of my father's new job for me was that it made me an RK—Rabbi's Kid—which meant that everyone spoiled me because they wanted to ingratiate themselves with the rabbi. I had so much candy given to me it is a wonder I still have teeth.

Being an RK also came with responsibility. When I was nine years old, I tried smoking. I do not remember where I got the cigarette, but I stole away to the basement bathroom of my father's synagogue to light up and take a puff. I thought it was tasteless, even kind of gross. Suddenly a man walked in. He stopped when he saw the cigarette in my hand. I immediately threw it to the floor and stomped on it, but I knew that I was in big trouble. My face had probably turned green because of the tobacco I had inhaled, but now it was ashen.

"I will tell your father," the man threatened, "unless you promise never to smoke again."

I was shivering. "Oh, no. Don't tell my father. I promise I will never smoke again."

It is a promise I have kept to this day.

When I was sixteen years old, my father suffered a heart attack. Even today a heart attack is nothing to sneeze at, but back then there was no such thing as a bypass operation that got you back on your feet quickly. My father's doctor put him on bed rest for six months. His synagogue could not possibly afford to hire another rabbi during his convalescence, so I was pressed into emergency service.

I was young, but I knew my way around a synagogue. I had been going every day, pretty much all my life. I went every morning and every evening. I knew the prayers and the rituals. There was not even a real discussion about my taking over. Everyone was shocked at what had happened to my father, and they were focused on making sure he got better, so there was no fuss over me. I just stepped in like it was the most natural thing in the world.

I did not have the credentials to preside at a funeral or a wedding—I was not a rabbi, after all—so rabbis from other synagogues helped out on those occasions. But it fell to me to make sure regular services were conducted properly, to run religious classes, and to deliver sermons. I could quote the Bible easily enough and I could tell stories about Abraham's relationship with God, but I knew there was more to being a rabbi than familiarity with the Bible, so of course it was intimidating at times to stand before the congregation. Who was I to draw life lessons for people who had seen much more of life than I had?

In truth, it was a good experience because I got a free pass on a lot of stuff. I was so young that if one of my sermons bombed, it was not a problem. People would say, "What do you expect from a kid?" On the other hand, if I managed to deliver a sermon everyone liked, they said, "Great. He's so good."

Those six months were my first taste of rabbi work, if I can call it that. I had many conversations with my father during this period, and he assured me I was doing well. He never asked me to follow in his footsteps, and to that point I had not settled on any future occupation, but this experience made up my mind for me. I liked it a lot. I was going to become a rabbi. Nothing was going to deter me.

I finished high school and started my rigorous rabbinical studies at the Rabbi Jacob Joseph Yeshiva. At the same time, I pursued a secular education at the City University of New York. It made for long days. Up before the sun to say morning prayers, on the subway to rabbinical school for classes from 9 to 5. Then back on the subway to Manhattan for more classes from 6 to 10. I would not get home until after 11. But I kept my head above water.

At the rabbinical seminary there was one field where I had an advantage—public speaking. I had no fear whatsoever standing up and delivering a speech or a sermon because nothing would ever be so frightening as being a teenager speaking to a congregation of adults. If I could get away with that, I knew I would be fine.

After four years, I graduated as a rabbi. I was twenty-two and ready to face the world. At first I did some teaching, like my father had done, but it became clear to me that it just did not pay enough, especially if I was ever going to get married and have a family. I needed to find work in a synagogue. I was not actively looking, though. Truthfully, I was actively looking for a wife. You may think it would have been wiser to get a job, get settled, and then find a wife, but many synagogues at the time would not hire a rabbi who was not married.

Little did I know that I had already met the woman who would become my wife. When I was growing up, my father and I would sometimes go off for a weekend together. Once, when I was seventeen, we went to a kosher resort in Bethlehem, New Hampshire. Don't ask me why there was a kosher resort there—there are hardly any Jews in New Hampshire. That weekend we met a large family from Montreal who were also visiting the resort. I said hello to one of the daughters, Naomi. She seemed nice enough, but I thought nothing of it.

Years later, her name was suggested to my father as a possible match for me by a mutual acquaintance. At the time, Naomi was teaching kindergarten in Montreal. She came to visit relatives in New York, and a meeting was arranged. You have to understand that in our circles a date was more than having a good time. Matrimonial possibilities were always at the forefront. "Is this a viable match?" was a question always on our minds. We connected on a meaningful level that night. We had a second date in Montreal, and that went well too. On our third date, I proposed to her and she accepted. I found out much later that she had always told her family she never wanted to marry a rabbi. I guess I swept her off her feet.

"I've met the lady of my dreams," I told my parents when I came home.

They had some perfunctory questions: "Are you sure? Are you rushing into this?" But they could see my excitement, and they shared my joy.

Naomi and I started to make plans to get married and live in New York. I knew money would be tight since Naomi did not have a job in the US and I was teaching only part-time in a Jewish school. Finding a place to live that we could afford was not a cheery prospect, but I was determined to find better work. One day I saw an ad in a newspaper called the *Jewish Press*. A synagogue in Ottawa, Congregation Machzikei Hadas, was looking for a rabbi. I knew little about Canada at that point, aside from the fact that it had produced the wonderful woman who was about to become my wife. It was 1967, but even all the Centennial celebrations had not caught my attention. I was like every good American, living in the American cocoon. But I did know that Canada had a good reputation, and so I did not hesitate to answer the newspaper ad.

Still, I was only twenty-three years old. I knew my age would work against me. I had done some interviews with other synagogues that had not led anywhere. I remember one in Rhode Island that seemed promising. In the end, they said, "All good, but you're just too young."

I had an idea on how to overcome this problem. Every summer, there is a three-week period when Jews are prohibited from shaving. At the end of the three weeks, I always had a scruffy beard that I immediately shaved off. But this time, with the interview in Ottawa coming up, I decided that I would trim the beard, not cut it off. I left myself with a goatee.

As I suspected, during the interview, my age was brought up.

"Maybe someone a little older could provide better advice and guidance because he'd have more life experiences," they said.

I looked around the table at the six or seven people on the hiring committee. "I'm going to get older every day, so if you think being older is better, I can promise you I will improve every day."

That seemed to impress them. I saw some smiles and felt I had said just the right thing.

The interview ended, I was asked to leave the room, but told not to go too far. Just a little time went by before I was called back and the chairman spoke words I was only too happy to hear: "We'd love to have you."

Here I am in 1967. I had just moved to Ottawa and was sporting what would become my signature goatee.

Later, a member of the hiring committee told me, "I saw a picture of you before you had the beard, and let me tell you that if you had come to Ottawa without the beard, you never would have gotten the job."

I have the goatee to this day.

I called Naomi as soon as I left the synagogue. I told her we did not have to worry about living in a basement apartment in New York. I had a new job, and it came with a house! We would be living in Ottawa, just two hours away from her home in Montreal.

My second call was to my parents. They were obviously happy for me, though I sensed some ambivalence from my mother because she had been hoping I would live close to them in New York. Every Jewish mother, in fact probably every mother, is a little sad at the thought of her children moving away.

Naomi and I were married just a week before we moved to Ottawa. When we arrived in this new city, we had no idea how long we would stay. The congregation was great. The people were great. It was as good as any rabbinate ever gets. It was almost too good to be true. There were just ninety or so families in the congregation at first, which is not very many. We were invited to people's homes. We invited some to our house. I got to know almost everyone because of course I went to services every morning and every afternoon. I'll admit, though, that it took a while for Canada to become home. For the first six months I would drive about ten minutes out of my way to the Château Laurier hotel every morning to pick up a copy of the *New York Times*. But year after year, the synagogue was very good to me, and Canada was very good to me.

In 1985, I became a Canadian citizen. Once I was reasonably certain that I would spend the rest of my life in Canada I thought it was the correct thing to do, if for no other reason than to express gratitude to Canada for the "use of its space."

Oddly, no sooner had I become a Canadian than I received an offer from a congregation in New York to become its rabbi. Naomi and I had to make a quality-of-life decision. Being a rabbi in Ottawa was not without its challenges, but we knew it was a relative paradise compared to the hurly-burly and high-powered stuff that goes on in New York. We did not want our kids to grow up in a house full of tension because their father was under constant pressure and bringing it all home with him. We chose tranquility, and I do not regret that decision for a minute. As a good Canadian, I said no to New York.

I was very comfortable doing what I could for my congregation and my community, but out of the blue there was suddenly a big opportunity. In 1991, I got a call from the Dominion Command of the Royal Canadian Legion, the organization that supports military veterans and is in charge of the annual Remembrance Day ceremony at the National War Memorial. They told me there was a rabbi who came every year from Montreal to do the benediction at the ceremony. He used to come to Ottawa on November 10, stay at the Château Laurier, and

With Naomi in 1999.

then the next day, walk out of the hotel, cross the street, and come to the cenotaph. But now he was retiring and they were looking for a new rabbi, preferably someone local so they could eliminate the expense of the overnight hotel stay. Apparently, I was the only rabbi in the city who was a Canadian citizen. Was I interested?

I did not think twice before accepting. To me, they were not offering me a job; they were presenting me with a great honour.

In the days that followed, I let the full weight of this responsibility sink in. Beyond being born on D-Day, I had no military credentials at all. The closest I had come to carrying a weapon was having a water-pistol fight as a kid. Even my connection to Remembrance Day was minimal. We always have a Sabbath of Remembrance at our congregation on the Saturday before Remembrance Day, where we say a memorial prayer for all veterans who passed away, but on November 11 itself, all I had ever done was watch the ceremony on television. But now I was ready to throw myself into it holus-bolus.

That first speech I wrote for Remembrance Day was probably the most difficult. Though I was confident about my ability to speak in public, only a fool would think confidence alone is enough to get the job done properly. My father once told me, "For speeches of two hours I need five minutes of preparation. For speeches of five minutes I need two hours of preparation." He was exactly right. There is great pressure to make sure that your words connect with everyone who is listening, both on Confederation Square and watching on television. When I deliver a sermon in the synagogue, I never use notes. If I forget a point, I just put it in a little later. It is much more important to make eye contact with the people in the audience, rather than bobbing up and down reading from a script. But at the Remembrance Day ceremony, there was a limited amount of time—then a minute and a half—so I decided to write everything out.

That first year, I knew generally what I wanted to say. I wanted to show gratitude to our veterans from the entire country. I wanted to speak about the obligation we have as a country to show our appreciation for the fact that we are free because so many others had been willing to sacrifice their lives. I wanted to be inclusive, of course, mentioning English Canadians, French Canadians, and Indigenous peoples. And I wanted to include the families, especially the wives, of those who fought. They were patriots as well. They endured all the uncertainty. Where is he right now? Is he all right? When he comes home, will he be damaged physically or spiritually or psychologically? Will he come home at all?

Of course, as a rabbi, and as a Jew, I felt particularly obligated to remember. Six million Jews were killed in the Holocaust, including my mother's and father's families. The courage of Allied veterans saved our people from even further destruction and catastrophe.

Yet I did not want my remarks to be particularly religious. I made a conscious decision to keep things general so all Canadians could relate to what I said. Not because I am a heretic. I just did not want anyone who was listening to me to say, "He's not talking to me because he's speaking a different language." I wanted to make sure I was speaking the language of all Canadians—religious and nonreligious—so that everyone would feel that the act of remembering was a sacred obligation but not a religious one.

I wrote the speech. Then I tweaked it. I practiced it, which was a first—I wanted to make sure I did not go over my time. I got reactions from people. And I was ready.

Which brings me to that moment, standing in front of the National War Memorial.

I began to speak.

Ninety seconds later it was over, and I was greatly relieved. I really did not know how I had done. The reaction on site seemed encouraging. Lots of handshakes and "well done" comments. When I got home, Naomi, who had been watching on TV, told me it had gone well. In the next few days, several members of the congregation said they were proud that "their" rabbi had taken the national stage. The lasting feeling I got from that first ceremony was that I had been blessed with a chance to meet authentic Canadian heroes face-to-face, and I hoped I had let them know their country would never forget what they did.

* * *

In 2001, Remembrance Day changed. It went from remembering and honouring the heroes of distant wars to acknowledging and paying our respects to those being deployed to Afghanistan in the aftermath of the terrible Al Qaeda attacks in the United States.

It had already been a difficult year for me. My beloved Naomi died of breast cancer in May. She was just fifty-five years old. Then, on September 11, 2001, I was at my synagogue leading the regular Tuesday morning women's learning class when we heard rumours that something had happened in New York. Someone brought in a television set and, as we watched the footage, we forgot about the class. We were horrified that something like this could happen, but it did. A few of the women remembered the day John F. Kennedy had been assassinated in 1963 and said they had not been so shocked since then.

I had lived in New York, but if this had happened in Cleveland or Kalamazoo, I do not think it would have made any difference. The horror of it was overwhelming. I knew my parents were safe because they had moved to Israel by then, but I felt no sense of relief. Thousands of people had died. We went through the tragedy together at the synagogue. We all viscerally reacted to it as human beings.

In the days immediately following, there was a lot of anger in the larger community of Ottawa. And some of it was misplaced. There was strong anti-Muslim sentiment. No one should jump to the conclusion that the entirety of any people is the enemy because of the actions of a few. The actual perpetrators were our enemies—murderers who set out to kill as many innocent people as they possibly could. But the thing we have to be careful about is not to generalize, and unfortunately in the heat of the moment and the passion of the moment, it was something we saw happening. I was part of a group of clergymen who worked with the mayor's office and with the police to condemn and blunt any vigilante nonsense. We said that any attack on any religion was unacceptable, that it was an attack on all religions.

When it came to preparing my remarks for Remembrance Day that year, September 11 consumed me. Even if I had wanted to forget, it would have been impossible. To have the enemy actually penetrate into our safe haven shattered all our illusions. Before this, it had been easy to think that terrorism was something that happened on the other side of the world, that it would never come here, that we did not have to worry about it, that it was someone else's problem, not ours. Suddenly we realized things had changed. We were vulnerable. It was an attack on the free world and the values our soldiers had given their lives to protect in the past.

By November 11, Canadian troops had already been deployed to Afghanistan, and I wanted to make sure we honoured them. Looking out over the crowd gathered, there was something different in the air. We were used to remembering wars of the distant past, and maybe we had been lulled into believing Canadians would never again be asked to die on foreign battlefields. If that was our collective hope, we knew then it was a futile hope. I wanted to say that in this new war our country was standing up for familiar and important principles.

"A generation ago we defeated the forces of hatred, cruelty, tyranny, and racism," I said to the crowd that day. "But the war against these ravaging intrusions on human decency is not over. Now our younger generation has been sent overseas, fully aware of the dangers but equally fully committed to stand on guard for us, to protect the values we cherish, and if necessary to fight for them."

A few years later, in 2007, our troops were still fighting in Afghanistan and they were also dying. Most Canadians were too young to remember our earlier wars, but the war in Afghanistan galvanized the country and brought the conflict right into our homes. Every time a Canadian was killed in faraway Afghanistan, the media was saturated with the news, making the loss feel close to home. In September, a stretch of Highway 401 running from Trenton, Ontario, to Toronto was renamed the Highway of Heroes as a tribute to Canada's fallen soldiers. In the lead-up to Remembrance Day, I sensed a mood of quiet support not only for our veterans but also for the young men and women currently serving in our armed forces. The military wasn't "them," it was "us"—our precious sons and daughters serving far from home because their country asked them to. People have a great capacity to take things for granted, but hearing about young Canadians dying at war shook us from our apathy.

I thought there was something out there that amounted to more than support. I thought it amounted to love for our troops.

There was very strict protocol with regard to the Remembrance Day ceremony, but something was missing. Thousands of people surrounded Confederation Square, listening to speeches and watching processions but not participating. I had an idea to get them involved.

I went to Steven Clark, then in charge of the Remembrance Day ceremony for the Royal Canadian Legion and now its national executive director, and explained that I wanted to ask the tens of thousands of people in the crowd to join me in saying "We love our troops." I thought that saying those words out loud would bring the sentiment from the subconscious to the conscious.

"This is a little bit of a break from protocol, but will you allow me to do it?" I asked. "Will you let me lead the crowd to respond at the end of a few sentences?"

When he said yes, I knew I was walking out on a limb. Canadians are famously reticent to show their patriotism. What if everyone just stood there silently? I decided it was something I would not even contemplate. I thought people wanted to speak from their hearts.

With General Hillier in 2007.

On that Remembrance Day, my speech built to the climax. I asked the crowd to say that four-word sentence, and they were more than ready.

"We love our troops," they roared.

"Because of their selflessness," I finished, and the crowd applauded. "We love our troops because of their unswerving love of Canada. We love our troops because of their bravery and dignity in combat. We love our troops because through them, we gain a more vivid, vital appreciation of all the veterans who fought on behalf of Canada for global freedom."

There was enthusiastic and spontaneous applause after each sentence. Everywhere I looked I saw smiles. The message was above politics, so the prime minister and the opposition leaders nodded as one. On a day when veterans were lost in somber recollections of friends who did not return, some of them even smiled. "We love our troops" seemed to have struck a resonant chord, and connected Canadians emotionally with our venerated past and our heroic present.

I found out later that General Rick Hillier, the chief of the defence staff at the time, said, "I think today is going to be remembered for that line."

* * *

We can thank God that we have never had an attack in Canada like the Americans did on 9/11. But there was a day in October 2014 that affected us profoundly. It was the day twenty-four-year-old Corporal Nathan Cirillo was murdered while on sentry duty at the National War Memorial.

I was in downtown Ottawa that morning for a meeting, and I remember how uncertain we all felt when we heard the news of a gunman firing shots on Confederation Square, running across Wellington Street toward Parliament Hill, hijacking a vehicle, driving it to the base of the Peace Tower, and shooting his way into Parliament's Hall of Honour, where he engaged in a gun battle until the sergeant-at-arms killed him.

9/11 was not far from our minds, and we could not help wondering if this was a random attack or the beginning of something much bigger? Looking back, knowing that just one man was the perpetrator, it may seem like we all overreacted, but this was an act of hate, one that had taken the life of a bright, dedicated young man. More than 4,000 people came to his funeral. Those of us who watched it on TV were heartbroken to see Cirillo's five-year-old son, Marcus, walking behind his father's casket, wearing the regiment's cap.

That the murder had occurred at the National War Memorial was a punch to the gut. This is the place where we commemorate and extol and venerate people who have given their lives to our country; this was the place where Corporal Cirillo was standing guard, where he had been killed. It was a violation. The entire country felt that way.

I had already started writing my speech, but I knew I had to start over. Sitting there at my desk, I struggled with what to say. What was the right reaction to this? What was the right thing to do when the unthinkable, the unfathomable, had happened? As a nation, we were stricken with grief.

It would be easy to get angry, but I wanted to encourage others not to be defined by those who try to upset us, but to be defined by our better selves. The sad truth was that nothing we did would bring Corporal Cirillo back, but maybe each of us could do something to perpetuate his memory. Maybe we could do something positive to help others, to make sure that he did not die in vain. And that is what I spoke about.

"We are shaken to the core, but shaken toward firm resolve," I said. "If anything, we are shaken from apathy, toward actively promoting our sacred values. We are united not because of a common enemy. We are united because of a common and shared resolve that Canada remain defined by its warmth, its kindness, its harmony, its culture of embrace."

It would be easy to say that was a very special Remembrance Day. In truth, they are all very special.

Since my first speech in 1991, I have noticed that Canadians have a greater sense of appreciation of our military. You do not need a much better gauge than looking at the number of people who come out to the Remembrance Day commemoration in Ottawa. When I started I was able to walk easily from wherever I parked to the War Memorial, but now when I walk, it is almost like I need someone to clear a path because there are so many people. They are two, three, and four deep, even as early as I get there, well before the ceremony is supposed to start. It is all part of a general sense among Canadians that veterans deserve our thanks. You see parents bringing their children and linking the future of our country to its past.

We call a pilot who shoots down five enemy aircraft a hero. But it is not the killing that makes him or her a hero. What makes a person heroic is the fact that he or she was willing to sacrifice their life for the well-being of others. We glorify the heroism of those who fought. Hating the very idea of war does not mean we should shrink away from showing gratitude to those who went to fight. They responded when they were called on to stop the world from descending into permanent darkness. These are the people who made our freedom possible.

So if the few words I deliver on November 11 carry that message, I am happy. And I have done my job if the veterans feel appreciated. That is worth everything. If they know that the rest of us understand that we are always in their debt, they will know that they did not fight for nothing. They will know that their suffering, their losses, their hardships, and their sacrifices were not in vain, and they have not been forgotten.

Having a role on Remembrance Day is something I never considered in my wildest dreams, but I am ever so thankful that the Legion asked me. It has truly been a blessing, and it brought me right into the mainstream of what we are all about as Canadians. It changed the focus of my job as a rabbi. I have been able to serve my immediate Jewish community but also to reach out to the country as a whole.

On Remembrance Day, as I get ready for the ceremony, I am so grateful to be part of this country. I think about how so many individuals sacrificed so much to make my life possible. We are all indebted, but with that debt comes a great opportunity to keep our country true to the path on which they put us. We may not have to pick up arms and fight on the battlefield where guns are pointed at us, but we should be willing to contribute what we can to the greater good, and to make a difference. None of us should take today's Canada for granted, because without the heroism of those willing to die for our future, we could very easily not have it.

Rabbi Reuven Bulka wrote more than thirty-five books and too many articles to count in scholarly and popular journals and had regular programs on television and radio and served on Jewish and interfaith

groups. An active and engaged citizen, he advocated for organ donations through the Trillium Gift of Life Network, which he chaired for
eleven years, served on the board of Canadian Blood Services—he donated blood 369 times—chaired the Ottawa Regional Cancer Foundation Courage Campaign, founded Kindness Week in Ottawa, and
was the president of Kind Canada Généreux. For all that and more,
he was inducted into the Order of Canada. He was the rabbi emeritus
of Congregation Machzikei Hadas and called Canada home. He lived
in Ottawa, Ontario, with his wife Leah, with whom he shared children in many generations, until his death in 2021.

J. W. (BILL) CAMPBELL
Providing Life's Necessities

I was born poor, but I was brought up in a good family with good values. Years later, just by moving around town, I could see there were an awful lot of people who were poorer than I had ever been.

If you know anything at all about Prince Edward Island, you know that it's small. It makes up about a tenth of one percent of Canada's landmass. Our size, and the fact that we're on an island, makes us different from pretty much any other place in the country. We're so small that, while it's not true that everyone knows everyone else—we have about 160,000 people on the Island—it is true that there's a special connectedness we feel to each other. I was born in Manitoba, but since I came to PEI when I was just six months old, I'm an Islander through and through.

I grew up in Miscouche, on the western half of the Island, the son of a corporal in the Royal Canadian Air Force, and with a mother who was a devout Roman Catholic. I was the oldest of eight children, six boys and two girls. It was never easy making ends meet in our family. My father worked an extra job at the canteen at the local hockey rink and managed a golf driving range in the summer, but with ten mouths to feed, it was hard to scrape by. When I was about twelve years old I got a job working nights as a pin boy at the bowling alley. Those were the days before pins were reset by machine. Instead, someone like me jumped between alleys with every roll of the ball, taking away the dead pins, rolling the ball back, setting up a new rack. I got four dollars a night, working from 6 to 11. I also had a paper route, delivering seventy-five papers every day to the families that lived in the personal married quarters on the base where we also lived. I gave some of my earnings to my mother to help the family budget.

Looking back, I realize my early years gave me a firm understanding of how hard life could be, even for the hardest-working, best-intentioned people you could find. I'm sure that influenced the man I became, though it's also true that I almost took an entirely different path.

In the early 1960s, I was teaching at Miscouche Regional High School, where at nineteen years old, I was barely older than some of my students. It was a Catholic school, and the Mother Superior asked me to organize meetings where grade eleven and twelve students could listen to visiting priests and nuns talk about becoming priests or nuns. The speakers came from everywhere. The Sisters of Notre Dame, the Sisters of St. Martha, the Oblate Fathers, and many others all made beautiful presentations, and after each one, interested students would walk to the front to discuss the possibilities of joining the order.

One day, a priest from the Franciscan Friars of the Atonement showed up. They're often called the Graymoor Friars after the church grounds about 80 kilometres north of New York City. The priest gave a wonderful talk about Christian unity, which appealed to me because I had long thought it was ridiculous that some people were Catholic and some were Protestant. There wasn't any animosity between Catholics and Protestants when I grew up, but as Catholics we were certain there was no way for a Protestant to get to heaven. Thank God even those prejudices have now vanished.

I guess I was the only person in the room who found the presentation compelling because I was the only one who went up to talk to the priest at the end.

*Here I am in the middle with my younger sister and
two brothers on our tricycles in 1956.*

"I'm the guy who organized the meeting," I said. "And I'm interested."

He seemed surprised. "You're interested?" Then he asked two more important questions. "Are you married? Do you have a girlfriend?"

"I've been going with a girl for five years."

"Oh, you've got to do something about that."

"Yes, I will. I'll do something about that."

I went to talk to my girlfriend to tell her my new plan for life. It did not go well. She was very upset, and I can't blame her. "We've been together for five years, and now you tell me you need to be a priest?" She actually left the Catholic Church because she was so angry with me.

I had quite a struggle with my decision, to be honest. I asked myself many times, "Am I crazy? What am I doing? I gave up a good teaching job. I gave up a girlfriend. Did I really have to go to New York to be with God? Wasn't He in PEI?"

A photo from my time as Brother Melvin in 1966.

It was with some sadness that I packed my bags for New York.

At the monastery, I was given a new name. I wanted a manly, muscular name like Mario. Instead, I became Brother Melvin. Despite the disappointing name, I enjoyed life at Graymoor that first year. I especially liked our trips to New York City once or twice a month to visit museums or art galleries. I even met the archbishop of New York, Cardinal Francis Spellman.

My second year wasn't as easy. It was my novitiate year, a year of serious study, prayer, and preparation that would determine if I was really called to be a priest before I took my vows. We were up at five every morning and spent long hours praying, and that was the only time we spoke, other than designated recreation periods. As an avid talker, I found the vow of silence particularly difficult.

One of the breaks from this concentrated religious life was regular mountain hikes. One day when we were climbing, we saw two women out on a ridge, yelling for help. We weren't allowed to talk, so we couldn't yell back. The Father who was leading us made his way to the women to find out what the trouble was. When he returned, he was forced to speak to us.

"Brothers," he said. "Does anybody here know anything about a Coleman stove?"

I was so anxious to talk to a woman, or anyone, I put up my hand in a flash. "I'm from Prince Edward Island and we use them on a regular basis down there." It was the truth. Years as a Boy Scout were about to pay off.

"Okay, Brother Melvin, go on over and see if you can help them."

I set off, eager. When I got to them, I said hello and then looked at the stove. It took about two minutes to see the problem: they had a dial turned the wrong way. But it took me about two hours to tell them that.

The Father Superior checked in every so often. "Brother Melvin, have you solved the problem yet?"

"I'm working on it, Father."

I had the greatest chat with these two ladies because I was free to speak. It was like winning the lottery. When I came off that mountain, I couldn't suppress my doubts any longer. Could I really spend the rest of my life like this? I knew the answer was no.

The Fathers gave me every chance to change my mind. Even as they drove me to the train station to go home they kept stopping along the way. "Are you sure, Brother Melvin? Once you get on that train, it's goodbye forever." But I was sure.

The hardest part was going home to my mother. She had put all her bets on my becoming a priest. I knew she was disappointed, but she didn't show it or put me down. She said all the nice motherly things to let me know that she still loved me dearly. She said it was "God's will" that I not become a priest, and He must have another plan for me.

If that was true, I had no idea what His plan was. I represented PEI on the Centennial Caravan that crossed the country in 1967, worked in the advertising department of a local newspaper, and then found a job selling life insurance for a while. I was living in a boardinghouse in Charlottetown, and on Friday nights I would get on a bus to go back to Miscouche. I noticed a very pretty girl on the bus every week. I found out later she was taking a hairdressing course in Charlottetown and, like me, going home on weekends. She stayed on the bus longer than I did, another forty minutes to Alberton. I thought I'd never have a hope with her.

It turned out that my mother and this girl's sister played bingo together, and as they talked it came out that they both knew someone taking the Friday night bus. One thing led to another. My mother told me the girl on the bus thought I had a nice look and talked about me. This was a revelation. The next Friday on the bus I got as close to her as possible, smiled, and said, "Hi." Alice-Faye and I were married six months later.

I decided to go back to school to upgrade my teaching credentials, and I became a grade six teacher at Elm Street School in Summerside. I loved that year. I enjoyed teaching that age group, eleven- and twelve-year-olds.

To this day, I can still go into a restaurant and someone will come up to me and say, "Are you Mr. Campbell, my grade six teacher?" They tell me it was the best experience they ever had in school. For whatever reason, they liked me and never forgot me. Maybe I was too easy on them.

At the time, the premier of PEI was Alex B. Campbell. He's no relation, but my father and I had both done some campaign work for him. One day, out of the blue, he called me. "Bill, my executive assistant wants to go back to university for a year to get another degree. Would you like to join us?"

It sounded like a good opportunity, but my first reaction was to say, "I already signed a contract to teach another year. I made a commitment."

He didn't see that as a problem and invited me to dinner with him and the superintendent of education. I told you PEI is a small place. That night, I felt like a pea sitting between two giants.

Premier Campbell started the conversation. "Mr. Superintendent, we'd really like to have Bill for a year, if we can get him."

The superintendent looked at me. "I think it would be an honour to have one of our teachers working in the premier's office. Don't worry about your contract. When you finish your work in Charlottetown, we'll make sure there's still a place for you at school."

By the time we'd finished dessert, I had agreed to move to Charlottetown to work in the premier's office. But there was one hitch. Alice-Faye had just accepted a job as a hairstylist in Summerside.

She proved to be flexible. She took a job in Charlottetown instead. In 1974, she opened her own salon at the new Charlottetown Mall and became "Charlottetown's First Lady of Hair" to many people. She also became the mother of our only child, Vanessa Rose.

When my year in the premier's office was over, I didn't return to teaching. Instead, I went back to university, worked for the provincial government for a while, and then went to work as an employment counselor for the federal government. I liked the work. I was finding jobs for people and I loved helping people. But when I was moved into the fraud division, finding people who were cheating the system, it wasn't much fun at all. People didn't cheat because they were bad. Most just wanted to put food on the table for their families. That's why I remain a proponent of a guaranteed annual income in Canada.

I became consumed with helping those who were falling out of step with society because they didn't have enough money. This was what I needed to use my voice for. I was born poor, but I was brought up in a good family with good values. Years later, just by moving around town, I could see there were an awful lot of people who were poorer than I had ever been.

In 1984, I was invited to a meeting at St. Dunstan's Basilica, where a group was hoping to start a soup kitchen. I didn't know a lot about what might need to be done, but I was enthusiastic about the idea. "I'm an employment counselor. I see people every day that don't have jobs and don't have enough to eat. There are indeed hungry people in this town. We need a soup kitchen, and we can do this."

The other people at the meeting liked my spirit so they put me in charge of raising money. I knew a great many people from my time at the premier's office. I'd phone somebody and say, "I know you're sitting at a desk all day. While you're sitting, why don't you think up some ideas for raising money to get a soup kitchen here in Charlottetown?"

Sure enough, they'd show up at our Thursday meetings and they did have good ideas. One well-off retired couple who were originally from New York started a group of donors called "angels" who would contribute a dollar a week—$52 a year—to keep their angel status. Through this program and many others, we raised hundreds of thousands of dollars. That's how we got things going.

By 1986, we had enough resources to start a food bank where, once a month, people could get groceries: basic food, fruits, and veggies. Most of the people who came to us were what you might expect—men living on the street because they couldn't find work. But there were also women, many of whom had children to feed. Sometimes they were the victims of deadbeat dads—the guys had just walked away after a divorce or separation. A lot of single mothers came to us for the sake of their kids. Even today, more than 35 percent of our clientele are under the age of eighteen.

We were also seeing the working poor. I remember that even as an adult I used to send money to my mother to help her buy a dress for one of my younger sisters, or shoes for one of my younger brothers. People could be working hard, but they couldn't make ends meet because their housing costs were high. I'd ask them, "How much do you pay for rent?" Then, "How much money do you make?" Some were paying more than half their income to keep a roof over their head. I knew that left little for anything else, for food, clothing, or recreation.

I thought it was time to do something about that, so when I got a call one day from the CBC about the food bank, I ended up on TV shooting my mouth off. "There are a lot of people in this town who are being gouged by landlords," I fumed. "They're paying too much money for rent. No wonder they don't have enough left to buy food."

Turns out, the regional director at Canada Mortgage and Housing Corporation (CMHC) was watching. He called me the next day. "How come you never come talk to us?" he asked. "Why don't you come in and let's see what we can do."

When I sat in front of him in his office, his first question was direct. "So, what is it you want?"

"I want a six-unit building. It'll be a crisis centre," I said, gaining momentum. "I'm running into too many people who have some crisis in their life. Maybe they just got out of jail, or maybe it's something else. Their relatives are mad at them, they're totally rejected, they have no place to go. I need a shelter for these people. Give them twelve months to fix their current situation, get a job, get out in the community, and do something to convince everyone they deserve another chance."

The man from CMHC listened, then he said, "I'll make a deal with you. You build a co-op. I'll let you split off six units into a separate building and you can call that your crisis centre."

At first, I didn't appreciate the value of a co-op. It was a completely foreign concept to me. But I didn't hesitate. "It's a deal." I do a lot of things that others consider risky. I just do it. I'm prepared to make mistakes.

I got a lawyer who was willing to donate his time to set up a private housing corporation called Kings Square Non-Profit Corporation. I asked people to join the board of directors; we oversaw the construction of a 23-unit co-op, then trained the tenants to manage it. Our crisis centre was right next to it.

Now we had to furnish it, but we had no money for that.

It was time to gamble. I went to a furniture store and bought $26,000 worth of chairs, beds, tables, and lamps, and charged it on my own personal credit card. I was determined to give the people in crisis a home, a place where they could feel safe and comfortable for twelve months while they integrated back into the community.

The guys on the board told me I was crazy. But I was still a fervently faithful man. I said to the board members, "Don't worry about it. This is something that is meant to be. The money will come from somewhere."

A little while later, a Charlottetown dentist passed away and left us $60,000 in his will. Vindication! I enjoyed going back to the board and telling them, "You have to have a little faith."

I was still working for the federal government, but I admit I was becoming a pain in the ass. People were dropping in all the time with donations for the food bank, and the media came in to do interviews. When Ottawa wanted to cut staff by offering early retirement packages, I thought the time was right to stop dividing my attentions. I jumped at the offer.

Now I had more time to do some real work for the soup kitchen and the food bank. And I had caught the building bug. I didn't want to make a cent myself. I was just trying to provide affordable housing to people, and I knew I could do wonders if I wasn't on the payroll. I still didn't know much about building houses, but that didn't stop me. My job was to find the people who had the skills to build a bloody house. I only had to get out there and get talking, which came naturally to me.

I connected with some good people who had land they were willing to sell at a reasonable price. With help from a consultant, I negotiated with them, got CMHC and the province to put up some money, and took out a bank mortgage at a good rate for the rest. We hired the contractors and built a 20-unit apartment building and set up an affordable housing program. If someone's income was below a certain threshold, they paid 25 percent of what they made. I'm not sure who decided that 25 percent is the magic number, but it seems to work. If you don't spend more than that for housing, you can still pay for the rest of life's necessities.

We built on that success, literally. At one point, when we had four buildings on a street, city hall phoned us and said, "We have to develop a lane there. What should we name it?"

One of the lawyers on our board of directors thought we should recognize my contribution by calling it "Bill Campbell's Lane."

"Oh no. We can't do that," they said at city hall. "We already have a Campbell Road and a Campbell Boulevard."

So our lawyer asked, "Well, how close can we come to Bill Campbell's Lane?"

"How about Bill's Lane?"

I said, "Call it what you want. I don't need that, but thank you. I appreciate the fact that you think I've done some work that deserves recognition."

And that was that. There's a piece of Charlottetown named for me, though somewhere along the way, someone dropped the apostrophe, so now it's Bills Lane.

As much as we've done, there's still more to do. We have a waiting list a mile long to get one of our apartments. We're building 60 more units now, but I have about 400 applications on my desk. Many are from single mothers. Just recently, a woman with four little kids came to me in tears.

"What's wrong?" I asked her.

"My husband couldn't make enough money to provide for us so he just gave up. He said, 'To hell with it' and he's just left us."

I'm determined to find her an apartment, but I know that for every family that gets in, six are going to be out in the cold. It's incredibly frustrating how difficult it is to beat poverty.

Surrender is not in my nature. I keep trying to get more people to step up to the plate. Affordable housing should be a right from birth, and we've got to figure out a way to create government policies that will end the commodification of housing. I understand that landlords need to make a profit, and they have a right to, but people shouldn't be homeless because of that. At the very least, we have to do something about landlords who are gouging people. While more and more people are beginning to see things this way, change isn't coming fast enough to suit me.

I'm always thinking, some would say scheming, for ways to alleviate poverty. In 2002, I read about microcredit. In the developing world, small, collateral-free loans were really doing wonders to lift people up economically, and I started wondering if that could work in Atlantic Canada. After I went to a couple of microcredit summits in the United States and Europe with about 3,000 delegates from all over the world, I got it into my head that the next summit should be in Prince Edward Island. Bringing the world to our island would be like nothing that had ever happened here.

I went to talk to Pat Binns, who was the premier at the time. "Bill," he said. "If you can bring something like that to PEI it would be incredible."

Turns out, it was incredible. As in impossible. When I invited the microcredit people from Washington to Charlottetown for a look around, they said, "You couldn't hold the queen of Spain's security detail here, let alone bring in thousands of delegates."

So I went to Nova Scotia to talk to Premier John Hamm. He was interested enough to give me $250,000 to try to get the summit to Halifax. It was a start, but I knew I needed a million dollars before anybody would take me seriously.

I called the Atlantic Canada Opportunities Agency in Moncton. (ACOA is the economic engine the federal government uses to distribute money throughout the Atlantic economy.) I got exactly nowhere. One bureaucrat told me, "You want us to give you a million dollars to put on a conference for a bunch of basket weavers from South America? I don't think so." I got mad at him, of course. That wasn't the idea at all. He didn't have a clue about microcredit.

In 2015, I received the Order of PEI for my work in the community. On the left is
Premier Wade MacLauchlan, and on the right, Lieutenant Governor Frank Lewis.

Then my luck changed. One day, my member of Parliament called
me. "Bill, are you still trying to get that microcredit thing in Halifax?
Well, Prime Minister Paul Martin is at the Charlottetown airport right
now, sitting all by himself in a little room waiting for a jet to come pick
him up. Go see him."

I thought it was a long shot, but with nothing to lose, I raced out to
the airport. I knew the airport manager—I told you PEI was a small
town—so I ran to see him. "I know the prime minister is here. Can you
let me into the room where he's sitting?"

"No, I can't do that," he said. "But I can walk away." And with that,
he turned and left. I went and knocked on the prime minister's door.

A voice on the other side called out. "Come in."

For about twenty minutes, I gave Paul Martin my sales pitch. I explained to him how powerful microcredit was. I gave him the history of how it was used in developing countries, how women were being targeted with the smaller loans and how they were creating enough money to bring their families out of poverty and malnutrition. "Families are struggling here too," I told him. "Maybe we could educate people on the value of this tool and see if it can work here in an industrialized economy. If we have a global summit in Halifax, we'll spread the word."

The prime minister got pretty excited. He called an assistant over and told me to repeat everything I had just said. I left with a good feeling.

A couple of weeks later the same bureaucrat I'd been talking to in Moncton called me on the phone. "Mr. Campbell," he said. "We have revisited your file, and we find merit in it."

In November 2006, we had a four-day conference in Halifax.

After that, it was time for me to test out my theory that microcredit could do some good right here. With some money from Ottawa, I started a little nonprofit company called Canada Microcredit Educators Group. We began by lending money to new immigrants to help them upgrade their education credentials to Canadian standards. It might be a doctor from the Congo or an engineer from Romania. The retention rate of newcomers in PEI is low because there's not enough opportunity for them. I thought if I could help level the playing field for new Canadians, they could compete with the people who were graduating locally in different trades and professions, and then maybe end up staying here in PEI.

The loans range from $3,000 to $20,000. Three thousand dollars may not sound like a lot, but if someone doesn't have access to cash or a good credit rating, they're in trouble. People aren't going to lend them any money at all. They need somebody who will say, "Here is a collateral-free loan. I trust you."

I was happy to see that the microcredit system works. My default rate? Zero. Every single person has paid back their loan.

Looking back, I don't think I could have done as much had I become a priest. I married a fantastic wife who gave me the freedom to do things I love. I have absolutely no regrets. The spirituality that was started and seeded in me through organized religion has now evolved. I feel like the kingdom of God isn't in church; it's within all of us.

There is nothing that gives me more of a thrill than giving to others. Sometimes people say no, they don't want to accept anything from me. To that I reply, "Why are you depriving me of an opportunity? If I can give you something with the right heart, I'll get it back ten times over. Why are you stopping me from doing that?" The Bible says, "The poor you will always have with you." I don't believe that has to be so.

J. W. (Bill) Campbell is the president and founder of Kings Square Affordable Housing in Charlottetown, PEI, a not-for-profit housing project that provides subsidized accommodations for 100 families. Another project contains 12 geothermally heated town houses plus one 8-unit apartment building, and another 60-unit project is under construction. He was instrumental in bringing Habitat for Humanity to PEI. He is also the president and founder of Canada Microcredit Educators Group, has received the Canada Volunteer Award and Medal of Honour, a CMHC Concept and Design award, and is a member of the Order of Prince Edward Island. He lives in Charlottetown, PEI, with his wife, Alice-Faye.

JESSICA GROSSMAN
The Reason I'm Alive

*I would sometimes wonder why this was happening to me,
but I never wanted my life to be over. In truth, I was too sick to
think about how my life was going to change. . . . If I had a
lucid moment, all I could think about was the pain I was feeling.
A change was needed, no matter what it would bring.*

By the time I was thirteen years old, I had lived through five years of on and off—mostly on—severe abdominal pain. Agony was probably a better word to describe it. At times it felt as if knives were stabbing into my intestines, and I couldn't eat, I couldn't sleep, and I couldn't go to school. For the better part of two years, I had been in and out of hospitals, had been poked with needles, and had undergone hundreds of tests. It was on the last of those long hospital stays that a surgeon came into my room for what I now call "the day that saved my life."

My body, awash in pain-killing drugs that had dulled my senses, made it hard to follow everything the doctor was saying. One part penetrated the mist. He said that if I didn't agree to undergo life-altering surgery, I would soon be dead. I was just a teenage girl, and I wasn't ready to die.

* * *

The stomach pain started when I was a kid. I grew up eating what any kid eats—hot dogs, pizza, chicken nuggets, lots of candy and sweets— but at eight years old, I'd cramp up almost immediately after even half a meal. At first, the pain was manageable, but it eventually worsened to the point that I stopped eating. When I said no to chocolate cake and ice cream, my parents knew something was seriously wrong.

My dad's brother has had Crohn's disease since he was thirteen, so to my parents it seemed the most likely answer. Crohn's is a bowel disease that causes inflammation of the digestive tract, which can in turn cause abdominal pain, severe diarrhea, fatigue, weight loss, and malnutrition. Researchers haven't figured out why some get it, but studies suggest that genes play a role.

When I lost five pounds—a lot of weight for a growing kid to lose— my mom took me to our family doctor, who ran tests to identify the cause of the pain. One was a barium enema, a procedure where a well-lubricated tube was inserted into my rectum and pumped a liquidy metallic substance (barium) into my colon. The barium coated my intestines so doctors could get a clear X-ray picture.

I think that if I had been older I would have felt embarrassed, but I was in so much pain that there wasn't room for emotion. Despite the situation, one thing sticks in my mind: the wall of photos of the radiologist's family. Mom, dad, sister, brother, dog . . . all staring back at me with the biggest shit-eating grins. It was ironic. Apparently, that was supposed to distract me from what was going on up my butt.

But I could hear the radiologist saying to his colleague, "Oh, yes, I see something there. Look at that, uh-huh."

When it was over, they told my parents that they were 99 percent sure I had Crohn's disease. Even with those findings, the doctors wanted to be absolutely sure and X-ray the upper part of my digestive track. To do that, I had to drink the barium. It tasted awful, but a nurse told me that mixing it with Orange Crush would make it taste better. It didn't.

That X-ray, and some blood tests later, confirmed the diagnosis. I had

Crohn's disease. It was incurable. If I was lucky, I'd be able to manage the disease with medication. They put me on something right away, which was fine by me. I was anxious to get on top of the disease. While I hadn't been born when my uncle was diagnosed, I knew what he had been through, and he was alive. My mindset even then was: we can handle this.

For a kid who had never swallowed a pill, my prescribed pills could not have been larger. "Horse tablets," my dad called them as I tried to take my first one. It wasn't coated and fell apart into little, chalky balls that stuck to my mouth. I didn't figure out how to swallow it cleanly for two weeks.

After my diagnosis, I was referred to SickKids hospital in Toronto and assigned a pediatric gastroenterologist. Diet is one of the first steps to managing Crohn's, so she recommended I avoid stringy vegetables (good-bye asparagus!), popcorn (damn), and berries with seeds (double damn), among other things. At nine, I was old enough to understand the serious-ness of the matter, but not old enough to grasp the sacrifices my family had to make. My mother, bless her heart, used to peel strawberries for me so they wouldn't have seeds. The dietary adjustments worked, and I felt normal again for a little while.

That was, until the summer after grade six. I was set to go to summer camp for the first time, but when I got the stomach flu I missed the first week. After I recovered, my parents drove me to camp and said goodbye.

For the first two days, I was all right. I went swimming, met new peo-ple, and tried to acclimatize to camp. It was on the third night that the pain hit me. The stomach flu was a dream compared to this agony. Our cabin was at the bottom of a small hill and the girls' bathroom was at the top; all night, I made multiple trips back and forth in the dark. I was exhausted and couldn't get out of bed the next morning, or the day after that, or the day after that. Except to go to the bathroom. This was no stomach flu.

After a few days, my camp counselor, who wasn't much older than I was, transferred me to the medical cabin, hoping someone there would know what to do. I remember hearing the camp doctor whisper to the nurse about how ill I was and the faint sounds of a one-sided phone conversation with my parents. They had thought that once the flu passed, camp would be good for me—it would get me out of my shell and help me make friends. Maybe it would have happened, but Crohn's came to camp too.

After I got home, I spent almost every waking moment on the toilet with nothing but blood coming out the other end. The rest of the time I was passed out on the couch with my younger brother, Jason, watching TV.

My parents, realizing what was happening to my body, didn't panic (or at least, it didn't look like they were panicked) and took me to SickKids hospital for what would be the first of many long hospital stays. I don't remember much of this first visit because I was passed out 95 percent of the time. My body was losing liquids, bloods, and enzymes on an almost hourly basis, and I was a puddle of flesh and bones lost in a giant hospital bed. My body was starting to reject life. And the pain. It never went away.

While this first hospital stay is a foggy memory, I do remember bits and pieces.

One thing that's burned into my memory is the day I woke up to something puncturing my chest. I let out a blood-curdling scream. No one had told me they were going to do a procedure, and here were four people standing over me poking a giant needle into my chest.

I know now that they were trying to put in what's called a central line. I hadn't been eating, so all my nutrition was coming through an intravenous line (an IV), which the doctors inserted into my veins in routine places, either on my wrist or my hand or my arm. Those only last for a few days at a time and I needed something more stable. Ergo, the central line—a long, thin, flexible tube inserted through the chest into a large vein near the heart. Unfortunately, my scream stopped them. I never did get that central line.

Instead, the doctors went another route and put me on steroids to calm the inflammation. After a few weeks, my pain subsided enough that I was able to eat real food again, which was great. But I hadn't known that a major side effect of the drug was weight gain. I went from being 52 pounds to 152 pounds and my face became a round moon. I looked like an alien with a giant head and small eyes. My parents kept assuring me I was still their beautiful daughter, but I wasn't fooled. For a twelve-year-old girl hitting puberty, this wasn't what I imagined my life would be. I felt like I was turning into a monster.

While I was able to eat again, there were restrictions that made school lunches especially difficult. I was on what I called "the all brown, no fun diet." No vegetables. No fruit. No dairy. No sugar! Brown bread was allowed. Peanut butter was allowed, but my school was peanut-free. I never liked tuna, so what was left for sandwiches?

My mom, always looking for ways to make my life as normal as she could, found dairy-free cheese slices at the store.

"You can take this for lunch," she enthused. "You'll put a slice on a piece of bread, pop it into the microwave at school, and you'll have a nice melted cheese sandwich. You like melted cheese sandwiches."

Indeed, I did. But as I soon discovered, any resemblance between the white substance she had bought and real cheese was coincidental.

At noon on my first "cheese" day, I walked to the school lunchroom and popped my meal into a microwave. After forty-five seconds the white slice hadn't melted at all—it even felt room temperature to the touch. I thought maybe the microwave was broken, so I put it in a different one for another forty-five seconds. The bread came out warm but the "cheese" was the same hard slice as when it went in.

"Are you done?" a kid behind me asked.

"I think both microwaves are broken."

He didn't take my word for it. And he was right. His noodles came out steaming hot, and my sandwich went in the garbage.

I wasn't really eating, but I was gaining weight thanks to the drugs, and my pain came back. I tried to stick it out, but the nightly bathroom excursions kept me up, so my days at school were spent sleeping on my desk. After a few weeks of waking up to a teacher telling me to go to the office, I was once more in the hospital with new medication and, this time, the "zero food diet," where I got my nourishment through an IV. The hope was that the new medication would work and the IV would keep me nourished while allowing my bowels to rest.

I stayed in the hospital for two weeks. There wasn't much to do besides the homework the teachers would send by way of my brother-turned-messenger-boy, and watching television. TV binge-watching when you're a preteen sounds like a dream—until you can't eat and realize just how many food commercials there are. I'd be watching a program and a commercial for Pizza Hut would pop up. I never even liked Pizza Hut, but there I'd be, drooling over their cheesy crust. I'd change the channel and the screen filled with Big Macs and fries. I couldn't escape it.

After they took out the IV, I was sent home with new medication and new hope, but nothing changed. Two weeks here. Three weeks there. I would be at school, then home, then back at the hospital in a cycle that never seemed to end. I was so fed up with my blood being taken every day that I refused unless they numbed the area. Every visit, I had a colonoscopy. I don't know what all those tests did for me because I only got worse.

My dad, who worked from home, often spent his days by my hospital bed. When he wasn't there, he was researching Crohn's, learning much more than he knew when his brother was diagnosed and hoping to find new, even experimental treatments that could stop my suffering. He was a realist who never bullshitted me, so he didn't hesitate to tell me that the experimental poop transplant he read about wasn't accepting patients my age.

Eventually, after running out of new diets to alleviate the pain, my medical team decided to completely cut off my ability to ingest food for a significant amount of time, and only feed me through a naso-gastric (NG) tube, which would be threaded into my nose and down the back of my throat into my stomach. I had seen other kids in the hospital dealing with them and they always looked awful, so I had done everything in my power to avoid an NG tube. But after convincing me it was the only option, a nurse inserted the tube and turned on the machine, then left the room as liquid nutrition pumped into my stomach. Within five minutes, I vomited and the tube came out. There I was, a tube taped to my face, still threaded through my nose but now dangling out of my mouth as it churned out white liquid.

My dad dragged a giant rubber garbage can from under the sink, and I sat there for over an hour while the liquid spewed gracefully to the bottom of this Rubbermaid bin.

Throughout this experience, my parents were often worried about my mental health and would send in a social worker. The first time she sat down across from me, she said, "I'm here to be with you. I just want to sit with you and we can talk."

I lashed out. "I know why you're here. I can see your badge. You're a social worker. You're here to understand my feeeeelings," I said sarcastically. "I don't need you. I'm fine."

The only photo of me in the hospital was from a time in 2001. I was eleven years old, eating pizza after I hadn't been allowed to eat for eight days. From left to right: my aunt Sheryl, me, my dad, and my brother Jason. My mom is behind the camera.

I was fine. To this day I still remember being fine. I didn't need to talk to anyone. She visited at least seven times throughout my two-year hospital stay, but I never talked.

When I finally went home, they paired yet a new medication with a liquid-only diet of Ensure meal-replacement shakes. Ensure is meant to provide complete, balanced nutrition for people at risk of malnutrition, but they're basically just sugary, highly caloric, artificially flavoured milkshakes in a can. While it was something I could ingest on my own, those drinks made me want to hurl—and still do to this day.

I stopped going to the lunchroom because I didn't want to be around food I couldn't eat, so I stayed in the classroom sipping my Ensure. After a while, the teacher would pick a student to keep me company, but their unhappiness at being forced to sit with me made me feel nothing but alone.

Maybe it was the taste of the Ensure or maybe it was because I had to have eight a day—and nothing else—but I couldn't do it. I'd take a number of cans to school, but only drink a few, if any. At the end of the day, my dad would ask, "How many did you drink?"

"All of them." I'd smile.

"Let me see your shake tracker," my dad would ask. He had made me a custom spreadsheet with check boxes for the number of cans I drank throughout the day. I couldn't get anything by him.

By the end of that school year, the pain was worse. There were no good days anymore, and that summer SickKids might as well have been sleepaway camp because I slept there most nights. The doctors ran new tests and tried new drugs, including a cancer drug that made me lose some hair and burned when it was injected into my forearm every week, which made me scream. I once saw a nurse coming through the doorway to my room, ready with the injection, and I threw a stuffed animal at her. My parents made me apologize.

I was running out of options, and my condition continued to deteriorate. I wouldn't do another NG tube, and my veins were shot from the flood of harsh chemicals. Finally, the doctors decided to give me nutrition through a PICC line, which is basically a semi-permanent IV inserted into a vein in my upper arm that fed directly into my heart. I would get everything—protein, vitamins, carbs, fats, and minerals—through my bloodstream, by-passing my bowels entirely, but without ruining my veins. It was a major procedure done under anesthetic, and I eventually left the hospital with this giant tube sewn into my skin and protected by a bandage that I had to keep clean. Oh, and my very own IV machine to use at home.

That September—my fifth school year dealing with Crohn's—I fell into a dull routine. After spending the day at school, where I couldn't eat anything, I'd come home for a bit of TV before I had to be "plugged in." At 7 o'clock every night, I'd go down to my room in the basement so my parents could plug my PICC line into a bag of nutrients. The IV pole was too tall to fit in our stairwell, so once I was hooked up, I couldn't go upstairs. Since it took twelve hours to feed me, I was stuck down there like a troll. When I'd wake up at 7 a.m., I'd wait for one of my parents to disconnect me and then get ready for school to start another cycle.

At this point, I hadn't eaten a real meal in almost two years and I was only getting sicker and bleeding more heavily. I couldn't concentrate on anything but the excruciating pain that was growing increasingly un-bearable. It was like nothing I had experienced before.

I turned thirteen, beginning my teenage years as a listless sick child. In October, I celebrated my bat mitzvah, which marked my transition to a woman in the Jewish faith, and my parents couldn't have been happier. I looked like a sausage in a prom dress. I ended up back in the hospital the next day, for what would be my last trip.

At the hospital, I spent the majority of the day asleep and my wak-ing hours in pain. I barely got up to go to the bathroom—a normal routine for someone with advanced Crohn's—but I hadn't eaten any-thing in months so there was nothing to come out. They gave me a pump that released narcotics into my system every time I pushed a big, shiny red button for my pain. I pressed it almost fifty times an hour, even though it only released the drugs once an hour. The days passed, the pain grew worse, and the narcotics grew stronger. Everything got hazier. The world was disappearing.

This went on for four months—four months that I can't even remember. Until the doctors tried one more attempt to give me a somewhat normal life.

It started with my parents coming into my room. "It's time to make a decision," they said, not making any attempt to keep the mood light. Even in my state, I could tell this was serious.

Then the surgeon came in and introduced himself as a family friend—he was—whom I apparently already knew—I didn't. I could barely see faces at this point.

"Your intestines have been so tormented and inflamed you now have what we call toxic megacolon. Your colon can't expel gas or poop from your body. If gas and feces stay in your colon, your large intestine may eventually burst. If that happens, the bacteria normally present in your intestine will release into your abdomen. That can cause a serious infection and it will kill you."

My brain was mush, but I tried to follow what he was saying as he proposed how to keep me alive.

"The only solution is to remove a large part of your intestines. You won't ever go to the bathroom like you do now. You'll be given an ostomy bag."

He described the bag and how it worked and told me his wife had one. His wife, whom I also apparently knew.

As he continued his pitch, my mind wandered back to a conversation I'd had with my parents years ago when they had mentioned a neighbour who had an ostomy. They hadn't gone into any detail, and I hadn't understood what they were talking about. "He has to go to the bathroom in a bag?" I thought. My seven-year-old imagination conjured up a Loblaw's grocery bag taped to his stomach. Six years later, that was going to be me.

My brain snapped back to the present as best it could.

"Ultimately, it's up to you to decide if you want the surgery," the doctor said.

Looking back now, that wasn't true. My parents had already made the decision, but they gave me the illusion that the choice was mine. I still thank them for it.

I remember thinking, "What a stupid question. Obviously I'm having surgery." Out loud, I said politely, "Yes, okay."

In the three days before the emergency surgery, the hospital tried to get me psychologically ready. They sent a kid around my age who had an ostomy to talk to me about it. The surgeon's wife also came in wearing tight black jeans to make her point. I remembered her face as soon as she walked in the door. "I have an ostomy and you can't tell." She also assured me it wasn't a Loblaw's grocery bag.

While I was sad that I was going to have surgery, I wasn't depressed. I would sometimes wonder why this was happening to me, but I never wanted my life to be over. In truth, I was too sick to think about how my life was going to change. I was in a daze. I didn't do research. I didn't ask questions. If I had a lucid moment, all I could think about was the pain I was feeling. A change was needed, no matter what it would bring.

There were no good parts to the surgery, but I was lucky that it was laparoscopic. Instead of slicing me open down the middle of my abdomen, as is customary, they made three small incisions on my belly and one through my belly button. They pushed a camera inside through one hole and tools through the other two, and pulled my intestines out through the third. They cut out the six feet of my intestines which looked like they had been mauled by a large cat, took the healthy end and folded it over like you would a sock, and sewed the edges to the outside of my stomach, giving me a stoma. This stoma was where I would excrete waste and where the ostomy bag would go. This rosebud, as doctors like to call it, is what saved my life.

I wasn't as lucky when I woke up from the surgery too soon. The doctors were still pushing me out of the operating room when I suddenly came to and started screaming at the top of my lungs from the pain. I pleaded for painkillers, promising the money I had just made from my bat mitzvah. No deal. They had already given me some, and I needed to wait for them to kick in. And then, oh boy, did they kick in.

It was about four days before I regained full consciousness and then I was in recovery for about two weeks, which took longer because I had been sick for so long. I was still in need of drugs for the pain, still not eating. I was barely walking. I needed a few blood transfusions. I even hallucinated at times.

But, slowly, there was improvement.

I started to walk. I got up to shower. A nurse showed me how to change my ostomy bag. I changed it myself.

One day, the doctors told me I could eat. "You can have anything you want," they said. It had been a long time since I had heard those words. "Sushi," I said. "I love sushi. I want sushi."

My dad and my uncle went to get me sushi, and when I saw the cucumber rolls, I couldn't wait to taste them. I picked one up, put it in my mouth, started chewing, and then . . . nothing. I hadn't had solid food in nearly a year, so my mouth had no idea what to do with it. I couldn't swallow. I was sitting there with a chewed cucumber roll in my mouth and was stuck for what to do next. I had to teach myself how to eat again, but you can bet I finished those cucumber rolls.

As they weaned me off the most powerful painkillers, my mind cleared and I was even able to do some schoolwork. One day, I started a science test (open book, of course) and a nurse came along with a mild pain pill. She didn't tell me what it was, and I was distracted so I didn't ask. The next thing I remember was waking up with my head on the test and a pile of drool on the paper. I finished writing, gave it to my mother, who gave it to my brother, who took it to school. When the test came back the teacher had circled the drool and written, "I hope you're okay."

And then, finally, it was time to go home. Life, for once, seemed normal. Sure, I now went number two in a bag attached to my abdomen, but after everything I had been through, that was nothing. There were no more painkillers or medication. After living so long in agony, I was finally pain-free. It was almost unbelievable how quickly the stomach pain disappeared. After all, the pain was only from the surgery. The pain of the disease went with the intestines they pulled out of me.

I returned to school for the last four months of grade eight, and with fake cheese, milky shakes, tubes coming out of every orifice, and the fog of narcotics still a recent memory, I was happy to rediscover the joy of life, but most of all, the joy of food. I would come home after school and grab a bag of corn chips, grate real cheese on top, put them in the microwave— watch them actually melt—and eat them before dinner. After dinner I'd have ice cream or cake or candy or all three! I ate not because I was hungry but just for the pleasure of eating, which I had lost for so many years.

For three months, an ostomy nurse came to my house about once a week to make sure I was changing the bag properly. I had to learn how to sleep with an ostomy and how to dress with an ostomy, but none of that was too difficult. I didn't have any fashion sense, so I still dressed like a weirdo, ostomy bag or not. I found it difficult to walk up and down stairs because I hadn't moved that much for such a long time, but I was feeling fine and sleeping well. Anything I had to deal with now just didn't seem like a real problem.

My parents were still worried about my mental state, so they took me to an ostomy support group meeting. To this day, I remember walking in, looking around, seeing that the median age was at least sixty, and walking right back out. "I don't fit in here," I said to my parents, and we left. There was also an ostomy support group at SickKids that I reluctantly joined. I really didn't need it—I wasn't embarrassed or ashamed—but at least they were my age.

My classmates, who had known me for most of my life, also knew that I had been away so much over the last two years. On my first day back, I headed to the front of the room to answer all their questions about my absence.

"You all know I've been gone. Now I'm back because I've had surgery that has made me better. I have an ostomy now." I was told to keep an extra ostomy bag in my locker, so I brought it out and showed them how it worked. They all seemed pretty nonchalant about it, which suited me just fine.

At lunchtime I went to the bathroom, and some girls were really interested. "Does it hurt?" "How often do you change it?" "Does it smell?" The best question was "Do you stick your finger in it?" I glared at the girl who asked it, then shot back, "Do you stick your finger up your butt?" I still giggle about it to this day.

High school was harder. I moved from a private school to public school, and I didn't know anyone. Making friends was difficult because I hadn't developed many social skills while isolated in the hospital. When I stood with a group of girls, I had no idea how to join their conversation. I would say something I thought was cool, and they would look at me as if I had just told them that their mom was ugly.

Nothing clicked. I was eating everything now, and eating too much. So I piled more weight on top of what I had gained from the steroids and from the years of perfectly calculated nutrients (which hadn't taken into account that I could barely move to burn calories). I was a weird kid. If somebody had followed me with a camera back then, I'd be burning those recordings today.

I hated everything about myself—except my ostomy. In a lot of ways, my ostomy saved me. It was unimaginably liberating to be free of pain. I was comfortable with my ostomy and I found my confidence because of it. "This is me," I'd say to anyone who would listen. "This is why I'm alive."

Years later, I found out that the doctors had approached my parents about an ostomy a year earlier and they had said, "Over our dead bodies will our daughter have an ostomy bag."

As they watched me go through a year of debilitating pain, they felt very guilty about their decision. My mom is still tortured by that. I don't blame her, though. I know a lot of parents who can't bring themselves to say yes to an ostomy bag. It speaks to the stigma and shame around it.

My parents naturally hoped there was a less radical solution. It wasn't unreasonable for them to say, "No, let's try something else." But looking back, we know that nothing else helped.

For four years, I tried to raise awareness about ostomy surgery and Crohn's disease at school. Whenever we had a science week, I would set up a booth to talk about Crohn's. I didn't talk specifically about my ostomy, but I had the pictures from my surgery (yes, the photos that were taken while I was on the operating table!). The principal thought they were too graphic so I covered them up, but when people stopped at my booth, I'd ask them, "Would you like to see some gross pictures?"

Most said, "Sure." Then I would uncover them and they would recoil. "What the hell is that?" It was an effective opening to explain Crohn's disease.

I took this desire to advocate into grade twelve, where a marketing class sparked a whole new adventure. One of my last projects of the year was to create a media campaign about a topic I found interesting. I obviously chose the ostomy.

This time I didn't want to have to hide my photos. I wanted something that could be put on buses and billboards. The idea was to show me for who I really was—a young adult with an ostomy who didn't look like all those sixty-year-olds I had met at that support group. I hired a photographer, booked a studio, and took a bunch of photos of myself wrapped only in a white sheet and showing my ostomy. Then I added statistics about how many people in Canada have an ostomy. I didn't get a great mark on my project, but the idea never died.

That summer I went to a camp in Alberta for kids with ostomies. I brought the project with me, and a volunteer took an interest in it. His name was Rob Hill. He had climbed Mount Everest with his ostomy and started an organization called IDEAS, the Intestinal Disease Education and Awareness Society. He told me he wanted to do something with the photos, but I didn't hear from him for another couple of years.

By that time, I was in my second year at Western University in London, Ontario, where I was also in a sorority. (At the recruitment night, we had played a game where I had to tell them two truths and a lie. One of my truths? "I poop in a bag." My roommate told me they wouldn't let us in, but they did, and a few years later I was president of the sorority.)

When I told Rob that I thought he'd forgotten about the photos, he said he hadn't.

"You were just seventeen back then," he said. "We wanted to wait until you were nineteen because the photos were pretty sexy. I really want to turn this idea into something."

I felt good about that. Here was a guy who seemed to know how to get things done, and he saw potential in me. We agreed that I'd come out to BC once school ended for a new photo shoot and to talk about setting up a campaign built around a website.

Rob had a new idea too. "You're going to have a blog."

This was 2009, so I said, "What's a blog?"

"You just write about things. It doesn't matter what exactly, just whatever you think is interesting."

But nothing in my life goes in a straight line. In February, before I started blogging, my dad got sick. At first, he thought he might have Crohn's too, but it turned out to be much worse. He had myelofibrosis, a rare bone marrow cancer.

It was terrible news, but my family doesn't wallow very well. If there's a problem we're going to find a way to solve it. We all looked at his disease as something we had to deal with, and we were going to get right on it.

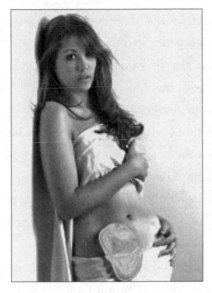

This is the photo I took for my high school media campaign assignment. I added stats about Canadians with ostomies for the final project. It was the start of what would become Uncover Ostomy.

During those years when I had been sick and staying at home, my father had been my constant companion. He would never sit still, always searching for a better answer. Now it was my turn, and I was on his case. He needed a bone marrow transplant to survive, so I turned my attention to finding a donor.

In 2009, to find a donor, you had to search through Canadian Blood Services' worldwide registry of volunteers, but the only way to get new donors registered—and widen the chances of a match—was to ask people to request a kit and test themselves at home before mailing it back. It was not a very scalable model for our purposes, so we looked elsewhere.

With the help of an organization in the United States, we set up a bone marrow drive where we tested more than 1,400 people in seven hours in the hopes of finding a match. We also raised $80,000 to pay for it. My dad, passionate about changing the world—something he instilled in me—but burdened by his disease, spoke to the board of directors at Canadian Blood Services and told them how unfair it was for his family to have to find that kind of money because of their outdated system. They agreed, and in the coming years they took the example we set and started running bone marrow drives across the country, eliminating that financial burden for people who were already worried and desperate.

Once my dad received his bone marrow match (which is sometimes impossible), he was admitted to the hospital for a transplant. That's when I started to blog. But I didn't write about me; I wrote about my dad. Ironic, I guess. I had been the sick one for so long, but now it was my dad's turn, and I had to be there for him. He thought the blog would be the best way to tell our family and friends how he was doing, so they wouldn't pester my mom. He also thought it was fun and would often say, "Be sure to put this in the blog."

Meanwhile, I booked my trip to Vancouver for the ostomy photo shoot, excited to build the ostomy campaign, still high on the success of my dad's campaign. Now that my dad had his bone marrow match, his transplant got scheduled for what was supposed to be my second day on the west coast.

"I'll cancel," I told my dad. "I'll do this later."

He disagreed. "Don't be crazy. You go do what you planned. I'll be fine. We can Skype."

And we did. I watched the transplant live on Skype from Vancouver, which I thought was fitting given my dad had wanted pictures of my ostomy surgery. I saw them put the bone marrow in through an IV while my mom and brother were in the hospital room. It wasn't very exciting until my dad started vomiting violently, at which point I thought it was time to sign off. My mom reassured me later in the day that everything looked good.

For the rest of the week, I did the ostomy stuff in Vancouver with Rob and his team. We came up with the name Uncover Ostomy and replicated the pictures from my high school project showing my ostomy, except I wasn't covered in a sheet, I wore a tank top and jeans.

I flew back home four days after my dad's transplant. I spent most of my time at his bedside in the hospital. At first, he did well. He'd make jokes, talk to us about what he wanted to do when he "escaped," and calmed my mom down on a daily basis, which was no different than usual. Eventually, the spark of happiness turned into a spark of confusion. He told us he had to escape the spies who were after him and needed my brother and me to help. He yelled at us for arguing with each other when my brother was actually down the hall. The doctors adjusted his meds but slowly he lost his ability to speak to us. When we asked him questions he just nodded. The doctors told us his vital signs were stable. Over the next few days, he became more aware of his surroundings and more talkative, but he was sleepy for long periods.

Then, three weeks after the transplant, his condition began to deteriorate rapidly. The marrow match was fine, but the chemotherapy he'd been through had taken a huge toll on many of his organs and they were failing.

Just looking at him, I knew he was dying, and the very thought was overwhelming. He was alive, but by most definitions it wasn't a life. He couldn't open his eyes. He couldn't talk. For three days, we wondered when it would finally, mercifully, end.

Then he was gone. He was forty-two. I was nineteen.

I was devastated.

In the weeks before the transplant, I had often sat with my dad in our kitchen, and he told me he knew I was a strong woman. Now that he was gone, it was time to prove him right.

A week after his death, I celebrated my twentieth birthday with friends and started my classes as if nothing had happened. My dad would have been mad if I hadn't. He was always the guy who, when I showed him a 95 percent on a test, asked me where the other 5 percent was. This was what he had raised me to do.

Shortly after, Rob told me that he was ready to launch the website. I knew it was time.

We went public on World Ostomy Day, October 3, 2009, with a website and a Facebook page. The reaction was immediate. Some people thought it was cool, but the majority of people were upset. In the first twenty-four hours, I heard:

"Why are you doing this?"

"We don't need to talk about this."

"This is something we keep secret."

"You don't have the scars of someone with an ostomy, so you're just a model pretending to have one."

That wasn't what we were expecting.

I frankly thought the complainers were crazy. Did they really think someone would pretend to poop in a bag? I called them "outrage enthusiasts," people who complained because they could. Not everyone was going to love what we were doing, but I thought opposition would come from people who didn't know what an ostomy was, not from those who had them.

Soon, though, the blog became popular. My posts whined about having to study for my university courses, vented about the terrible guys I dated, talked about going to frat parties. The blog was a hit because it wasn't about the ostomy. It was about a girl who happened to have an ostomy. Readers became invested in my life. They would send advice when I broke up with the same guy for the twentieth time. They would warn me about bad behaviour.

Information and the ostomy photos were there too. My mission was always to get people to think about ostomy as normal, but no one was going to be interested in ostomy if all I wrote about was the surgery and how I use the bathroom now. It was better that I wrote about going out for a great dinner. When I did that, people would say, "Wow! She has an ostomy and she can eat like that."

In just over ten years, I've had more than 500,000 hits on my website, and the most frequent thing I hear from ostomates who come through the site—that's the word for people with an ostomy—is that they worry about

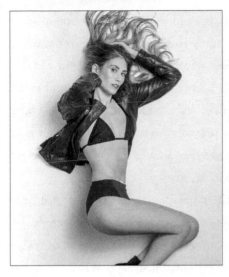

My life is possible because of my ostomy, but my life doesn't revolve around it. For the ten-year anniversary of Uncover Ostomy, I did a photo shoot to illustrate just that. The focus here is me, not my bag. TYLER BOWDITCH/ BAILEY NOELLE TRUDGEON

how other people will react to their ostomy. When I got mine, I was so young that I wasn't dating yet, but when women and men in their twenties get an ostomy the thought of changing how they date is terrifying.

So many people write to me that they are afraid to tell their partner about their ostomy. I always respond that if their partner isn't going to accept them, they need to find a different one. They can't keep it a secret forever.

The first time I dated, I was very scared. I sat the guy down and said, "I have to tell you something." I explained to him that I had this thing on my stomach and finished by saying, "It's the reason I'm alive." Then I ran to the bathroom before he had a chance to say anything, scared of what it would be.

I thought he might just leave and I'd never see him again. Two minutes later he texted me. "Are you hiding?"

That relationship didn't go anywhere, not because of the ostomy but because he hid that he already had a girlfriend. He chose to cheat with me—a woman with a bag! Apparently, pooping in a bag isn't quite the dating filter you'd think it would be.

Many ostomates are depressed that this is where they ended up, and they see it as a sad thing that has happened to them. I hear about wives having to empty their husband's ostomy bag because they don't want to look at it and about husbands whose wives have divorced them because of it. I hear about people who have been single since surgery and aren't sure why. I am sure why—it's because they're ashamed. Most people have no idea what an ostomy is, and if a person who has one talks about how much they hate it, everyone else thinks they should hate it too. You've got to love yourself for someone else to love you.

Everybody has something in their life that is less than perfect, me included. But there are so many worse things than having an ostomy. It's seen as shameful and scary only because nobody talks about it; nobody's normalized it. But we're normal people—we just happen to have to use the bathroom differently. Other than that, we're like everyone else.

Growing up, I had so many "issues" that I never allowed myself to think about what I might accomplish one day. It was always, what's the next thing I'm going to have to deal with? And how am I going to get through it?

These days, I don't spend a lot of time looking back on where I've been and how far I've come. I have a wonderful husband, I run my own company, I act and model professionally, and I do what I can to help others. I look forward to what I can do next because that's all I know.

My thirteen-year-old self faced a life-changing decision when thinking beyond the immediate pain was almost impossible. Choosing to have ostomy surgery is a decision I'll never regret. The life I've led ever since, and the life I lead today, is very persuasive proof.

Jessica Grossman is an actor and model, and she runs a digital marketing agency. Since her ostomy surgery on January 30, 2003, she has been in good health. She lives with her husband in Toronto, Ontario. Visit her website and read her blog at www.uncoverostomy.org.

PAT ATKINSON

A Life of Service

Some people become politicians because they enjoy the status.
I became a politician because I liked helping people. I liked solving
problems. I liked picking up the phone and figuring out how to get
people through what can sometimes be a tangle of government
regulations. I liked government responding to individual citizens.
That was the joy of politics—helping people.

My first name is Patricia, but everyone calls me Pat, and in Saskatchewan my last name is famous. My father, Roy Atkinson, was born in
Springwater, Saskatchewan, on his family farm where they grew wheat,
oats, flax, and barley. Since 1906, Atkinsons have run the farm, and today
it's transitioning to a fifth generation that farms organically.

My father grew up in the Depression, which wasn't kind to farmers,
many of whom went bankrupt while other businesses thrived. This
prompted my dad to become an outspoken advocate for the farming
community. In 1962, he became president of the Saskatchewan Farmers Union, and seven years later he, along with others, founded the
National Farmers Union and served as its president. He fought with
a passionate fierceness to protect farmers' economic interests and way

of life, and he was willing to take on any politician who dared stand in his way. Decades later, in 2002, he was invested into the Order of Canada for all he did on behalf of Canadian farmers.

My father was always busy. I remember in 1967, the Centennial year, he drove our family—my mom, my two sisters, my brother, and my cousin—across the country to Montreal for Expo '67, but when he got a call about some farming dispute in Vancouver, he flew off, leaving my mother with five kids to see the fair on our own. After he dealt with the issue, he flew back to drive us home.

To many farmers, my father was a hero. To me, his daughter, he was the man who always pushed me to succeed. He didn't hand out gold stars for effort, he was more concerned with results. He wasn't one to give praise. If you got an A on your report card, he'd wonder why you didn't get an A+.

It's natural for people to think he's the reason I got into politics. He played a role, of course, but it's my mother who deserves most of the credit.

My mother, Bette Aylward, was born in a farming community south of Lydden (now Duperow), Saskatchewan, into a large family of Irish Catholics who had moved from Prince Edward Island. She also grew up during the Depression. There was no high school in Lydden, so my mother had to go into the town of Biggar, about 30 kilometres away, to Biggar High School, where the principal was Woodrow Lloyd.

Now there's a name in Saskatchewan history. In 1944, Woodrow Lloyd won a seat for Premier Tommy Douglas's Co-operative Commonwealth Federation (CCF)—the forerunner to the New Democratic Party (NDP)—and became the minister of education in the province. After Douglas resigned to become the party leader, Lloyd was elected premier and instituted Douglas's universal health-care plan, Medicare, making Saskatchewan the first province to do so. But back then, he was just my mother's high school principal, and she really liked him.

She told me that her father would drive to Biggar to take her home and Mr. Lloyd would always let her go a little early because in those days the roads were bad and it took a long time to get back to the farm. Historically, the Aylward family was Liberal, but Mr. Lloyd's kindness led my grandparents to become CCFers at a time when Irish Catholic supporters were very unusual. My mother grew up to be a political spark plug, and she put all her energy into getting Mr. Lloyd elected as a member of the legislature in that 1944 campaign. You can draw a direct line from my grandparents to my mother to my place in the NDP.

My dad didn't join the NDP until much later in his life. As the leader of farmers' unions he represented people of every political persuasion, including rock-ribbed Conservatives and die-hard Liberals. Some were his best friends. He avoided party politics, but he taught me how to debate all the current issues. It used to drive people right around the bend to come to our dinner table because my father would always challenge their thinking. You had to have your facts lined up if you were going to discuss anything with him. The intensity of our conversations used to scare some of my cousins.

My mother was a great listener. But when she spoke, everybody paid attention. She wasn't as out-there as my dad, but she was very smart. In fact, I think she was a lot smarter than Dad because she knew people. She taught us how to listen to what people were saying, and she understood that she didn't have all the answers, whereas my dad was certain he did.

Up until 1962, my mother was a strong Catholic. That's when, as premier, Woodrow Lloyd introduced Medicare and the doctors went on strike. He persuaded them to settle after twenty-three days, but the province remained fractured. When my mother heard a priest say that people who supported Medicare were communists, she was outraged. As a mother and a farmer, she knew that a lack of health insurance hurt her family. And of course she knew Mr. Lloyd was no communist. After that, my mother never went back to mass.

She kept a firm grip on her children's comings and goings. She didn't want her three daughters in cars going up and down gravel roads getting into trouble. When I was about twelve years old, someone in the community got pregnant at a very young age. That was a signal to my mother that it was time to move to the big city of Saskatoon. Her job was to make sure her daughters were educated and never economically dependent. We were not going to get pregnant too young and forgo a university education. She herself had been a teacher, but she had to quit when she had me because in those days you couldn't teach if you were married with a child. I think she always regretted that she didn't go back to teaching.

I certainly wanted an education. I had big goals. I bought a party membership and became part of the NDP youth movement. Mr. Lloyd had never forgotten our family, and from time to time he would come to our house, so I got to know him a little bit.

When I was in grade twelve, he asked me, "What do you want to do in your life?"

"I want to be a teacher like you," I replied.

"Well, then," he said. "You're going to have to get an education. You'll have to go to university."

That I did, and I graduated from the University of Saskatchewan with two degrees—one in arts and one in education.

I loved teaching. In university, I did an internship in a grade four class. The social studies curriculum was all about Saskatchewan and our pioneers and I wanted the students to learn experientially, so I brought in my great-aunt to talk about her time in Saskatchewan's pioneer days. We did drama lessons around the province's first years.

The principal came to me and said, "Your classes are making too much noise."

"That's because they're into what we're doing and they're excited."

He wasn't impressed.

I became quite worried that I was never going to be a good teacher. I thought kids should be active learners and not just sit and listen. I didn't fit into the regular school system, so when I graduated I didn't even apply for a job in the Saskatoon public or Catholic school systems. Instead, I went to work at an alternative school with young people who didn't fit either. These were students who had all kinds of behavioural problems, but I thought they had huge potential.

We used something called reality therapy. The idea was to give the kids a sense of who they were and to address the behaviour that was stopping them from finding their place in the world. My basic approach was to sit down with a student and say, "You have huge issues with authority that you have to overcome. You have to learn how to get to school on time, work while you're here, and then go home. This isn't about forcing you to go to school; it's about you getting an education."

That was always my focus—their education—because it was a first step toward making a decent living. But a lot of young girls at our school were getting pregnant and some were just fourteen or fifteen years old. I attended many of the births at the Royal University Hospital. This was a time when girls started to keep their babies instead of giving them up for adoption. I thought that if my students were to have any chance of finishing high school, we should have daycare in high schools. From a public policy point of view, it would be much better to have young people who were raising children on their own continue their education and become financially independent. There were people who thought this would encourage young people to have babies, so the idea didn't become a reality for a very long time.

Daycare was one of the issues that got me into politics. That, and education policy. Not everyone fit into the regular kindergarten to grade twelve system, and I thought there ought to be other options for young people to become educated. At the time, there was quite a bit of talk that these kinds of issues might move higher up in the agenda if more women were elected at various levels of government. If I really wanted things to change, I shouldn't wait for someone else to do it. Saskatchewan had an NDP government, but the member of the legislative assembly for my local riding, Saskatoon Nutana, wasn't going to run again. So I decided at the ripe old age of twenty-eight that I was going to enter the contest for the party nomination.

My main opponent was the executive assistant to the outgoing MLA, which was a big advantage, but he lived in Regina. I said we needed someone to represent us from Saskatoon Nutana who was active in the community and knew its needs. I didn't think I could win, but I wanted to get my ideas in front of the party membership.

My biggest asset was that I knew how to organize. I had worked as a volunteer in earlier campaigns. I had also spent a year as an organizer for the National Farmers Union and had gone to Prince Edward Island and New Brunswick to sell union memberships to farmers, and I was pretty good at it.

I bought some dresses to make myself look older and enlisted my friends—they knew how to organize too—and we put together an efficient campaign. We sold a lot of new party memberships and then went door-to-door asking the new members to support me. I drew up sheets of papers about the current issues so that no matter what topic was brought up, I had a policy. When we finally got to the nomination meeting, there were so many members—over 800—who came out that it had to expand to two venues.

And then I won. I couldn't believe it. I had become the NDP candidate in Saskatoon Nutana for the 1982 provincial election.

The NDP always won the riding, so getting elected was pretty much a slam dunk. Except it wasn't. Grant Devine was the new Conservative leader, and he was very popular in my constituency. He had lived there, and he spent the campaign talking about cheap mortgage rates and eliminating the tax on gasoline, two very attractive promises.

I door-knocked like crazy, but I could see I wasn't going to win. Just before the polls closed on election night, I was told about a constituent who had indicated he would vote for me but now wasn't going to vote at all.

One of my campaign people said, "Pat, you've got to go talk to him."

My dad drove me over to the voter's house, and I persuaded him to vote. We whisked him to the polls and then back home.

"Well, kid," my dad said. "You're going to go to the legislature."

I looked at him. "No, Dad, I don't think so. It'll be close. But we're probably a hundred or so votes short. I don't think we made it."

I was right. I lost by 155 votes.

I didn't realize how competitive I was until I lost. My mother was a competitive athlete, so I blame her. I immediately said to myself, "You're doing this again because you liked it. And next time you're not going to lose."

I stayed active in the party and in the community, and in 1986 I was nominated again to run in the provincial election. I was out on the street six days a week, stopping only on Sundays. I knocked on every door I could before the election—once, twice, even three times. And it paid off. I was elected with about 60 percent of the vote and almost twice as many votes as the Conservative candidate. It felt amazing.

After I won, I came out into the hall and made my way to the stage at the front of the room as everyone cheered and shook my hand. My dad and mom were already on the stage, and when my mom shook my hand she was beaming. We had a big hug, and she whispered, "Oh my God. Wouldn't your grandparents be so pleased?" My dad was on that stage too, but he didn't say a word. I'm sure he was pleased, but he just wasn't demonstrative in that way.

I was an MLA. But an opposition MLA. The Conservatives had won a second majority government. The NDP leader was Allan Blakeney, who had been Saskatchewan's premier for eleven years and had become a respected national political figure, but most of the NDP MLAs were brand-new. We were in our thirties and had very little political experience. We were teachers and farmers and social workers and union leaders, but Blakeney showed us how to conduct ourselves in the legislature, especially when it came to opposing bills the party didn't agree with. Our focus in opposition was in exposing corruption, opposing the

With Premier Allan Blakeney just before he called the election for April 26, 1982.

privatization of public assets, and fighting severe cuts to health care. I was nervous at first—I had never spoken in the legislature before—but my years of debating around the kitchen table came in handy.

"You need to understand how to read a balance sheet," Blakeney told us.

What did we know about a balance sheet? Or about how to read provincial auditor reports? Or the provincial budget? He tutored us on all of this, and it was essential learning for the road ahead.

By the next provincial election in 1991, Blakeney had stepped down, having fought his political battle long enough, and Roy Romanow became our leader.

I had first met Roy when I was in high school. My mother had dragged me to an NDP tea somewhere. Roy saw me and asked, "What do you think of my suit?"

"Not much," I replied.

Now I thought very highly of him because he led the NDP back into power with a majority government.

I was easily reelected in my constituency, and I expected to be asked to go into the cabinet. Finally, I would have a chance to make some real change. But the most pressing issue was the provincial deficit, which had ballooned to $15 billion.

Roy called me up and offered me the speaker's chair. The speaker's role is to remain neutral and ensure that parliamentary debates are conducted properly and fairly. I wasn't interested in being a referee—I wanted to join in the debate. Hadn't all those conversations around my family table prepared me for just that?

"Who is going into the cabinet?" I asked.

Roy wouldn't tell me, so I said, "I can't imagine myself in that three-cornered speaker's hat. Besides, I'm an activist. I have ideas and now that we're the government, we can implement some of them."

"You'll get a cabinet minister's salary. You'll get a car."

"I have never been motivated by money," I countered. "And I have my own car."

He didn't give up. "I talked to the lieutenant governor"—a friend of mine—"and she thought it was a great idea. You would be the first woman speaker."

"I don't care. I'm not into the rules and procedures of the legislature. I don't want to tell people to be quiet. I don't want to tell people they talk too much. I am an activist. And I have ideas."

I was left out of the cabinet. I was disappointed, but I think I know what Roy was thinking. Because of the deficit, he knew we would be forced to do a lot of cutting, and for someone like me, so eager to expand services, it would be like getting shot in the foot. I didn't get elected to cut things. I got elected to have better schools, to get more daycare programs, to change the human rights code to protect gays and lesbians, and to improve the lives of people living in poverty.

The cuts were gut-wrenching. We cut pensions. We cut support programs for farmers. We had excruciating caucus debates that went on for long periods of time as we tried to get our heads around the foul-tasting medicine we had to deliver.

*Delivering more than 10,000 Saskatchewan signatures
on a petition that stopped the privatization of SaskEnergy
by the Grant Devine government.*

Almost a full year later, Roy's chief of staff came to see me about join-ing the cabinet. "There are still more cuts to come," he said. "Are you okay with the tough things the government has to do?"

"I will never break from cabinet solidarity in public," I told him. "But I will ask tough questions inside, and people need to be able to answer them. I have defended all the cutbacks so far. Ask some of the members already in the cabinet. They'll tell you I have defended our policies at my constituency town halls and it's never been a tea party."

I don't know if I gave him the answer he wanted, but it didn't take long to find out. I was soon called to a meeting with the premier and asked to go into the cabinet, where I was put in charge of seniors and social services.

Now that I was in the cabinet, I felt a much heavier burden of responsibility. Not only were there real issues to address in my portfolio, but I didn't want my time in Regina to take away from my constituency in Saskatoon. Every Friday, I went home to walk down the street and see people. We had a group that met every Friday at five at our local watering hole and I was there to talk to people.

It wasn't enough to know just my own constituency or my own portfolio—I had to acquire a broader perspective of the province. My dad was a reader, and he always told me that reading was the way to ensure you knew what you were talking about. I read reams of material so that I would be prepared to take part in every discussion and debate around the cabinet table.

In Regina, I lived in the home of a woman named Doris Winters. Doris had been both Woodrow Lloyd's and Allan Blakeney's secretary. I guess she always needed every dollar of her salary, so she had chosen not to contribute any of her income to a pension plan. Now she didn't have a large income. My rent was enough to allow her to stay in her two-bedroom apartment, and she was good for me because she kept me grounded.

Sometimes I would come home bummed out, and Doris would say, "Oh for God's sakes, Pat, do you think people sit around and think about the legislature? They're going on with their lives. You're taking this far too seriously. Now I'm going to have a little drink of vodka. What would you like?" She was fabulous. But of course an evening cocktail didn't make the province's financial troubles magically disappear.

Our cabinet meetings were dominated by the budget process, and we hashed out what we were going to do about the big deficit we had. We simply didn't have enough revenue to make ends meet. We increased taxes. We created a deficit-reduction tax. We increased the sales tax. But you can only tax people so much.

We had to find money elsewhere.

We tried to raise money by selling bonds, but no one bought them. That was scary. If no one would lend us money, we would go bankrupt, which had never happened to any province in all of Canadian history. In early 1993, we were on the brink and might have had to declare bankruptcy if the prime minister, Brian Mulroney, had not stepped in with emergency financial assistance.

The hard times still continued. We took a lot of heat. People thought we were betraying NDP principles. Even my mother was upset about some of the things we did. None of this was easy. The low point came when we converted fifty-two rural hospitals to health centres. The public thought we closed them.

In September 1993, I was promoted to the more senior role of education minister just as teachers were negotiating a new contract. The school trustees wanted to do all the bargaining, but they were dealing mostly with provincial tax dollars, and there were precious few of those. There was no way we were going to hand over the negotiations to the school trustees.

As a former teacher, and as the daughter of a teacher, I respected the profession. I went to the convention of the Regina Teachers' Association with a prepared speech, but I could sense a restlessness in the room, so I threw away the speech, made a few remarks, and then said, "Go ahead now. Ask me anything you like."

One of the things that came up was that teachers were paying out of their own pockets for school materials for their students. I didn't doubt for a minute that that was true. "It's not just a problem for teachers," I told them. "Lots of people who work in the human services field use their own money to support kids or families." It was a hard conversation, but I had it. A good number of teachers came up to me and thanked me for being honest. I always tried to be honest even if the truth was hard to hear.

Still, in the end, it took a long while to get an agreement that everyone was happy with.

In 1998, I got a call from another member of the cabinet telling me I was going to be invited to be the health minister. "More like the minister of absolute hell," I thought. At that time, we were still closing hospitals and people were livid. We also had five collective agreements to negotiate. I knew it would be tough, but I was prepared to accept the job.

The first thing I did was exactly what my mother used to do— listen. I was still the education minister, but I hit the road to meet with the people directly affected; it was unfair that we were making these decisions without facing them first. I had some experience facing large crowds, as I had gone to Kerrobert, a town in west central Saskatchewan, when there was a huge meeting protesting the closure of the Dodsland Hospital. It was a place where my dad knew everybody and everybody knew my family. There were a thousand people there, and I sat and listened as they gave me what for because their hospital had been closed. One man got up and said that if everybody thought bringing Medicare into Saskatchewan had been a dogfight, it's going to seem like a birthday party compared to the blowback this time.

I had a clear message. I explained how our balance sheet looked with the revenue coming in on one side and the money we were spending going out on the other side. "If we're going to deal with the debt, we can't have all our yearly deficits just piling up. We have to figure out a way to match revenue to expenditures."

As education minister I also went to Englefeld in the eastern part of the province where we were closing a school. Again, I tried to listen, then explain the situation. It didn't go well. A crowd surrounded me. I was okay, but afterward on the way out of town, we had to stop the car on the side of the road because I was nauseous. Those weren't happy times. I remember my dad telling me, "Never give up." And also, "Never cry in front of anybody."

As the years went by, I continued fighting for the people of Saskatchewan any way I could, and there was no letting up. I woke up at 6 a.m. most days. I made my coffee and had a piece of toast. Before 7 a.m. I was at the legislature, where I sat in the cafeteria and read three newspapers. By 8 a.m. I was in my office before anyone else got there. There was always a pile of letters. Staff people read the mail and wrote replies, but I also read every letter and every response.

I hated the words "but" or "however." I didn't like it when we said, "Thank you for writing. You've made a very good point, but . . ." There was no humanity in those responses. They sent the wrong message. I insisted that if someone put a question to us, we were going to answer that question. We weren't going to ignore it. It took a while for the staff to understand that we weren't going to tiptoe around the issues. They were well-meaning, but our constituents deserved more respect.

The rest of the day was often spent meeting with stakeholders, attending cabinet committee meetings, and reading cabinet material. Those were very long days.

By 2001, our government had turned years of deficit budgets into balanced budgets. We reduced taxes and started investing again in

My family on my parents' fiftieth wedding anniversary in 2002. I'm on the far left in the back row next to Michael, my mother and father, and Leta; in front of me are Bob and Wenda. KIRK FONG

health care and education. I had been in charge of some hard portfolios for a long time—and was on every committee in the cabinet—and I was tired. There was so much rumbling around in my head, and it was physically and emotionally draining. It was a good time to go. The new premier, Lorne Calvert, whom I was good friends with, agreed, and for two years I was a backbencher.

After the NDP was reelected in 2003, Lorne told me, "You're coming back into the cabinet." By that time, I had recharged my batteries so I said, "Okay." I became minister of the Crown management board, public service, and immigration. Crown corporations provide Saskatchewan residents with everything from telephone to natural gas to insurance, and the future of the publicly owned companies was a major campaign issue. We had promised the public that we would provide the lowest-priced basic package of utilities in the country and maintain public ownership.

In 2007, the NDP had been in power for sixteen years, and the conservative Saskatchewan Party had a new leader, who was very popular. We knew our time was up, but I did get some things done. Just before the election, Lorne appointed me the finance minister, and after all the years of counting nickels, we finally had some money to spend. My mother had taught me that if you had some extra money you paid off your debts, so I paid down the province's debt by about half a billion dollars.

When the new government came in, they started spending the money like there was no tomorrow. At a time when we were making record-high royalty revenues, the province was going to go further into debt. We couldn't be spending money we didn't have. Even social democrats like me believed that. I couldn't forget how awful the 1990s had been and how hard we had worked to get the finances of the province in order. I couldn't watch what was happening.

So I decided I wouldn't run in the next election. I was done. In 2011, I left politics after twenty-five years.

Some people become politicians because they enjoy the status. I became a politician because I liked helping people. I liked solving problems. I liked picking up the phone and figuring out how to get people through what can sometimes be a tangle of government regulations. I liked government responding to individual citizens. That was the joy of politics—helping people.

I remember a seventeen-year-old girl who used to hang around my constituency office when I was first elected. She was very smart, but when she had a baby it looked like a higher education was out of the question. I steered her into university, where she earned a master's degree.

I remember a woman with serious health problems whose natural gas was turned off one cold winter day. A neighbour called me, and I went over to find her huddled in the kitchen with the electric stove on. I contacted SaskEnergy and made an arrangement so she could pay what she owed a little at a time every month. I loved doing that kind of thing. Politics had been tough. But the rewards made it worth it.

In 2016, my father died. When my sister and I went to clean up his apartment, she found a little box with a note inside and called me over. "Pat, you have got to see this."

It was a note that dated back to my first years in politics, when I was an opposition member. Dad had gone to the legislature to watch the question period from the visitors' gallery. A Conservative member of cabinet, Lorne Hepworth, had written him a note and sent it up. Here's what it said:

Roy,
As you can imagine, I don't agree with your daughter's ideology.
Having said that I must say she has distinguished herself as a very
capable legislator even in this, her first term. I am sure you are
very proud of her and you should be.

My dad never told me about that note, but he kept it in a special box all those years, and now I have it. That is about the closest I ever got to a compliment from my dad.

My father and my mother were different in so many ways, but each of them taught me how to serve my fellow citizens. My mother taught me to listen, and she planted my roots in the NDP. My father was a fighter, a brilliant orator, and really smart. He also told me that I would lose some battles, but he advised me to lose with grace and if I ever got mad to never let the other side know I was mad. I'm the daughter of two fine people who, I like to think, made me a daughter of Saskatchewan.

Pat Atkinson is the longest-serving female MLA in the history of Saskatchewan. She won her first election for the NDP in 1986 and stepped down in 2011. During that quarter century, she sat both on the opposition side of the legislature and on the government front bench. She held at least fourteen different cabinet portfolios under two NDP premiers, Roy Romanow and Lorne Calvert, including some of the most senior portfolios such as education, health, and finance. She lives in Saskatoon, Saskatchewan.

MANNY KOHLI
True Riches

There's a common stereotype that businesspeople are
hard-hearted and calculating. Everything comes down to dollars
and cents. Every decision can be made by looking at the numbers.
If you can make a move that makes you richer, you make
the move. If not, you pass. But that wasn't me.

Fashion has been in my blood from the day I was born. I grew up in Kapurthala, in India's Punjab state. My father had a shop, Kohli Cloth House, in the main market of the city, where he sold loose fabric, and every month I would look through the store for new fabric to make a new pair of trousers. Once, I got some fabric for a pair of bell-bottoms and took it to the best tailor in town to get them made. Then I waited for the call that they were ready. I was the happiest person on earth when I tried them on—they were perfect.

When the father of one of my good friends came home from a trip to the United States with a pair of denim jeans, I loved what I saw. I had never seen denim before, but I dreamed of one day getting a pair of my own—that wouldn't happen for many years.

At age fifteen, I took my first vacation to Kashmir. I spent the evening at a lake.

In 1980, my father went to Montreal to visit his brother and attend his nephew's wedding. He was immediately taken by the city's beauty and thought that perhaps one day he might go back and live there. When he came home, the wheels started turning.

By then, my older brother and two older sisters were already living on their own in England, so it was just me and my parents. My father wasn't a hundred percent sure that Canada was right for us, so he decided to apply for a visa to visit Canada, not to live there. When my uncle in Montreal was scheduled for heart surgery, we had an excuse to go and see if we wanted to move there permanently.

The three of us went off to the Canadian High Commission in New Delhi, about 400 kilometres south of our home, to be interviewed. We all stuck to the story. We were going to visit a sick relative in Montreal, and then we were coming back. After all, my father said, he had a business in India. My mother said she was a happy housewife. I said I was finishing high school and planned to go to college in India. A lot of people were having trouble at that time getting a visa to Canada, but we got it.

In April 1982, we boarded the plane, knowing that if things worked out, we might be living in Canada for the rest of our lives. I was eighteen years old, going abroad for the first time, excited and also a bit nervous. I was leaving all my friends behind. All I really knew was that I wanted to buy my first pair of denim jeans, a pair of boots, and a bunch of fashion magazines. I intended to be very fashionable and stylish.

We landed at Mirabel Airport, about an hour north of Montreal. At one time, Mirabel was supposed to be the largest airport in the world, but at just six years old, it had already become a white elephant, well on its way to being abandoned as a passenger facility, reduced to cargo flights only. I didn't know any of this, of course.

All I could see when we touched down on the runway was endless fields of snow in every direction. I had never seen snow before, and now it was everywhere. I was expecting to see Montreal, a big, bright city. Instead, it seemed as if we had landed in an isolated village cut off from civilization. Things didn't get any better when we cleared customs and drove to my uncle's house in Brossard, on the south shore of the St. Lawrence River. It was also cursed with unlimited quantities of snow.

For the first two or three days in Montreal, I was in tears. Not metaphorical tears, real tears. Fighting with my parents became the norm. "What did you like here?" I asked my father. "What the hell am I doing here? It's too damned cold. I have no friends. I have no life. Why did you bring me here?"

I was very lonely. There were about three quarters of a billion people in India back then. It was so lively. The whole city where I lived was my friend. I had a Vespa scooter that I drove around like a hero in the movies. I wore beautiful outfits. People knew me. Twenty times a day, people would wave and say, "Hi, Manny. How you doing, Manny?" In Canada, I saw a few hundred people in a week and not one greeted me.

My brother, Harpal, was living in Manchester, England, where he ran an electronics business. I pleaded with him to let me come stay with him. He agreed to take me in, and so my first experience with Canada lasted just three or four months.

England was fantastic, especially compared to the cold and barren wasteland I left behind. I missed India a bit, but not that much, because in Manchester there were so many Indian people. I probably would have stayed there forever, except for two things.

First, the British authorities wouldn't grant me immigration status. We hired a lawyer to try to change their minds, but that didn't work.

And second, I got married. To a Canadian. Daisy was born in India, but she had moved to Montreal when she was three years old. My parents knew her parents from India, and everyone thought we were a good match. I was just nineteen years old, but I agreed to marry, mostly for my mother's sake.

When I was growing up, my mother had missed the weddings of all my siblings because they had been in London and it just wasn't possible for her to travel from India to England in time. I remember how sad she was to miss these important moments in her children's lives. And now, because I wasn't allowed to stay in England, it looked as if I might have to go back to India and, one day, she'd miss my wedding as well. But if I married now, in England, she would be there. After all, it was a much shorter flight from Montreal to London than from Montreal to India.

After the wedding, there were no legal obstacles for me to return to Canada. Frankly, I wasn't looking forward to Montreal, given my first encounter. Even though I was married and had responsibilities, I was still just a kid. But a kid with some experience in electronics, and my brother had generously written a cheque for $50,000 to help me start my own business. When I tell people about that money, they assume my brother gave me a loan. But it wasn't a loan. We Indian people are very family oriented. He felt it wasn't only his money, it was all of his family's. He said, "You can't be empty-handed when you land in Montreal."

My life in Canada awaited.

Daisy and I bought a five-bedroom house where we'd live with my parents. We didn't know much about life, and we were happy to be surrounded by family. We got to know each other better, and I can honestly say that our relationship got stronger every day.

In 1985, my father and I opened our first electronics store on Montreal's legendary St. Laurent Boulevard, the main street that divided the city between East and West. We called the store Sitone, and business took off from day one, when we sold $10,000 worth of merchandise.

Every few weeks, I used to drive to New York with one of our employees and fill up a truck with VCRs, blank videocassettes, and Sony TVs and then come back. Twelve to fifteen other electronic stores on St. Laurent Boulevard started buying from me wholesale. Harpal decided to join us in Canada, and soon we had two divisions. My brother and I worked upstairs, selling wholesale, while my father was downstairs with eight employees looking after the retail division. These were boom times. I was so busy I didn't have time to notice that Montreal was still too cold in the winter.

There's a common stereotype that businesspeople are hard-hearted and calculating. Everything comes down to dollars and cents. Every decision can be made by looking at the numbers. If you can make a move that makes you richer, you make the move. If not, you pass. But that wasn't me.

In 2000, I went to a wedding in Winnipeg and met a fellow Montrealer, Inder Bedi. We made polite conversation. I told him I was running an electronics store, and he told me he was running a small business producing handbags and wallets using only animal-free and recycled products. He called it Via Vegan. I thought that was interesting, but truthfully, I didn't give it a second thought. We did make a strong connection, and Daisy hit it off with his wife as well. Back in Montreal, we became friends and went out to restaurants, to clubs, and for drinks, and visited each other at home.

One day, Inder invited me to come see his business. It was indeed very small. He had about 400 square feet of space. I looked around for about an hour, examined a few handbags. I thought to myself that he needed more variety, more styles. He had maybe five. I knew that at our electronics store, for example, we sold forty different styles of Walkmans. Customers liked choice. But all I said to Inder was "Very nice" a couple of times and left.

Three days later, he told me he was looking for a partner to help him build his business—he had very little money and experience. Inder did have a good idea—making handbags without using leather—he just didn't know how to make money from it.

"Maybe I can be your partner," I told him. I was totally joking. After all, I had a thriving business of my own. But I did dream of having a fashion company. In the back of my mind I thought, just maybe this was the opportunity.

Over the next two or three months, Inder called pretty much every day. He had latched on to what I thought had been a comment made in jest. "How are you, Manny? Did you think about it more?" He needed a partner really badly. Eventually, we sat down at a Chinese restaurant. "Okay," I said. "Tell me, what do you want?"

Inder looked me in the eye, and then he asked for a huge amount of money for half the company.

"You're crazy," I told him. "No one is going to give you that much money. You don't have enough sales to justify that asking price. If you seriously want that much, forget it. I'm not interested."

But Inder didn't leave it at that. He kept calling until one day I said, "I'll tell you what. Send me your financial statements. I'll send them to my accountant in Toronto, and we'll see what he says."

A few days later, Inder came to my office. We settled into our chairs, and I put my accountant on a speakerphone. I asked him to tell us what he thought.

His voice was clear as a bell. "Manny, are you kidding me? This business is nothing. Why would you want to be part of this?"

"Let's say I have a vision," I said. "How much should I pay Inder for half of the company?"

"Zero," he said.

I started laughing. "Inder," I said. "Did you hear that? He said 'zero.'"

That should have been the end of it. Logic told me to walk away. But the truth is, I did have a long-term vision, so I decided to offer Inder $10,000. The next day he said, "Okay, done deal." I was in the fashion industry, where my heart had always wanted to be.

I liked that our company didn't kill any animals to produce our beautiful bags and accessories. Purely by coincidence, that same month I became a vegetarian. I had always eaten a lot of chicken and fish, but barely any greens. When I began developing some physical issues, a naturopath recommended less chicken, more veggies. I resisted but eventually agreed to eliminate chicken first, and then fish. I felt so much better. I felt more energized than ever. (Eventually I became vegan, which meant giving up my beloved leather shoes.)

I love fashion. I love dressing up. I bought a new cape
and posted this image on Instagram.

I left Sitone to my brother to run and threw myself into this new endeavor. Inder agreed that I had more experience than he did, so he let me take the lead. First, we expanded our workspace. Sometimes, when you have a tiny space, it stops you from thinking big. We went from 400 square feet to 2,400 square feet. Then I said, "We need a catchy name."

We spent a couple of days, maybe a week, banging some names around. We came up with a name we both loved: Matt & Nat. It was easy to remember and it was open to interpretation—could be Matthew and Natalie, could be something else. Later, we decided it meant Material and Nature. That fit because we were a vegan company. The lining or MATerial in every handbag was made of recycled plastic bottles to protect NATure.

We designed everything in Montreal, manufactured in China in small factories that were in line with our ethos—we regularly verify that their operations are up to our standards—and aggressively pursued growth. We went to shows in Toronto and then New York and sold tens of thousands of dollars' worth of our handbags. We signed sales reps in Toronto, Vancouver, Dallas, New York, and Atlanta. Our trajectory looked good.

Of course, Inder and I had our disagreements. He didn't like some of the prices I set. There was a bag, for example, called Buddha. He wanted to sell it for $36. I said, "No, we'll put it at $24." That still gave us a healthy margin, and I was interested in growth more than anything. We needed more customers, and to do that, I felt we had to deliver something special *and* affordable. If you want to catch a fish, you have to use the right bait. At our very first show with Buddha we sold about 500 units. The second show another 500 units. Eventually, we sold half a million of them. It was a simple bag priced at $24.

Until 2008 it was boom, boom, boom for us, then the financial crisis and the ensuing crippling recession hurt us very badly. For the next five years, our sales declined every season. Instead of making millions, we were just getting by. Inder had calculated that we'd never get back to where we were, and he wanted to cash out. I felt that we could ride out the rough patch and turn the company around. This was still my passion, and I believed that making sustainable fashion was important.

I told Inder I would happily buy him out, but I felt the price he gave me was ridiculously high for what the company was now worth. If I sold out to him, I wouldn't have asked for so much, but he was unmoved. I knew I had transformed his business. When I became his partner he was renting a one-bedroom condo for $400 a month. By 2008, he had built a beautiful $2 million house. Now we had hit a stumbling block.

My accountant warned me. "Manny, don't buy him out. It's not a good deal."

I consulted with a couple of friends who all said the same thing. But for the second time, I decided to ignore common sense, ignore the hard logic, and go with my gut. It was telling me to buy him out, at his price, because with hard work, we'd make it.

The turnaround didn't take long. I told our creative director we had to grow the collection, and the very next season we put out six new styles and ten new colours. It took off like crazy, and sales grew by a few million. Next season, we had fifteen new styles and colours, and that took off too. Back-packs became hot so we went from one style of backpack to six. We kept growing and growing. Today we have ten times more sales than we had when I took over the company. We went from eighteen employees to 200.

We still sell lots of handbags, but now we also sell shoes and boots, jackets and coats, sunglasses and candles. I can't take credit for every brilliant idea. Our customers often point us in the right direction. They love to interact with us on social media, and we get messages on Instagram and Facebook and too many emails to count. For example, a few years back, I got an email that said, "Matt & Nat, you are so stupid. Why don't you have vegan footwear?" It made me laugh because it made so much sense. Why didn't we? I went to a marketing meeting and the salespeople confirmed that they were being asked the same question, so I hired a young footwear designer who came up with eight styles. We put seven into production and sold out in four weeks. Today no vegan company has as wide a range in shoes as we do.

Matt & Nat is a Canadian business success, but I like to think it's more than that. It's an ethical and sustainable business success.

From the very beginning, I was keen to let people know how we did things. Some people would laugh and say, "I don't care if you're killing animals or not." But most people appreciated what we did. Anybody who is vegan knows our brand and buys our brand. That's 25 percent of our customers. The other 75 percent are not vegans or vegetarians. They love our products for the design and the quality.

Our designs are clean and simple. Personally, I don't buy anything that is very busy, so our bags reflect that vision. We also make sure our bags are practical. Women have so much stuff to throw in the bag that we make a lot of compartments to help with organization.

The vegan leathers we use, PU (polyurethane) and PVC (polyvinylchloride), are beautiful. People won't buy a product just because it's eco-friendly. It also has to look and feel great. PU is less harmful for the environment than PVC, so we try to use that whenever possible. In addition to being vegan, we look for sustainable materials to incorporate into our designs: recycled nylons, cork, and rubber. All our linings are made of 100 percent recycled plastic bottles, about twenty-one for every bag we produce, which adds up to about 9 million bottles a year.

I built the brand from quality materials. Otherwise I'd be in big trouble. Customers can go to other stores and buy less-expensive bags, but those bags will break down in a few months. The fabric might tear, or the zipper will stop working. I have customers tell me they've had bags for ten years. They don't break down. When they buy a new pair of shoes, they like to buy a new bag, but they tell me they don't have a reason to throw out the old bag, so there's no room in their closet.

In 2014, my brother opened a restaurant in Montreal, so my parents, Daisy, and I attended the grand opening.

Once you're running a successful and profitable business, it's easy to say it's not about the money, but from the beginning I was never in it for just the money. It was a lifelong dream to work in fashion, and it still is. And if money was all I wanted, I could have sold out by now. I had an offer from somebody in New York that would have paid me ten or fifteen times more than what I paid for the company. I turned it down because my vision is not just to fill pockets but also to do good for the world. That's true riches.

One of the founding principles of my religion, Sikhism, is the performance of *sewa*, or service, and it directs us to give part of our income to charity.

In 2017, we launched a bag style called Hope. It's a handbag that comes in one style and one colour. We make exactly 1,000 of them every year, and we sell them only online with the promise that every penny of the purchase price goes to charity. Initially, when someone bought a Hope bag they could choose to direct the money to one of ten charities that supported humanitarian and children's causes, animal rights, and health and medical advancement. Now we just have the Hope Bag Fund, which we use to donate the money to causes that are in need. In recent years, we've contributed to Vital Voices, an international organization that invests in women's leadership efforts around the world; SOS Bolivia, a children's charity; Khalsa Aid, to deal with the consequences of flooding in Punjab; and the World Wildlife Fund and RSPCA in New South Wales, for Australian bushfire relief efforts. Every year, we have sold all of the 1,000 bags, which means we've collected more than a quarter of a million dollars.

Looking ahead, I'd like to get more personally involved in our giving. We look at Haiti and see that kids need schoolbags to go to school. We look at India and see millions of people who are homeless and need blankets and shoes. I'd like to deliver these things with my own hands. I can go to Haiti. I can go to India. For every smile I see, I'll smile on the inside.

Matt & Nat is now recognized around the world as a vegan and eco-friendly brand doing its part to protect our fragile planet. It's the company of my dreams in the city of my dreams. Yes, there was a time I hated Montreal, but just like my father, I fell in love with this beautiful city—with its strong French and European influence, it's one of the best places for fashion. And now it's my home. Our products are 100 percent vegan, and I am 100 percent Canadian.

Manny Kohli is the president and CEO of Matt & Nat, based in Montreal. He has received the Sikh Foundation Award, the Canadian Art and Fashion Impact Award, and the Ernst & Young Entrepreneur of the Year National Special Citation Award for values-based innovation. He lives in Montreal, Quebec.

HOPE SWINIMER
Wild at Heart

I didn't wake up one day and say, "I'm going to do wildlife rehab."
It just grew, took on a life of its own, and I went along for the ride.

Everything in my childhood was connected to the natural world. I saw fish pulled from the sea and meat hunted from the woods. My friends and I were outdoors most of every day. We spent our time in tree houses and in forts, hiking, riding bicycles, and swimming. On summer days, we would check to see what time the tide was coming in so we would know when to be at the wharf so we could swim.

I grew up in Argyle, a little fishing community on the southwest tip of Nova Scotia in the 1970s. My dad was one of the few people who wasn't a fisherman, but he did work on the water. He was part of the crew of *My Bluenose*, a passenger and vehicle ferry that traveled between Yarmouth, Nova Scotia, and Bar Harbor, Maine. It obviously wasn't anything like the famous *Bluenose* racing schooner it was named for, but it provided reliable service for many years and was an important part of the local tourist economy.

Less than 30 kilometres away, Yarmouth was the closest town where you might find things like music and theatre, but kids like me hardly ever went there. We stayed in our beautiful village of Argyle and made do with very little in the way of cultural activities until high school. We didn't have one of those in Argyle, and back then, it was thirty to forty minutes each way on the school bus to Yarmouth. Today there's a highway between the two towns and the trip takes half the time.

I was the third child in a family of four. As a kid, I was shy and reserved. I had some good friends but wasn't the most popular girl by any means. It's just the way I was. I was a good listener, and observant too.

I preferred to spend my time outdoors. From an early age, I was fascinated with nature. I had a mouse named Shorty for three years and built him a little wheel he could run on. The whole neighborhood knew when Shorty was on it because it was so squeaky. I also collected caterpillars and put them in a jar with holes punched in the lid. Now I know how cruel that was, but like most children, I didn't realize I was taking them from their natural world and treating them like toys. I just wanted to study their beauty. In grade six, I always had a notebook with me where I would list the different animals that I saw and write interesting facts about them. I got into trouble when the teacher said, "You should be doing schoolwork, not stuff that isn't in the curriculum."

A little later, I discovered that I liked numbers and found such joy in getting them to balance. In grade ten, I thought I might be an accountant, but also a farmer so I could get outside. As it turned out, this wasn't too far from what I ended up becoming.

We were rather poor. If my dad didn't bag a deer during hunting season for our freezer, the winter would be a little harder for us. It made me sad to see the deer hanging in the barn, but I understood that it was going to feed us. At the same time, I knew I could not kill an animal.

When I finished high school at sixteen, neither my family nor I had any money for me to go to university, so I went to a business college three hours away in Truro. It was a lovely place to live, but I missed the smell and sound and view of the ocean. It was the last place I ever lived that wasn't on the water.

This is Skidder, my very old horse. . . . He is now in his fortieth year and doing great!
PAM McKENZIE

I got through my basic accounting courses and learned enough to get an office job at a company that sold trucks and trailers. I continued working toward becoming a certified general accountant by taking correspondence courses. I also had my eye on working with animals and started taking courses to become a certified veterinary practice manager (CVPM), someone who looks after the business side of a veterinarian's practice. Then the company where I worked went bankrupt.

The timing worked out for me. The Dartmouth Veterinary Hospital was hiring for a new management position. There were three vets at the hospital, and they had previously divided up the accounting, the human resources, and the purchasing between them. Now they wanted someone to take over all of that so they could focus on the doctoring. In those days, there weren't many CVPMs, so I had a leg up.

That job changed my life and started me on an unforgettable and fulfilling path in animal rescue.

Until then, I had never seen a bird of prey up close. But the provincial department of natural resources had asked our hospital to help them save injured birds. The usual practice was for an injured bird to be euthanized, but there were some good people within government that didn't want to see that happen, so they would bring the birds in and our doctors would fix them up for free.

Although the vets had been doing this for years and had seen hundreds of bald eagles, every time one came in the door they got so excited and passionate and they did everything they could to save it. They did surgery on wings, beaks, eyes, and talons.

I found their work inspiring, and it made me think about all the other injured animals out there besides birds of prey. We'd get calls all the time from people who found an injured squirrel or hare. When people see an animal in distress, the first thing they think of is calling the vet. "What should I do?" they'd ask. At first, the short answer was, "Nothing. There's nothing to do."

Except I hated that answer. I thought there were always things you could do. It was just a matter of education. I had to educate myself to know what to do, so I could educate others. That's how I started studying wildlife rehab techniques. Pretty soon, every time a call came in, our front desk would say, "It's another one for Hope."

If someone saw a wounded animal—a robin or raccoon or fox—on the road and called our hospital, I'd tell them, "Bring it in." Only then, with the animal already on the way, would I ask the doctors to fit it into their schedule. They were so good about agreeing. They were unbelievably kind to me and willing to put up with all my quirks. Before you knew it, they were treating songbirds and seabirds and marine life and everything imaginable from seal pups to slightly injured black bears.

I rarely got into trouble for bringing in an animal. But there was the skunk episode. One day, I got a call from a couple who saw an injured skunk as they were driving. I could hear them having a fierce argument.

"We're going to take that poor animal to the vet," said the wife.

"There's no way we're taking that animal into the car," the husband insisted. "We didn't hit it."

"No, we didn't," the wife agreed. "But look at all the cars just driving by now. No one's stopping to help."

The wife won the argument, and soon enough they were on their way to me with a skunk. I went to the back of the hospital to find one of the doctors, Ian McKay.

"Doctor, can you help me? I may have made a mistake, but there's a skunk coming in. It was hit by a car. Might be dead on arrival, but can you come over to the parking lot with me to see?"

Dr. McKay looked at me kind of funny because it was, after all, a skunk. I don't think they really wanted a skunk in the hospital, but he followed me out to the car. The skunk was in terribly rough shape. We brought it in and set it up in an isolation area, where Dr. McKay very skillfully saved its life. Over the next two months, we nursed it back to reasonable health, but it wasn't going to recover enough to be released into the wild, so we decided the skunk could be used for education purposes instead.

"We should de-scent him," Dr. McKay said.

"Okay," I said. "I'm up for that."

When the day arrived for the procedure, I walked into the operating room to see Dr. McKay with a book in one hand and a garbage bag in the other. "What's going on?"

"You're going to assist me. You're going to be my tech," he explained.

"Doctor, I'm not a technician. I'm a manager."

"Yes, yes. But you're going to help me with this one."

"Okay, if you say so. What's the garbage bag for?"

"Cut a hole at the top and put your head through. It's your surgical gown."

We went into surgery, and he propped the book open because he had never de-scented a skunk before. It was a very hot summer day, and we had no air conditioning. I sweltered in that garbage bag as I tried to hold the forceps and keep the work area clean—the whole time I felt like I was going to pass out at any moment. It was an experience that I'll never forget.

When the operation was over, Dr. McKay was very proud of himself because everything had gone well—by the book, so to speak. The book said that once the anal glands were out to pop them into a bowl of bleach to kill the odor. That accomplished, he decided it was time to brag a little bit.

Dr. McKay carried the bowl with the glands and the bleach into the main work area of the hospital where everybody gathered around to hear the story of the surgery. There was a bit of a smell, but it wasn't bad.

Then, like a slow-motion disaster movie, he stumbled, and the glands tumbled from the bowl to the floor and exploded. What a smelly mess! Needless to say, there were no more skunks after that.

But other animals kept coming. To the point where we didn't have space for all of them to recover. One day, a robin that had been attacked by a cat came in, and after the doctors fixed it up, they turned to me. "Hope, why don't you take this robin home? Here are the meds it needs. You care for it."

That worked rather well, and I began to take home more animals.

I ended up getting my basic wildlife rehabilitation certification from the International Wildlife Rehabilitation Association and received a very good job offer as a wildlife rehabilitator in Ontario. But when I thought about leaving Nova Scotia, I realized I simply couldn't. I knew I wouldn't be happy unless I could look out my window and see the ocean.

In that first year, I probably took in twenty or thirty animals. I had a spare room at home where I could keep them. I'd wake up a little earlier than usual to feed my patients, give them their medicine, and clean their cages. Then I'd put in a full day at the hospital before coming home again to another round of feeding, medicating, and cleaning. It was a lot of work, but I found it worthwhile and rewarding.

I started taking home animals that needed to be cared for more often than morning and night. Some had to be fed every four hours. So they came to work with me, which made for even longer days. I'd get up at four in the morning and do my rounds. After that, I put the neediest patients, usually twenty or so, into the back seat of my car. Then I showered, dressed, and drove to the hospital, where the vets gave me a room in the basement for the animals. I'd do a feeding before I went to my desk to start the workday. After four hours, I'd take a break, run downstairs to feed again, then come back up for another four hours of work. My eight-hour day usually meant twelve hours at the hospital, unloading the car, setting up the basement, a couple of feedings and cleanings, and then loading the car again at night.

And I still had my patients at home, so as soon as I got home from work I had to do the medical rounds and clean up again. When it was all done, it was time for bed.

That was my life for years. It was pretty intense, and it got to the point where I physically couldn't keep up with the demand. I also knew it wasn't good for the animals to travel back and forth so much. But I couldn't turn away a broken creature.

I didn't wake up one day and say, "I'm going to do wildlife rehab." It just grew, took on a life of its own, and I went along for the ride. It was never my plan to run a wildlife rehabilitation centre, but I felt called to rescue animals, so I learned more and more about what I would need to do to set up a rehabilitation centre in Nova Scotia.

One thing was clear—I needed more space. In 1997, I took out a map and drew a circle around Halifax-Dartmouth that reached out about thirty-five minutes by car. I needed to be a certain distance from the city so I'd have more land but close enough to where everyone lived because a lot of the injuries wildlife suffered were due to conflict with human activity. I also worked in the city and I didn't want to spend all my time driving. Seaforth was right on the coast, just on the edge of the thirty-five-minute ride. It's also the most beautiful place in the world, with enough land to be able to set up cages outside.

I had made a bit of a name for myself as the local rescuer of all animals, and people began donating small amounts of money to help me out. I did some folksy fundraising events, but most of the finances were coming from my paycheck at the vet hospital. This was a labour of love for me.

I called it the Eastern Shore Wildlife Rehabilitation and Rescue Centre, which made it clear where we were and what we did, but the name was way too long. No one was using it. People would just refer to the centre as "Hope's place" or "the place Hope runs." They knew me, but not the facility. People couldn't even squeeze it all onto a cheque if they were making a donation. So my boyfriend and I started kicking around ideas for a better name, and he came up with "Hope for Wildlife." It had two meanings, and it seemed just right, even brilliant.

Then, one day, there was a knock on my door that threatened everything. It was someone from the Nova Scotia Department of Natural Resources.

"What you are doing is illegal," the man informed me. "You are not allowed to help a wild animal in any way. You must cease immediately."

I invited him in to discuss it. "Okay, so what do we need to do to make it legal?"

"That's a good question," he said.

"I've had training," I explained. "I've gone away on a lot of courses. I've visited rehab centres in other places." I showed him all the books I had. "I know what I'm doing. Besides, your department has been bringing injured birds of prey into the veterinary hospital for years. How come you're allowed to help wild animals, and I'm not?"

"That's a good question too," he allowed.

Thank heavens he didn't shut me down on the spot. Instead, he agreed to look into what could be done to make me legit. It took two full years, but the province finally issued the permit so I could run the first legal wildlife rehab centre in Nova Scotia.

But that didn't bring peace between me and them. Even now, twenty-five years later, the Natural Resources people show up, with guns no less, block our driveway with their trucks, and embark on a complete inspection of our property. It once happened five times in a single year. That's the hardest part—trying to get the respect and understanding of provincial authorities. We're the only province in Canada that does not allow the long-term rehabilitation of black bears or moose or adult deer. Before I die, I want to get Nova Scotia in line with the rest of the country and the rest of the world.

My goal is to return every animal we get back to its natural habitat, but it's not always possible. About 40 percent are so badly hurt they have to be euthanized. People hear that and they conclude that our "success rate" is about 60 percent. I tell them, "No, euthanizing an animal is a success. That animal was suffering on the side of the road with three broken legs and a broken pelvis. It was never going to get better, so we scooped it up and it's been euthanized quickly and humanely."

I hate to think of an animal suffering, but if we can provide an animal with a good quality of life for a certain time, we should save it. When we release an animal back to the wild, it's always with a mixture of joy and worry for me. Will they last two days or twenty years? Recently, a deer was killed by a car down at the end of our road. It had an ear tag, identifying it as a deer we had cared for. We dug it out of the ditch and loaded it onto the back of our truck. He was beautiful and had done well in the wild. We checked our records and found we had released him three years earlier. This fawn, who never had the care of a mother, went out and lived comfortably in the wild for three full years. That's good enough for me.

Let me tell you about an otter we once had named River. A man brought him to the farm in one of those big white milk buckets, which he set on the deck and said, "Take this."

I lifted the lid. All I could see was a big head and a little tiny body. It was a river otter, an aquatic mammal famous for playfully sliding down mudbanks or snowbanks. It was the most beautiful thing in the world, but it looked so scared.

I looked up from the bucket and asked the man, "What happened to its family?"

"I've been watching it for about a week," he answered. "There's some-

*This is our rehabilitation centre in Seaforth, where there is land, forest,
and water for all the wildlife we care for.*

thing wrong with its hind end and it couldn't keep up with the family, so
I'm bringing it to you."

"Okay," I said. "We'll take care of it."

The truth was I knew nothing about otters at that time, but it's like
that in my world. Science has identified more than a million species of animals, so it's inevitable that one is going to come in that I've never treated
before. That means hitting the books to figure out what to do, what kind
of milk to give it, how to get it to suckle, and stuff like that.

River turned out to be a very interesting animal to rehab. We got him
X-rayed, and it looked like he had been grabbed by a bald eagle because he
had puncture wounds right along his spinal cord. We nursed him through,
though he was always a handful. He became very territorial and aggressive, even dangerous. It really opened my eyes to instinct and the power of
nature. River caused laughter, tears, and bite wounds. He got stronger and
stronger until, after about eighteen months, he was well enough to leave.

We did a soft release on River. That is, we let him go very close to
the facility. Some animals can be released in the middle of nowhere, but
not all. Deer, for example, are okay to drive into the forest because food

is readily available; they don't have to learn how to hunt it. They also have a natural flight instinct from predators.

But some animals have a lot to learn before they can fend for themselves, so we release them where we can keep a watchful eye on their well-being. We put River in our lake. It was great to see him coming up with fish every day, jumping over to the wharf, and eating. He would go away for a couple of weeks at a time and then come back.

One night I heard the sound of something running across my deck. I hurried down the stairs, pulled open the door, and River, whom I hadn't seen in several weeks, threw his front legs around my leg and just held on.

I shone a flashlight along the deck and, suddenly, in the beam of light, I could see another, much bigger, otter. River had obviously gone into another otter's territory and had been chased back to the farm.

River had huge puncture wounds on his face and body. He needed antibiotics for a couple of weeks. But he learned a life lesson about how territorial otters are. If he hadn't come back "home" he probably would not have lived through those infections.

After we released him again, we saw him less and less until he didn't come back at all. River made me realize how important it is to do rehab well. He taught me that it's rough in the wild, that nature is powerful and dangerous. Things can go right when we step in, and things can go wrong. And then they can go right again.

Eventually, I quit my job at the Dartmouth Veterinary Hospital and I moved to an even larger property—we call it "the farm"—still in Seaforth, that could better accommodate the rehab's immediate needs but also leave room to grow. Since 1997, Hope for Wildlife has rescued, rehabilitated, and released more than 40,000 injured and orphaned wild animals representing over 250 species. We have flight cages, barns for white-tailed deer, a hospital, a lab, and nurseries. We have a beautiful marine unit with three huge pools for seals and otters. We just keep building. Every year we assist more than 30,000 callers through our wildlife helpline, welcome thousands of visitors to our education facility for tours, give hundreds of offsite educational presentations to community and school groups, and collect a wide range of data from animals treated at our rehabilitation centre. For the first fifteen years or so, I worked alone, but now I have eight to ten year-round staff.

Of course, I still work off the farm. My full-time job is with the city of Halifax, running Homeward Bound City Pound, which shelters stray dogs and cares for critically injured cats, and I'm also on the board of directors and do the accounting for the Metro Animal Emergency Clinic, which provides care for pets when regular vet offices are closed. So very close to what I imagined I might do all those years ago in grade ten.

In 2003, I got a call from the Nova Scotia Agricultural College (now the agriculture faculty at Dalhousie University). One of their pine martens had given birth, then died, and they wanted to know if I could care for the kits. There were two: one male, whom they had named Hansel, and one female, Gretel. I was there in an hour.

Pine martens live in forests almost everywhere in Canada but are endangered in Nova Scotia. They're long, slender weasels, about the size of a mink, with large ears, short limbs, and a bushy tail. They are invariably called cute and adorable, though their survival depends on them hunting small mammals like mice and voles. In the wild, they might live eight to ten years.

When I brought Hansel and Gretel home, they were both ill with some kind of bug. Hansel soon died, but I managed to nurse Gretel back to health. I would have released her as soon as she was healthy, but because she'd been born in New Brunswick, wildlife authorities in Nova Scotia were afraid she was genetically different from local pine martens and wouldn't allow it. (That turned out not be the case, but gene testing didn't happen until many years later.) In captivity, Gretel still had a good life, and she taught many people at the centre about pine martens and their endangerment.

A lot of our staff were afraid to death of her because she would sometimes turn and attack, but Gretel had affection for me. She trusted me. If something was wrong, she came running to me. I still have a bit of shyness in me, but when I had Gretel with me I could talk to a million people. Children could touch her and feel her wonderful fur. Staff members were always shocked when they saw her gentle side.

While I don't like referring to Gretel as a pet—she was always very much a wild girl—I concede that by the common understanding of what a pet is, she was, loosely speaking, one. She lived with me for more than sixteen years.

One Sunday morning just after Christmas in 2019, I noticed Gretel wasn't herself. Usually a ball of energy, she was just lying about. I took her down to our hospital right away, but she couldn't be saved. A subsequent necropsy revealed that she had liver cancer. It broke my heart to lose her, but nurturing her and caring for her had brought me so much joy. If I hadn't chosen to pursue animal rescue, I'd have never met Gretel at all.

A lot of people still find it odd that we do what we do. I get asked all the time, "Why are you rescuing animals anyway? Shouldn't nature just take its course? Why the heck would you save a raccoon when there's hundreds of thousands of them?"

Here I am with Gretel, the pine marten I nursed back to health and my wild girl. PATRICIA HOMONYLO

Our goal is to show people that all of nature is connected and that it's all important—whether it's a starling or a mouse, a bald eagle or a deer. Yes, we know we're fixing up a red squirrel to put it back in the wild where it will be eaten by some other animal, but that's the ecosystem that we want to sustain. We want to teach people to care about it. Imagine a six-year-old coming in with a little squirrel that the cat brought home. If I said, "No, we don't rehab that," what message is that child going to absorb? She's got to understand she's part of nature too. I wouldn't run rehab any other way.

As for letting nature take its course—90 percent of the injuries we see have been caused by humans. The animal has been hit by a car, or a bird has flown into a window. We have created the injury. That's not nature. And it's not nature to see an animal suffering and dying on the side of the road. We've caused the problem; we'd better fix it.

I want to help every single injured animal that comes to us. At one point there were six billion passenger pigeons, and now there are none. Just because something is plentiful doesn't mean it's going to be around forever.

While my world never became as big as it might have, that's been my choice. Some people think I'm selfless for caring for the animals the way I do, but in my opinion, I'm the most selfish person in the world because I get to do what I love.

Each day has its routine, but there is always something new. Last year we had a black bear with a minor injury, and I cared for him five mornings a week, cleaning and feeding him. I tend to do a lot of the complicated cases like the baby porcupines, weasels, and beavers. Something about their very nature requires nurturing. But I always start my day early with a walkabout of the farm to make sure everybody is okay before my administrative duties get the best of me. I love to feed the fawns. It's peaceful. I have so many quiet moments, alone on the farm. I see a red squirrel or a flying squirrel or a starling or you name it and I feel amazed at the very sight. They're not less than us; they're just different from us.

My life is not glamorous, but it is beautiful. I see the joy in life—all life—every single day. As long as Hope for Wildlife continues, I'll be able to share the joy that is brought into my heart by all of nature's creatures.

Hope Swinimer founded the Eastern Shore Wildlife Rescue and Rehabilitation Centre, the first privately owned wildlife rehabilitation centre in Nova Scotia, in 1997, which was later renamed Hope for Wildlife. In 2019, she received an honorary degree from Saint Mary's University. She lives in Seaforth, Nova Scotia.

Acknowledgments

Peter Mansbridge

I'm often asked who my most memorable interview has been with. I've probably done close to twenty thousand interviews, so it's a tricky question. I could say Pierre Trudeau or Margaret Thatcher or Desmond Tutu. Or I could say Ringo Starr or Bobby Orr or Ferguson Jenkins or Robbie Robertson.

But I don't.

And that's because as exciting as it is to sit down with the famous people I get a chance to talk to, there's nothing quite as memorable as those with a name most don't recognize. I like to say they are ordinary people who have found themselves in extraordinary situations and therefore have unforgettable stories to tell.

Which brings me to this book Mark and I have written about some very extraordinary Canadians. Their stories are inspiring in so many different ways and it's been an honour to be involved in telling them. So I'd like to acknowledge all of them for being so open with us, and to the team at Simon & Schuster—thank you for giving us the platform to write about them. Especially to our gentle yet persistent editor, Sarah St. Pierre, and publisher, Kevin Hanson.

A special shout-out to my literary agent, Brian Wood, who got me involved with Simon & Schuster in the first place.

Of course also to my family for giving me the space to do a little writing.

And finally to my friend Mark, who, just as he did throughout my career, carried me on his back across the finish line.

Mark Bulgutch

Forty years in television news taught me that I couldn't do anything on my own. No matter how much I did to get a program to air, I had to rely on so many other people using their talents to make anything happen. Frankly, it was a joy to share my days and nights with exceptionally skilled colleagues (Peter among them), working on a common goal.

Writing a book (again with Peter) is a lonelier endeavour. But it would be foolhardy not to realize it also cannot be done alone.

There's an entire team at Simon & Schuster whom I never met, partly because of the COVID-19 lockdown when this book was written, edited, and printed, and partly because that's just how book publishing works. Unseen people take words on a computer screen and somehow turn them into a tangible thing called a book. One person I did meet was Sarah St. Pierre. She edited this book not only with sharp suggestions for improvement but with diplomatic delicacy that I'm sure would bring peace to the two Koreas. She has the remarkable ability to tell you how many things are wrong, while still reassuring you that everything is great.

You have read about a group of extraordinary Canadians in these pages. I feel grateful for the time they devoted to helping me get their stories straight. I'm glad extraordinary people can be so nice.

Finally, acknowledging that I can't do anything on my own would be hollow without naming my wife, daughters, and granddaughter. Rhonda, Melissa, Jessica, and Reid are why I'm so happy to wake up every morning.

About the Authors

COURTESY OF AUTHOR

Peter Mansbridge is one of Canada's most respected journalists. He is the former chief correspondent for CBC News and the anchor of *The National*, CBC's flagship nightly newscast, where he worked for thirty years reporting on national and international news stories such as federal elections, foreign conflicts, natural disasters, the fall of the Berlin Wall, 9/11, the 2014 Parliament Hill shootings, and numerous Olympic Games. From 1999 to 2017, he hosted *Mansbridge One on One*, a weekly program featuring conversations with world leaders, music legends, and sports heroes. Mansbridge has received over a dozen national awards for broadcast excellence, including a lifetime achievement award from the Academy of Canadian Cinema & Television. He is a distinguished fellow of the Munk School of Global Affairs and Public Policy at the University of Toronto. He is the former two-term Chancellor of Mount Allison University. In 2008, he was made an Officer of the Order of Canada—the country's highest civilian honour—and in 2012, he was awarded the Queen Elizabeth II Diamond Jubilee Medal. He is the #1 bestselling author of *Off the Record* and *Peter Mansbridge One on One: Favourite Conversations and the Stories Behind Them*. He lives in Stratford, Ontario. Follow him on Twitter @PeterMansbridge, visit him at ThePeterMansbridge.com, or listen to his weekly podcast, *The Bridge*, with Sirius XM Canada.

GARY GOULD

Mark Bulgutch is a journalist, educator, speaker, and the author of *That's Why I'm a Journalist* and *That's Why I'm a Doctor*. He worked at the CBC for forty years, eleven as the senior editor of *The National* and another ten as senior executive producer of all live news specials. He has taught at the Ryerson University School of Journalism for thirty-five years. A regular contributor of opinion columns to the *Toronto Star*, he has won fourteen Gemini Awards, four RTDNA Awards, the Canadian Journalism Foundation Award of Excellence, and the Canadian Association of Broadcasters Gold Ribbon Award. He lives in Toronto, Ontario. Follow him on Twitter @MarkBulgutch.